D1538123

CSS & CSS3

20 Lessons to Successful Web Development

About the Author

Robin Nixon is a prolific author on programming and web development (as well as psychology and motivation), with his books having been translated into numerous foreign languages—frequently topping the US and international computer book charts. He has worked with computers and technology for all his life, and began writing on the subject about 35 years ago.

He has authored hundreds of articles, and over two dozen books, and is a popular video and online instructor, with thousands of students taking his courses. Robin is also an accomplished programmer, developer, and entrepreneur, with several successful Internet startups to his name, from which he has learned a wealth of programming hints and tips, which he enjoys passing on in his expanding range of web development books, including the following titles:

- *HTML5: 20 Lessons to Successful Web Development* (McGraw-Hill Education, 2015)
- *JavaScript: 20 Lessons to Successful Web Development* (McGraw-Hill Education, 2015)
- *PHP: 20 Lessons to Successful Web Development* (McGraw-Hill Education, 2015)
- *Learning PHP, MySQL, JavaScript, CSS & HTML5* (O'Reilly, 2014)
- *Web Developer's Cookbook* (McGraw-Hill Education, 2012)
- *HTML5 for iOS and Android* (McGraw-Hill Education, 2010)

About the Technical Editor

Albert Wiersch has been writing software since the Commodore VIC-20 and Commodore 64 days in the early 1980s. He holds a Bachelor of Science degree in Computer Science Engineering and an MBA from the University of Texas at Arlington. Albert currently develops and sells software that helps web developers, educators, students, businesses, and government agencies check their HTML & CSS documents and their websites for quality problems, including many SEO (search engine optimization), mobility, and accessibility issues, with discounts made available to students. His website is at *HTMLValidator.com*.

CSS & CSS3

20 Lessons to Successful Web Development

Robin Nixon

New York   Chicago   San Francisco
Athens   London   Madrid   Mexico City
Milan   New Delhi   Singapore   Sydney   Toronto

Cataloging-in-Publication Data is on file with the Library of Congress

McGraw-Hill Education books are available at special quantity discounts to use as premiums and sales promotions, or for use in corporate training programs. To contact a representative, please visit the Contact Us pages at www.mhprofessional.com.

CSS & CSS3: 20 Lessons to Successful Web Development

1234567890   DOC DOC   1098765

ISBN   978-0-07-184996-8
MHID   0-07-184996-3

Sponsoring Editor Brandi Shailer	**Technical Editor** Albert Wiersch	**Composition** Cenveo Publisher Services
Editorial Supervisor Jody McKenzie	**Copy Editor** Megha Saini	**Illustration** Cenveo Publisher Services
Project Manager Anupriya Tyagi, Cenveo® Publisher Services	**Proofreader** Paul Tyler	**Art Director, Cover** Jeff Weeks
Acquisitions Coordinator Amanda Russell	**Indexer** Karin Arrigoni	**Cover Designer** Jeff Weeks
	Production Supervisor Jean Bodeaux	

To Julie

Contents at a Glance

Contents

Acknowledgments

Once again I would like to thank the amazing team at McGraw-Hill Education, with whom it is always a real pleasure to work on new book projects. In particular, I would like to thank my Sponsoring Editor Brandi Shailer, Amanda Russell for overseeing the project's development, Editorial Supervisor Jody McKenzie, Production Supervisor Jean Bodeaux, Copy Editor Megha Saini, and Jeff Weeks for the excellent cover design. Thanks also goes again to Albert Wiersch (whom I have had the pleasure of working with on a number of occasions) for his meticulous eye for detail during technical review.

Introduction

Why This Book?

The concept for this book grew out of Robin's extremely popular online courses in which thousands of students are enrolled. From their feedback it became evident that the reason for this popularity was that students love the way the material is broken down into easy-to-digest lessons, each of which can be completed in an hour or less. They also like the no-nonsense, jargon-free, and friendly writing style.

Now, working together, Robin and McGraw-Hill Education have further revised, updated, and developed his CSS & CSS3 course into this book, which not only will teach you everything you need to learn in 20 lessons (of less than an hour each), it also includes an average 15-minute detailed video walk-through for each lesson—comprising 5 hours of footage in total.

Watch the videos after reading the lesson to reinforce key concepts, or use the video as a primer to working through each print lesson. Used together, these course materials make learning CSS & CSS3 easier than it has ever been, and is the ideal way for you to add these essential skills to your web development toolkit.

 To view the accompanying video for this lesson, please visit mhprofessional.com/nixoncss/.

Who Should Read This Book?

Each chapter is laid out in a straightforward and logical manner as a lesson, with plenty of examples written using simple and clear CSS. Before moving on to each subsequent lesson, you have the opportunity to test your new knowledge with a set of 10 questions about what you have just learned. You can also work along with every lesson by watching its accompanying video tutorial.

Even if you have never used any CSS before, you will still learn everything you need from this book, because the first section provides a thorough grounding in what CSS is, what it can do for you, and how to use it. And if you have used CSS before, it will act as a great revision source to ensure you are fully up-to-date before moving on to learning all the latest additions to CSS3.

Between the lessons, the self-test questions, and the videos, this course will ensure that you become expert at CSS very quickly.

To save you typing them in, all the example files from the book are saved in a freely downloadable zip file available at the companion website: *20lessons.com*.

What This Book Covers?

This book covers every aspect of CSS, starting with basic syntax and language rules, such as where and how you include CSS in your web documents. Then the differences between styling elements by type, class, and ID are explained, along with how to refine the elements to which CSS will be supplied using selectors.

The term cascade (in cascading style sheets) is fully explained, as is how to create professional results with fonts and typography, and how to lay out compelling pages. All the CSS and CSS3 selectors are detailed, along with the new CSS3 ways to manage colors, backgrounds, borders, opacity, and more. How to transform and animate elements in 2D and 3D is also explained, with simple examples that you can easily incorporate in your own websites.

By the time you finish the book's 20 lessons, you'll have a thorough grounding in CSS, and be able to use it to ensure your web pages look as good as possible.

How to Use This Book?

This book has been written in a logical order so that each lesson builds on information learned in the previous ones. You should begin at Lesson 1 and then work sequentially through the book, proceeding to the next lesson only when you can correctly answer the self-test questions in the previous one.

If you already use CSS, you may wish to just browse through the first few lessons before tucking into the CSS3 section.

Lessons should take you less than an hour to finish, including viewing the accompanying video walk-through provided with each one. With over 5 hours of video in total, that's an average of 15 minutes dedicated to each lesson.

How Is This Book Organized?

The first section of this book covers everything you need to know as a newcomer to CSS, including these lessons: Introduction to CSS, Learning the CSS Rules, Applying Declarations to IDs and Classes, Accessing Selectors, Working with the Cascade, Selecting Fonts and Typography, Manipulating Color and Position, Handling Pseudo-Selectors and Using Shorthand Properties, and Understanding the Box Model.

The second section moves on to explaining everything that's new in CSS3, including these lessons: Introduction to CSS3, Using Selectors and Attribute Selectors, Setting Backgrounds, Attaching Borders, Controlling Box Shadows, Overflow, and Columns, Adding Colors and Opacity, Creating Text Effects and Changing the Box Model, Linking to Web Fonts, Making 2D Transformations, Applying Specific Transformations, and Directing 3D Transformations. The appendix lists all the answers to the self-test questions in each chapter.

How Is This Book Organized?

PART I

Basic CSS

Introduction to CSS

To view the accompanying video for this lesson, please visit mhprofessional.com/nixoncss/.

When CSS was invented it was based around a Document Object Model (DOM), a means of separating out all the different elements within a web page into discrete objects, each with its own properties and values. This led logically to the introduction of style sheets, enabling the content of a web page to be completely separated from its styling; it also made HTML documents easily modifiable by languages such as JavaScript to provide dynamic user interaction.

Because web pages use a DOM, it is easy for you to style every aspect of it using CSS. For example, each heading will be within pairs of tags such as `<h1>` and `</h1>`, and a single CSS declaration can set the styling of all such occurrences within a document, changing the font used, its size, any font decoration, and so on.

This lets you completely change the design of a page without altering the HTML. Some style settings can even apply dynamic effects to page elements, such as changing their color and other properties when the mouse passes over them, or create transition effects by using proprietary browser extensions.

The example files from this book are in a file you can download at *20lessons.com*. The files for this lesson are saved in it as *embeddedstyles.htm*, *example.htm*, *importedstyles.htm*, *importedstyles2.htm*, *styles.css*, *styletag.htm*, *usingclasses.htm*, and *usingids.htm*.

How the Document Object Model Works

The DOM separates different parts of an HTML document into a hierarchy of objects, each one having its own properties. The term *property* is used for referring to an attribute of an object, such as the HTML it contains, its width and height, and so on.

The outermost object possible is the window object, which is the current browser window, tab, iframe, or popped-up window. Underneath this is the document object, of which there can be more than one (such as several documents loaded into different iframes within a page). And inside a document there are other objects such as the head and body of a page.

Within the head there can be other objects such as the title and meta objects, while the body object can contain numerous other objects, including headings, anchors, forms, and so forth. For example, Figure 1-1 shows a representation of the DOM of an example document, with the document shown inside the outer window, and having the title `Hello`, a `<meta>` tag in the head, and three HTML elements (a link, a form, and an image) in the body section.

Of course, even the simplest of web pages has more structure than is shown here, but it serves to illustrate how the DOM works; starting from the very outside is the window, inside which there's a single document, and within the document are the various elements or objects, which connect to each other.

In the figure, values are shown with a darker background and in italics. For example, the value `robots` is the value of the property name, which is a property of `<meta>`, and so on. Although it isn't shown in the figure, the `<meta>` tag should have another matching property called `content`, which would contain a string specifying which robots (web crawlers) may access the web page.

Other properties are `href`, which has a value of *http://google.com* (and is itself a property of `<meta>`, and so on), and `<title>`, which has the value `Hello`. All the other items are objects or object argument names. If the figure were to extend farther down and sideways, other objects and properties attached to the ones shown would come into view. A couple of the places where these would appear are shown by unconnected dotted lines.

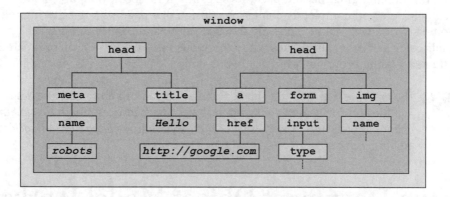

FIGURE 1-1 Example of a DOM showing head and body sections

In HTML tags you can generally use the single or double quotation marks interchangeably. Therefore `<a href="http://google.com">` is equivalent to `<a href='http://google.com'>`. Wherever possible, though, I tend to use single quotes because they don't require pressing the Shift key to type them in. Also there are sometimes occasions when you need two levels of nested quotes, where I would then choose double quotation marks for the outer string, and then apply single quotes within it, like this: `<p style="font-family:'Times New Roman';">`.

Representing this as HTML, the structure of the head section looks like this:

```
<head>
  <meta name='robots' content='index, follow'>
  <title>Hello</title>
</head>
```

And the body section of HTML might look like this:

```
<body>
  <img src='/images/welcome.jpg'>
  <a href='http://google.com'>Visit Google</a>
  or enter your username and password to continue...
  <form id='login' method='post' action='login.php'>
    <input type='text' name='name'>
    <input type='password' name='password'>
    <input type='submit'>
  </form>
</body>
```

Remembering that these two sections of HTML are part of the same document, we would bring them both together inside an `<html>` tag (preceded by a `!DOCTYPE` declaration), like this:

```
<!DOCTYPE html>
<html>
  <head>
    <meta name='robots' content='index, follow'>
    <title>Hello</title>
  </head>
  <body>
    <img src='/images/welcome.jpg'>
    <a href=http://google.com>Visit Google</a>,
    or enter your username and password to continue...
    <form id='login' method='post' action='login.php'>
      <input type='text' name='name'>
      <input type='password' name='password'>
      <input type='submit'>
    </form>
  </body>
</html>
```

Of course, all web pages are different, but they will usually follow this same form.

Correct HTML Structure and Nesting

To follow recommended HTML structure and to ensure your documents are readable by the maximum number of browsers and other clients, attribute values within tags should be contained in either single or double quotation marks like this: `<a href='http://yahoo.com'>`, even though nearly all browsers allow you to omit them, like this: `<a href=http://yahoo.com>`.

You should also close (end) every tag, and do so in the correct order. For example, you shouldn't close a document by issuing `</html>` followed by `</body>` because the proper nesting of tags would be broken by this reversal. The correct way to close a document is with `</body>`, followed by `</html>`.

About Cascading Style Sheets

Using CSS you can apply styles to your web pages to make them look exactly how you want. This works because CSS is connected to the DOM so that you can quickly and easily restyle any element. For example, if you don't like the default look of the `<h1>`, `<h2>`, and other heading tags, you can assign new styles to override the default settings for the font family and size used, or whether bold or italics should be set, and many more properties too.

One way you can add styling to a web page is by inserting the required CSS into the head of a web page between the `<head>` and `</head>` tags. So, to change the style of the `<h1>` tag you might use the following CSS:

```
<style>
  h1 {
    color     :olive;
    font-size :18pt;
    font-family:'Times New Roman';
  }
</style>
```

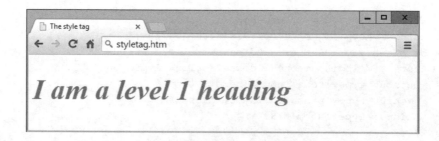

FIGURE 1-2   A simple document with a CSS-styled heading

Within an HTML page, this might look like the following (see Figure 1-2):

```
<!DOCTYPE html>
<html>
  <head>
    <meta name='robots' content='index, follow'>
    <title>The style tag</title>
    <style>
      h1 {
        color      :olive;
        font-size  :36pt;
        font-family:'Times New Roman';
        font-style :italic;
      }
    </style>
  </head>
  <body>
    <h1>I am a level 1 heading</h1>
  </body>
</html>
```

Importing a Style Sheet

When you wish to style a whole site, rather than a single page, a better way to manage style sheets is to completely remove them from your web pages to separate files, and then import the ones you need. This lets you use different style sheets for different layouts (such as web and print) without changing the HTML.

There are a couple of different ways this can be achieved, the first of which is by using the CSS @import directive like this:

```
<style>
  @import url('styles.css');
</style>
```

This statement tells the browser to fetch a style sheet with the name *styles.css*. The @import command is quite flexible in that you can create style sheets that themselves pull in other style sheets, and so on. Just make sure that there are no <style> or </style> tags in any of your external style sheets or they will not work. External style sheets must contain only CSS and never any HTML tags.

Importing CSS from Within HTML

You can also include a style sheet with the HTML <link> tag like this:

```
<link rel='stylesheet' type='text/css' href='styles.css'>
```

This has the exact same effect as the @import directive, except that <link> is an HTML-only tag and is not a valid style directive, so it cannot be used from within one style sheet to pull in another. Also, it cannot be placed within a pair of <style> and </style> tags.

Just as you can use multiple @import directives within your CSS to include multiple external style sheets, you can also use as many <link> tags as you like in your HTML.

Embedded Style Settings

There's also nothing stopping you from individually setting or overriding certain styles for the current page on a case by case basis by inserting style attributes directly within HTML, like this (which results in italic blue text within the tags):

```
<h1 style='font-style:italic; color:blue;'>Hello there</h1>
```

But this should be reserved only for the most exceptional circumstances as it breaks the separation of content and presentation.

Using IDs

A better solution for setting the style of an element is to assign an ID to it in the HTML, like this:

```
<h1 id='highlight'>Hello there</h1>
```

What this does is state that the contents of the <h1> element with the ID highlight should have the style applied to it that is defined in the following rule:

```
#highlight {
  text-decoration:underline;
  color        :orange;
}
```

Note the use of the # symbol, which specifies that only the element that has an ID of highlight should be styled with this statement.

Using Classes

If you would like to apply the same style to many elements, you don't have to give each one a different ID because you can specify a class to manage them all, like this:

```
<h1 class='highlight'>Hello</h1>
```

What this does is state that the contents of this element (and any other element that uses the same class) should have the style defined for the `highlight` class applied to it. Once a class is assigned you can use the following rule, either in the document's head section or within an external style sheet for setting the styles for the class:

```
.highlight {
  text-decoration:underline;
  color          :orange;
}
```

Instead of using a # symbol, which is reserved for IDs, class selectors are prefaced with a . (period) symbol.

 Note   You may wonder whether the semicolons used in CSS are actually necessary or if are they optional, as with JavaScript. The answer is yes and no. In order to separate multiple CSS statements on the same line, you must place semicolons between them. But if there is only one statement in a set of rules (or in an inline style attribute within an HTML tag), then you can omit the semicolon, as you can for the final statement in a group. However, to avoid hard-to-find CSS errors, you may prefer to always use a semicolon after every CSS declaration so that you can copy and paste them and otherwise modify properties without worrying about removing semicolons where they aren't strictly necessary or having to add them where they are required.

Summary

Now that you have learned some of the basics of CSS, in Lesson 2, I'll show you how CSS rules work, and how you can apply them in different ways.

Self-Test Questions

Using these questions, test how much you have learned in this lesson. If you don't know an answer, go back and reread the relevant section until your knowledge is complete. You can find the answers in the appendix.

1. What model is HTML based on?

2. What is the main purpose of style sheets?

3. What is the outermost object in the DOM?

4. What are the two main sections of an HTML document?

5. What types of elements are typically used in the head of an HTML document?

6. Within which tags are CSS rules typically placed?

7. How can an external file containing CSS rules be imported into a style section of an HTML document?

8. How can an external style sheet be imported into a non-style section of an HTML document?

9. How can a CSS style be directly applied to an element?

10. What is the difference between a class and an ID?

Learning the CSS Rules

To view the accompanying video for this lesson, please visit mhprofessional.com/ nixoncss/.

As with any language (and CSS is most definitely a language), there are rules and syntax that you must follow in order for your instructions to be properly understood. The way the rules work is based on the fact that web documents are built using the Document Object Model (DOM) in which every element of a page is treated as an object that can be uniquely addressed.

However, it is also possible to group objects together and address such groups collectively in a variety of different ways. Moreover, objects can be sub-objects of other objects, so you can reference all objects and sub-objects with one type of rule, or zone in on one particular sub-sub-object, according to what you are trying to achieve.

There are also different ways you can apply CSS rules to these objects (or elements), ranging from directly where the elements are created in the document, to within a special section of a document reserved for CSS rules, to external files containing sequences of rules. You can even combine groups of rules and apply them either to a single element or to a group of elements.

In other words, CSS is very flexible and easy to work with, but to do so you'll need to learn the basic syntax, which is explained in this lesson.

Selectors

Each CSS rule starts with a selector, which is the thing upon which the rule is affected. For example, in the CSS rule below, h1 is the selector that is being given a font size 200 percent larger than the default:

```
h1 { font-size:200%; }
```

Providing a new value to the `font-size` property of the selector ensures that the contents of all `<h1>` tags will be displayed at a font size of 200 percent relative to the default size. This is achieved by placing one or more declarations within the { and } symbols that follow the selector (in this case, `font-size:200%;`). The part before the : (colon) symbol is the property, while the remainder is the value applied to it.

Lastly, there is a ; (semicolon) to end the statement which, in this instance, is not required (but would be required if another declaration were to follow). For the sake of avoiding tricky to track down errors, in this book I always include the semicolons, even when they are not necessary.

IDs

Selectors may be element types such as `h1`, `img`, `p`, or `table`, or they can be ID or class names. ID names are ones you provide to an element by assigning a value to its `id` attribute, like this:

```
<img id='myphoto' src='photo.jpg'>
```

This element can now be uniquely referenced from CSS rules to modify its styles.

Classes

Class names are names you assign to an element by providing a value to an element's `class` attribute, like this:

```
<p class='intro'>
```

Any element that uses this class name can now be referenced from CSS. When a CSS rule is created for this class, all elements that make use of it will be modified.

There are also other types of selectors available in CSS, which you will discover as you progress through this book.

Multiple Assignments

You can create multiple property assignments in a couple of different ways. First, you can concatenate them on the same line, like this:

```
h1 { font-size:200%; color:blue; }
```

This adds a second declaration that changes the color of all `<h1>` headers to blue. You can also place the assignments one per line, like the following:

```
h1 { font-size:200%;
color:blue; }
```

Or you can space the assignments out a little more, so that they line up below each other in a column at the colons, like this:

```
h1 {
  font-size:200%;
  color    :blue;
}
```

This way you can easily see where each new set of declarations begins, because of the selector in the first column, and the declarations that follow are neatly lined up with all property values starting at the same horizontal offset. In the preceding example, the second (last) semicolon is unnecessary, but should you ever want to concatenate any such groups of statements into a single line, it is very quick to do with all semicolons already in place.

There is no right or wrong way to lay out your CSS, but I recommend you at least try to keep each block of CSS consistent with itself, so that it can be easily taken in at a glance.

These three examples are saved in the file *multipleassignments.htm* in the accompanying archive.

Comments

It is a good idea to comment your CSS rules, even if you describe only the main groups of statements rather than all or most of them. You can do this in two different ways. First, you can place a comment within a pair of /* and */ comment markers, like this:

```
/* This is a CSS comment */
```

Or you can extend a comment over many lines, like this:

```
/*
  A Multi
  line
  comment
*/
```

 If you use multiline comments, you should be aware that you cannot nest single-line (or any other) comments within them, otherwise you will get unpredictable errors.

Single-Line Comments

Although not in the CSS specification, I have tested the JavaScript form of single line (or to-end-of-line) commenting, and can report that it works on all major browsers. You may like to try it for yourself when you wish to quickly comment out a single rule, but be aware that it is not official, although since it is supported by all main browsers, perhaps it will become so.

Anyway, to make a single-line CSS comment, just place the tag // before the part of the line to comment out, like this (shown in bold):

```
float      :left;
//background:#eeeeee;
padding    :20px 20px 2px 20px;
border     :1px solid #888;
```

As I said, if you use this type of commenting, I'd recommend you do so only for a quick test that requires a single rule to be commented out, and then take out the comment as soon as you have made the test. To ensure full future compatibility, if you wish to leave a line commented out for any length of time, you should place it inside /* and */ tags. Also remember that your CSS will not validate with any double-slash comments left in it.

Style Types

There are a number of different style types, ranging from the default styles set up by your browser (and any user styles you may have applied), through inline or embedded styles, to external style sheets. The styles defined in each type have a hierarchy of precedence, from low to high.

Default Styles

The lowest level of style precedence is the default styling applied by a web browser. These styles are created as a fallback for when a web page doesn't have any styles, and they are intended to be a generic set of styles that will display reasonably well in most instances.

Pre-CSS, these were the only styles applied to a document, and only a handful of them could be changed by a web page (such as font face, color and size, and a few element sizing arguments).

User Styles

These are the next highest precedence of styles, and they are supported by most modern browsers but are implemented differently by each. In fact, these seem to be becoming a thing of the past; Google Chrome, for example, has even stopped supporting its *custom* *.css* file (editing the contents changes nothing anymore), although Microsoft's Internet Explorer browser still supports user styles, as shown in Figure 2-1.

However, there are plug-ins being released for the major browsers (such as Stylish) that will let you create your own user styles, so they are probably the best way to go about CSS customization at the moment.

Anyway, if a user style is assigned that has already been defined as a browser default, it will then override the browser's default setting. Any styles not defined in a user style sheet will retain their default values as set up in the browser.

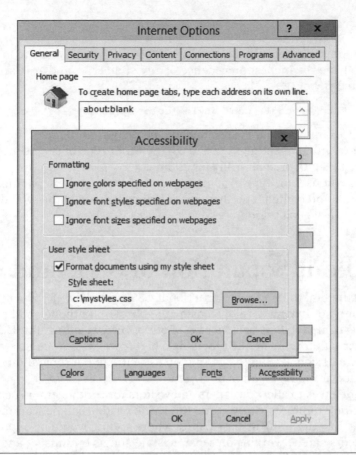

FIGURE 2-1 Applying a user style sheet to Internet Explorer

External Style Sheets

The next types of styles are those assigned in an external style sheet. These settings will override any assigned style, either by the user or by the browser. External style sheets are the recommended way to create your styles, because you can produce different style sheets for different purposes such as styling for general web use, for viewing on a mobile browser with a smaller screen, for printing purposes, and so on, and then apply just the one needed for each type of media.

Internal Styles

Then there are internal styles, which you create within `<style>` and `</style>` tags in HTML documents, and which take precedence over all the preceding style types. At this point, though, you are beginning to break the separation between presentation and content, as any external style sheets loaded in at the same time will have a lower precedence.

Inline Styles

Lastly, inline styles are where you assign CSS declarations directly to an element. They also have the highest precedence of any style type, and are used like this (highlighted in bold):

```
<a href='http://google.com' style='color:green;'>Visit Google</a>
```

In this example, the link specified will be displayed in green, regardless of any default or other color settings applied by any other type of style sheet, whether directly to this link or generically for all links.

When you use this type of styling, you are breaking the separation between presentation and content and therefore it is recommended that you do so only when you have a very good reason.

It's All About Separation of Style and Content

The fundamental thing to remember about CSS, especially if you come from a background of having developed using the obsolete (although still usable for backwards compatibility) tags such as <font> for controlling font faces and sizes, etc., is that rather than simply providing a better way to spruce up web pages, style sheets were designed from the ground up to facilitate the separation of layout and presentation from the creation of content.

The idea was to allow designers and writers to work together (possibly also alongside programmers) at the same time. The writers can be working on the main document, just dropping in class names where styling would be appropriate, and then the designers can be working on separate style sheets optimizing and tweaking the layout and, in fact, the entire look and feel (presentation) of a document, without affecting what the writer is doing with the content.

At the same time, a programmer could also be working on an external JavaScript file to provide the dynamic functionality needed by a website, although we won't be looking into that very closely in this book.

So the point with CSS is to try and think about the web pages you create more conceptually than precisely. For example, because I want to introduce simple CSS to start with, in this lesson I gave an inline example of changing the color of a link to Google to green. However, actually embedding color changes via inline CSS breaks the separation of content and style. So does the naming of classes with words such as color names.

Instead, right from the start, you should try to get into the mindset of considering what any part of a document does, or what it is for. For example, is it a heading, a news summary, an opinion piece, a quotation, a dispatch from a foreign correspondent, an advertorial, a special offer, or any of all the different types of content that make up a web page?

Once you have decided, place the content in a <div> or other element and give it a class name that describes the content. Then you can later write the CSS rules you need to present and style the content in the way you want, or you can hand that task over to a page designer.

So, in place of the previous example, the following is probably a better choice (with the `class` attribute shown in bold):

```
<a href='http://google.com' class='link'>Visit Google</a>
```

Then, as you'll see in Lesson 3, you can create a class called `link`, to which you can supply any CSS declarations you like, and which can be changed at any time without affecting the original link, which will automatically style the link for you according to the rules given.

Summary

You will now have a basic knowledge of CSS rules and syntax, the various types of styles available, and how to access them. In Lesson 3, we'll look into taking things a little further by addressing elements in groups by class names, and individually by ID names.

Self-Test Questions

Using these questions, test how much you have learned in this lesson. If you don't know an answer, go back and reread the relevant section until your knowledge is complete. You can find the answers in the appendix.

1. In CSS, what is a selector?

2. Following the CSS selector(s), which two symbols are used to contain the declaration(s)?

3. Which symbol separates properties from values in CSS declarations?

4. Is a semicolon necessary after CSS declarations?

5. How can you apply more than one CSS declaration to a selector?

6. How would you give the ID of `item1` to an element?

7. How would you assign the class `news` to an element?

8. How can you mark a section of CSS as a comment?

9. Ignoring browser default and user styles, what are the main types of CSS rules?

10. What CSS selector and rule could you use to set the font size for `<h1>` text to 300 percent of the default size?

Applying Declarations to IDs and Classes

 To view the accompanying video for this lesson, please visit mhprofessional.com/nixoncss/.

In Lesson 1 I very briefly introduced the concept of IDs and classes. Now let's look in detail at how you work with these mainstays of CSS design.

To recap, CSS supports the ability to style individual elements either by placing CSS inline with the element by supplying the declarations as a string value to an element's `style` attribute or, perhaps more simply (and certainly more in the spirit of separating content and presentation), by assigning an ID name to an element's `id` attribute, with which it can be accessed by any CSS rules that refer to it by ID name.

You can also choose to group a set of elements into a class by assigning a class name value to the `class` attribute of the elements. Any elements that make use of this class will then be affected by any rules that select them by class name.

 Actually there are other ways to style an element or group of elements, such as working through parts of the Document Object Model (DOM) an element at a time, but this can be quite cumbersome and is not recommended unless it's the only approach that will achieve the result you require.

Using IDs

The basic premise behind CSS is that it is better to separate out the styling and layout (presentation) of a web page from its content. There are some good reasons for this:

- When writing the main content of a web page, the author can concentrate on the text and not have to worry about the styling.

- Styling can be left until the very end of the development process, or can run in parallel because it doesn't interfere with the content.
- Web pages can be reformatted on the fly for use on different sizes of displays, in different types and sizes of fonts for people with visual impairment, or even to play out through speech synthesis for blind people.
- A print style sheet can be created that reformats a page such that it will print out well (most web pages sprawl out over many sheets of paper when printed without using such a style sheet).
- When newer CSS features and web technologies are developed, content can easily be repurposed to make use of them, thus presenting pages in the most modern manner.

Therefore, for no other reason than to help out your future self, I strongly recommend that you supply a class name for every different part of a document that you build, even if you don't currently plan on using them. That way you won't have to go back and retrofit them when you do wish to add particular styling.

And the same goes for any items that are unique or one-offs. They should be given an ID so that you can either style them now to display them well, or so that they are ready for you to do so in the future.

A Specific Case

For example, in the case of assigning IDs, suppose you are creating a news page with a photograph. If you place the photo in a `<div>` and give that `<div>` a unique ID, you can easily style a frame for the photo that can be changed at any time without going back and modifying the main document contents.

What's more, if your boss then asks you to turn the photo into a slideshow, you can probably write some JavaScript to access the ID and create such an effect without having to make any changes to the news item.

In this instance you might use HTML such as the following:

```
<div id='mainphoto'>
  <img src='picture.jpg'>
  <div id='caption'>Fishing boat at the beach</div>
</div>
```

And CSS rules to style the frame around the photo (and the caption) might look like this (see Figure 3-1):

```
#mainphoto {
  width      :320px;
  background:#eee;
  padding    :20px 20px 2px 20px;
  border     :1px solid #888;
}
#caption {
  font-style:italic;
  text-align:center;
}
```

FIGURE 3-1   Styling a photograph and caption

These rules could be placed either in a `<style>` section at the start of the document or as part of an external style sheet. The # characters that precede the names state that the names are to be applied to IDs.

The file used to create this figure is saved as *photo.htm* in the accompanying archive, and the files *photo2.htm* and *photo3.htm* contain updated versions, as detailed later in this lesson.

When you supply an ID name to an element, not only do you make that element easily accessible from CSS, but you also provide access to it from JavaScript, which can do even more dynamic things to the element.

IDs Are Single-Use Only

IDs are meant to apply only to a single element within a document and you are not supposed to reuse an ID in additional elements (unless you are very sneaky—and even then such use can be questionable).

However, in multiple tests I have found that you can use the same ID as many times as you like, in a variety of different elements, and in all major browsers. You can do this using `#rule` syntax, or the more complex `[id=rule]` selectors (see Lesson 4), and for all intents and purposes all of Firefox, Chrome, Safari, Opera, and Internet Explorer will treat these IDs as if they were a class, and all elements using the same ID will be modified by a rule.

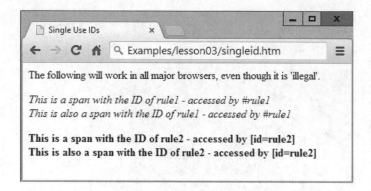

FIGURE 3-2   Reusing the same ID works in some instances but is "illegal."

The following example (saved as *singleid.htm* in the accompanying archive) shows "illegal" HTML that you shouldn't use, but which will work in all the main browsers (as shown in the Chrome screen grab in Figure 3-2):

```
<span id='rule1'>This is a span with the ID of rule1</span><br>
<span id='rule1'>This is also a span with the ID of rule1</span><br>
<span id='rule2'>This is a span with the ID of rule2</span><br>
<span id='rule2'>This is also a span with the ID of rule2</span>
```

And here's the matching CSS:

```
#rule1     { font-style:italic; }
[id=rule2] { font-weight:bold;  }
```

Evidently this means there must be a lot of people misusing IDs and so browser developers have gone to the trouble of writing extra code to support this illegal styling. But that doesn't mean that we will be doing the same, does it?

You see, there are potential pitfalls that can occur when you use IDs like classes:

- IDs are not defined as being interchangeable with classes in the CSS specifications, so even though browsers may currently support this usage, there is no guarantee that it will continue to be the case.
- JavaScript absolutely does not support this type of use, and only the first matching ID is picked up by it.
- Other developers working on documents that use the same ID in multiple places will be confused by the practice and find them difficult to maintain (the author may also get called a few unmentionable names under their breath).
- Why do it when classes are available?

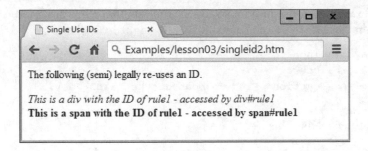

FIGURE 3-3   Reusing an ID name without it behaving like a class

By the way, I said you could reuse IDs in a sneaky way, so I'd better show you how with this HTML (saved as *singleid2.htm* in the accompanying archive), as shown in Figure 3-3:

```
<div id='rule1'>This is a div with the ID of rule1</div>
<span id='rule1'>This is a span with the ID of rule1 </span>
```

And with this CSS:

```
div#rule1  { font-style:italic; }
span#rule1 { font-weight:bold;    }
```

This works because one instance of `rule1` is applied to a `<div>`, and the second to a `<span>` element. These are then uniquely referenced in CSS by prefacing them with the element names `div` and `span`. However, this is still not good practice, will not validate, and can be confusing to anyone else maintaining your web documents.

What's more, this type of syntax will not work in JavaScript, because it will return only the first `<div>` element. What will happen here is that any `<div>` element with an ID of `rule1` will be affected by the first CSS rule (even though only the first such element should be), and any `<span>` with the same ID will similarly be affected by the second rule.

The long and the short of this subject is: Even if it seems to work, avoid duplicating IDs and make good use of classes (see the following section).

Using Classes

More often than not you'll find classes to be a more useful way to reference elements than via ID. This is because a class can apply to more than one element and so, once you have decided what parts will appear in a document, you can simply apply classes to these parts and all elements that are incorporated in them will display in the same way.

For example, in the previous section, the IDs that were assigned could just as well have been classes. In which case the HTML might look like this:

```
<div class='mainphoto'>
  <img src='picture.jpg'>
  <div class='caption'>Fishing boat at the beach</div>
</div>
```

And the CSS like this:

```
.mainphoto {
  width      :320px;
  background:#eee;
  padding    :20px 20px 2px 20px;
  border     :1px solid #888;
}
.caption {
  font-style:italic;
  text-align:center;
}
```

The result of this is identical to Figure 3-1, but it has the benefit that you can now reuse these class names with multiple photos on a page. You could even extend this code by supplying a class name to the photo, like this:

```
<img class='photo' src='picture.jpg'>
```

And add a new rule to restyle the new class (in this case to add a box shadow) like this (as shown in Figure 3-4):

```
.photo {
  margin-bottom:4px;
  box-shadow    :3px 3px 3px #888;
}
```

By the way, have you spotted the problem in the second example yet? Well, the first example was designed for a specific image that has a width of 320 pixels, and therefore a value of 320px was specified for the width of the <div>. This would be fine when applied to a class if all images are going to be exactly that width, but that's probably unlikely, and anyway is a rigid requirement to implement. It's far better to be flexible and allow for different image widths by replacing this rule:

```
width:320px;
```

with this one:

```
float:left;
```

You'll learn more about the float property later on, but all you need to know for now is that by floating an object you are choosing to allow it to be moveable. In the case of the <div>, instead of encompassing the entire width of the parent object

FIGURE 3-4   Adding a box shadow to the image

(which it does by default), the `float` property causes it to reduce its width to that of whatever it contains. It does this because otherwise (already being the width of the parent) it would be impossible for the object to move left or right by any amount.

The result displays identically to Figure 3-4 and all you need to do is ensure that you choose the correct value for `float` (such as `left` or `right`) that you want, and/or limit the width of the parent object.

Assigning Multiple Classes

In CSS you may assign as many classes as you like to an element by separating their names with spaces. For example, the following is quite legal:

```
<p class='content header news'>
```

Each of these class names can have a different purpose and they are not exclusive to each other. In this example perhaps `content` is used for the general styling of all content on a site, so this might affect the font family used. The `header` class might be used for headings and could set the font size and possibly its weight too. And the `news` class might incorporate a flash or other feature somewhere in the element to indicate that it contains news.

It is, of course, entirely up to you as to what your classes represent, but if you can, divide them into different types; then, instead of creating lots of different classes, such as `content-header`, `content-header-news`, `content-news`, `header-news`, and so on, you just design simpler classes and combine them at the point of use in a single `class` attribute, separated by spaces.

Accessing IDs and Classes with JavaScript

This isn't a book on JavaScript. However, it is so closely integrated with the Document Object Model (DOM) and CSS that it's important to show you how to access CSS properties from JavaScript.

If you don't use JavaScript, you can skip this section and move on to the following lesson, as the rest of this lesson focuses only on integrating JavaScript with CSS and the DOM.

To gain access to an element in JavaScript, you must call the getElementById() function on the current document, supplying the name of the element's ID as an argument, like this:

```
myobject = document.getElementById('idname')
```

The O() Function

The above line of code can be a lot to type in each time, however, so in the accompanying archive of example files (at *20lessons.com*), I have included a JavaScript file called *mainfunctions.js*, which includes the following O() function for far easier access to HTML elements:

```
function O(i)
{
  return typeof i == 'object' ? i : document.getElementById(i)
}
```

If you load in these functions at the start of a web document (preferably in the <head> section) as follows, you'll then be able to call on them whenever needed:

```
<script src='mainfunctions.js'></script>
```

Now you can replace the earlier rather long command with the following (where O stands for Object):

```
myobject = O('idname')
```

Or, to change the inner HTML of an object (for example) from JavaScript, you could use:

```
O('idname').innerHTML = 'Replacement HTML'
```

Or you could change an object created using the O() function, like this:

```
Myobject           = O('idname')
Myobject.innerHTML = 'Replacement HTML'
```

The S() Function

To allow quick access to the CSS styles of an element, the *mainfunctions.js* file also contains the function S() (where S stands for Style), which looks like this:

```
function S(i)
{
  return O(i).style
}
```

What the function does is simply append the style property to the object returned by a call to O(), so that now instead of using the following to set the text color of idname to blue:

```
O('idname').style.color = 'blue'
```

you can use this shorter code:

```
S('idname').color = 'blue'
```

The C() Function

Finally there's a function called C() (where C stands for Class), which you can call to return an array of objects for all elements that use the class name supplied to the function. It looks like this:

```
function C(i)
{
  return document.getElementsByClassName(i)
}
```

This code tests both for an element having a class name as its full class name property, and whether the class name is mentioned as one of a group of class names assigned to an element. So, for example, to return an array of objects representing all elements that use the class name heading2, you could call the function this way:

```
objarray = C('heading2')
```

You can then iterate through objarray[] just as you would through any array in JavaScript. For example, objarray.length will contain the number of elements returned by the call, objarray[0] will contain the first object, objarray[1] the second, and so on.

Using Hyphenated Property Names

A number of CSS property names are hyphenated (such as font-size or background-color). In JavaScript the hyphen is a reserved operator (for subtraction) so you cannot use them. Instead, you take the character following each hyphen and capitalize that character, and then you drop the hyphen.

Therefore, the property `font-size` becomes `fontSize` and `background-color` becomes `backgroundColor`, and so on, and they can be accessed in these ways (from longer to shorter):

```
document.getElementById('idname').style.fontSize = '24pt'
O('idname').style.fontSize = '24pt'
S('idname').fontSize = '24pt'
```

Or you can keep the property names as they are and use JavaScript's `setAttribute()` function like this:

```
O('idname').setAttribute('style', 'font-size:24pt')
```

Remember that if you are using `setAttribute()` it must be applied to an object (or the result of calling the `O()` function), and cannot be used on the `S()` function.

The following HTML (saved as *testfunctions.htm* in the accompanying archive) puts these three functions through their paces:

```
<div id='div1'>This is div1</div>
<div id='div2'>This is div2</div>
Plain, <span class='i'>italic</span>,
plain, <span class='i'>italic</span>,
plain, <span class='i'>italic</span>

<script>
  O('div1').innerHTML  = 'I am replacement HTML (view source)'
  S('div2').fontWeight = 'bold'
  obj = C(''); for (i in obj) S(obj[i]).fontStyle = 'italic'
</script>
```

The result of loading this example into a browser is shown in Figure 3-5. The first line had its inner HTML changed using the `O()` function. The second line was emboldened using the `S()` function. The third line had all instances of the word `italic` styled in italics using the `C()` function.

Why Use JavaScript?

Therefore, why would you alter CSS styles using JavaScript when you can do so from the `<style>` section of an HTML document or from an external style sheet? Well, the main reason is to let you create dynamic changes in a document after it has loaded. Some of these effects can be done through CSS using its built-in mouse hover features and so on, but for more sophisticated results you need JavaScript to access CSS properties in response to user interaction.

FIGURE 3-5   These CSS attributes have been modified using JavaScript.

Summary

This lesson has brought you up-to-speed on using IDs and classes both from the `<style>` section of a document and from external style sheets, and even from JavaScript. In Lesson 4 we move on to looking at the CSS selectors you can use to manipulate objects by ID and class.

Self-Test Questions

Using these questions, test how much you have learned in this lesson. If you don't know an answer, go back and reread the relevant section until your knowledge is complete. You can find the answers in the appendix.

1. What is the purpose of IDs in HTML and CSS?

2. What is the purpose of classes in CSS?

3. Can you reuse IDs in a similar manner to classes?

4. Which property can be used to make elements collapse to their contents' width and then line up horizontally with other elements?

5. Which CSS property enables the addition of a border to an element?

6. Which property lets you change the background color of an element?

7. With which property can you set the width of an element?

8. With which property can you set the style of text to italic?

9. How can you center text within an element?

10. How can you apply a shadow to an element?

Accessing Selectors

To view the accompanying video for this lesson, please visit mhprofessional.com/nixoncss/.

The means by which you access one or more elements is called *selection*, and the part of a CSS rule that does this is known as a *selector*. As you might expect, there are many different varieties of selector.

For example, you can select by the type of element to be styled (such as `<p>`, `<div>`, `<img>`, and so on), by whether an element is contained within another (is descendant), by descendant elements that are direct children (and not grandchildren, for example), by IDs and classes, by the attributes given to an element (such as the `target` attribute in a link), universally (matching anything and everything), and even in groups (where a rule applies to more than one target).

In fact, CSS is so well thought-out that whatever you wish to style, and in whatever relationship to other elements, you have the selectors you need to accomplish the result you desire. What you will learn in this lesson will become the fundamental knowledge you'll be using when developing using CSS.

The Type Selector

The type selector works on types of HTML elements such as `<p>` or `<i>`. For example, the following rule will ensure that all text within `<p>` and `</p>` tags is fully justified:

```
p { text-align:justify; }
```

You supply the name of the element (without the angle brackets that enclose it in HTML), and then place one or more rules following it (within a pair of curly braces). Therefore, you can also style the border of all `<img>` elements, for example, with the following rule:

```
img { border:1px solid #444; }
```

Or you could change the font size of all `<h1>` text like this:

```
h1 { font-size:26pt; }
```

The Descendant Selector

Descendant selectors let you apply styles to elements that are contained within other elements. For example, the following rule sets all text within `<b>` elements to red, but only if that text occurs within a `<p>` element (like this HTML: `<p><b>Hello</b> there</p>`):

```
p b { color:red; }
```

Descendant selectors can continue nesting indefinitely, so the following is a perfectly valid rule to make the text blue when it appears within bold text, that is inside a list element within an unordered list (like this HTML: `<ul><li><b>List item</b></li></ul>`, but not the following as the list is in an `<ol>` element: `<ol><li><b>List item</b></li></ol>`):

```
ul li b { color:blue; }
```

The Child Selector

The child selector is similar to the descendant selector but is more constraining about when the style will be applied by selecting only those elements that are direct children of another element. For example, the following rule uses a previously discussed descendant selector, which will change any bold text within a paragraph to red, even if the bold text is itself within italics (like this `<p><i><b>Hello</b> there</i></p>`):

```
p b { color:red; }
```

In this instance the word `Hello` displays in red. However, when this more general type of behavior is not required, a child selector can be used to narrow the scope of the selector. Therefore, the following child selector rule will set bold text to red *only* if the element is a *direct* child of a paragraph and is not itself contained within another element:

```
p > b { color:red; }
```

Now the word `Hello` will not change color because `<b>` is not a direct child of the paragraph (there is an `<i>` element enclosing it so `<b>` is a direct child of `<i>`, not of `<p>`).

The ID Selector

If you give an element an ID name (like this: `<div id='mydiv'>`), you can directly access it from CSS in the following way, which changes all the text in the `<div>` to italic:

```
#mydiv { font-style:italic; }
```

IDs are for working with sections of a document that will only appear once. For example, perhaps you have a ticker widget on every stock news page for a website about stocks and shares. It would make sense to identify this widget by ID to uniquely address it (from JavaScript as well as CSS).

IDs are especially necessary when you add dynamic functionality to a web page such as drag and drop, or certain mouseover effects, and so on. In which case you'll want to know exactly which element is being dragged at any one time.

Narrowing ID Scope

You can narrow the scope of action of an ID by specifying the types of elements to which it should apply. For example, the following rule applies the setting only to paragraphs that use the ID `myid`:

```
p#myid { font-weight:bold; }
```

In this example only paragraphs using the ID `myid` (like this: `<p id='myid'>`) will receive the new property value. Any other element types that may try to use the ID (such as `<div id='myid'>`) will be ignored.

Remember, also, that the ID should be applied only to a single element.

The Class Selector

When there are a number of elements in a page that you want to share the same styling, you can assign them all the same class name (like this: `<span class='myclass'>`) and then create a single rule to modify all those elements at once, as in the following rule, which creates a 10 pixel left margin offset for all elements using the class:

```
.myclass { margin-left:10px; }
```

In modern browsers HTML elements may also use more than one class by separating them with spaces, like this: `<span class='thisclass thatclass otherclass'>`. Older browsers only allow a single class.

Generally you should always use classes in your CSS and only apply ID rules in cases where a class will not work (such as where JavaScript also needs access to an element). That way you can be sure your code will be as bug-free as possible, more web standards compliant, and more likely to validate.

What's more, HTML and CSS written with classes is much easier to reuse because you can often simply use your classes again (possibly in conjunction with another class to modify it) as you extend your web pages.

Narrowing Class Scope

You can narrow the scope of action of a class by specifying the types of elements to which it should apply. For example, the following rule applies the setting only to paragraphs that use the class main:

```
p.main { text-indent:30px; }
```

In this example only paragraphs using the class main (like this: <p class='main'>) will receive the new style. Any other element types that may try to use the class (such as <div class='main'>) will be ignored.

The Attribute Selector

Many HTML tags support attributes, and using this type of selector can save you from having to use IDs and classes for referencing them. For example, you can directly reference attributes in the following manner, which sets all elements with the attribute type='submit' to a width of 100 pixels:

```
[type='submit'] { width:100px; }
```

If you wish to narrow down the scope of the selector to, for example, only form input elements with type='submit', you could use the following rule instead:

```
form input[type='submit'] { width:100px; }
```

 Attribute selectors also work on IDs and classes so that, for example, [class='classname'] performs in the same way as the class selector .classname. Likewise, [id='idname'] is equivalent to using the ID selector #idname. However, it's generally better to simply use ID and class names.

The Universal Selector

The wildcard or universal selector matches any element, so the following rule will make a complete mess of a document by giving a green border to all of its elements:

```
* { border:1px solid green; }
```

It's therefore unlikely that you will use the * on its own, but as part of a compound rule it can be very powerful. For example, the following rule will apply the same styling as above, but only to all paragraphs that are sub-elements (descendants) of the element with the ID boxout, and only as long as they are not direct children:

```
#boxout * p {border:1px solid green; }
```

Let's look at what's going on here. The first selector following #boxout is a * symbol, and so it refers to any element within the boxout object. The following p selector then narrows down the selection focus by changing the selector to apply only to paragraphs (as defined by the p) that are descendants of elements returned by the * selector. Therefore, this CSS rule performs the following actions (in which I use the terms object and element interchangeably:

1. Find the object with the ID of boxout.

2. Find all sub-elements (descendants) of the object returned in step 1.

3. Find all p sub-elements of the objects returned in step 2 and, because this is the final selector in the group, also find all p sub- and sub-sub-elements (and so on) of the objects returned in step 2.

4. Apply the styles within the { and } characters to the objects returned in step 3.

The net result of this is that the green border is applied only to paragraphs that are grandchildren (or grand-grandchildren, and so on) of the main element.

Selecting by Group

In CSS it is possible to apply a declaration block to more than one element, class, or any other type of selector at the same time by separating the selectors with commas. Therefore, for example, the following rule will place a dotted orange line underneath all paragraphs, the element with the ID of idname, and all elements using the class classname:

```
p, #idname, .classname {
  border-bottom:1px dotted orange;
}
```

Note Remember that to group selectors together, you must separate them from each other with commas. If you forget the commas, the rules will become descendant instead of group and you won't get the results you expect.

Figure 4-1 (which was created using the *selectors.htm* file in the accompany archive of example files) shows examples of simple HTML elements, the rules that are being applied to them, the selector types, and the result of applying each rule.

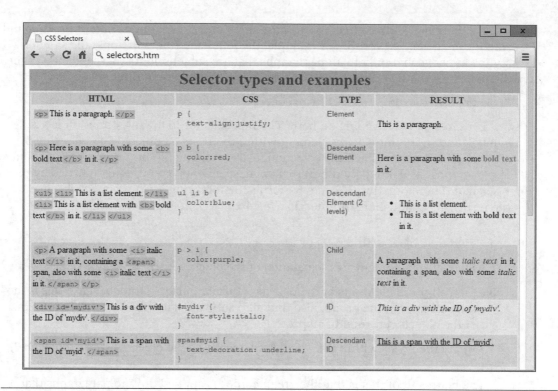

FIGURE 4-1 Example HTML styled with CSS, and the result of applying each rule

You may wish to load this file into your browser and scroll through the various examples and rules, comparing them with the results in the right-hand column.

For JavaScript Programmers

If you don't program with JavaScript, you can skip this section (don't worry; there won't be any questions about it at the end) and move on to the summary. Otherwise stick with me and I'll explain a few interesting details about the *selectors.htm* example and how it works.

Therefore, let's go through the document a section at a time, starting from the beginning:

```
<!DOCTYPE html>
<html>
  <head>
    <title>CSS Selectors</title>
    <style></style>
    <style>
      .tag {
        font-family     : monospace;
```

```
        font-size      :80%;
        color          :#a33;
        background     :#ada;
        margin         :0px 2px;
        padding        :0px 1px;
      }
      .rule {
        font-family    : monospace;
        font-size      :90%;
        color          :#80f;
      }
      .type {
        font-family    :arial;
        font-size      :10pt;
        color          :#933;
      }
      table {
        background     :#fee;
        border         :1px solid #ca8;
        border-spacing :3px;
      }
      caption {
        background     :#ca8;
        color          :#840;
        font-weight    :bold;
        font-size      :22pt;
        padding-bottom :5px;
      }
      td {
        padding        :3px;
      }
      th {
        color          :#440;
      }
      tr:nth-child(odd) {
        background-color:#edc;
      }
      tr:nth-child(even) {
        background-color:#fed;
      }
    </style>
```

This document is fairly standard in that it starts with a `<!DOCTYPE html>` declaration, and features an `<html>` and `<head>` tag, followed by a `<title>` element. But then there's an empty `<style></style>` pair of tags, which *is* unusual. This is here because the JavaScript will later fill that style section with some rules.

Next there's the set of CSS rules used by the document to style the table—all straightforward stuff, with some rule types you've already seen and some you haven't. We will get to all the rules in this book so bite your tongue and hold on to any questions—they will be answered. Although if you are curious about the final two rules (`tr:nth-child()`), they are how the alternating colors are achieved for the table rows.

Next, there's a large section of JavaScript in a `<script>` element, which I'll get to in just a moment. First though I want to show you the end of the document from the closing `</head>` tag onward:

```
  </head>
  <body></body>
</html>
```

It's not a lot, is it? That's because the `<body>` of the document is empty. Again, this is because the JavaScript will take care of populating it. Speaking of which, let's take a look at the programming behind this example that does just that.

Inside the `<script>` tags all the JavaScript is enclosed within the following structure:

```
window.onload = function()
{
  // The code goes here
}
```

The reason for this is that the JavaScript is in the `<head>` section of the document and it, therefore, could end up being started too early (before the document is ready), resulting in errors, or even nothing at all being displayed (because the `<body>` is empty and can only be created using the JavaScript). Therefore, by placing all of the instructions inside an `onload` event handler for the current `window`, the instructions will only be executed once the document is fully loaded and ready to run.

Therefore, let's now look at the first instruction:

```
examples =
[
  "<p>This is a paragraph.</p>",
  "<p>Here is a paragraph with some <b>bold text</b> in it.</p>",
  "<ul><li>This is a list element.</li><li>This is a list element with" +
    " <b>bold text</b> in it.</li></ul>",
  "<p>A paragraph with some <i>italic text</i> in it, containing a"       +
    " <span>span, also with some <i>italic text</i> in it.</span></p>",
  "<div id='mydiv'>This is a div with the ID of 'mydiv'.</div>",
  "<span id='myid'>This is a span with the ID of 'myid'.</span>",
  "<div id='myid'>This is a div with the ID of 'myid.'</div>",
  "<p class='myclass'>This is a paragraph using a class named"            +
    " 'myclass'.</p>",
  "<p class='main'>A paragraph using a class named 'main'.</p>",
  "<input type='submit' value='A submit button not in a form'>",
```

```
    "<form><input type='submit' value='A submit button in a form'></form>",
    "<div class='boxout'>A div using a class named 'boxout'. <span>A"     +
      " span within the 'boxout' div.</span> <span>Another span within"   +
      " the 'boxout' div, containing another <span>span within it</span>" +
      "</span></div>",
    "<div class='classname'>A div using a class named 'classname'.</div>"
]
```

This populates a new array called `examples[]` with 13 pieces of HTML, one for each of the rows in the table. This HTML will later be placed into the table in two different ways (once as HTML and once as what the HTML looks like after the CSS rules are applied).

Next comes code that populates a new array called `rules[]` with the matching CSS rules (one for each of the HTML examples):

```
rules =
[
    "p                       { text-align:justify;         }",
    "p b                     { color:red;                  }",
    "ul li b                 { color:blue;                 }",
    "p > i                   { color:purple;               }",
    "#mydiv                  { font-style:italic;          }",
    "span#myid               { text-decoration: underline;    }",
    "div#myid                { text-decoration: line-through; }",
    ".myclass                { margin-left:30px;           }",
    "p.main                  { text-indent:60px;           }",
    "[type='submit']         { color:blue;                 }",
    "form input[type='submit'] { color:red;                }",
    ".boxout * span          { border:1px solid green;     }",
    ".classname, #idname     { background:lightgreen;      }"
]
```

I've made liberal use of whitespace here to clearly lay out each rule and show what it does. CSS isn't bothered by extra whitespace, though—it simply treats it all as a single space.

Each of these CSS rules uses a different selector type, so next the new array `types[]` is populated with each of these types:

```
types =
[
    'Element',
    'Descendant Element',
    'Descendant Element (2 levels)',
    'Child',
    'ID',
    'Descendant ID',
    'Descendant ID',
    'Class',
```

```
'Descendant Class',
'Attribute',
'Descendant Attribute',
'Descendant Universal',
'Group'
]
```

Finally two more objects are created:

```
styles = document.styleSheets[0]
output = "<table><caption>Selector types and examples</caption>" +
        "<tr><th>HTML</th><th>CSS</th><th>TYPE</th><th>RESULT</th></tr>"
```

The object `styles` is set to reference the first `<style>` element in the document, so that each of the example rules can later be inserted into the object. It does this by referencing `document.styleSheets[0]`. The value 0 ensures that the first `<style>` section is accessed.

The string `output` is then set to the HTML required to build the start of a `<table>` element. It includes a caption and the four column headings. This will be later inserted into the `<body>` section of the document.

Next, there's a `for()` loop that iterates through each of the HTML examples in the `examples` array one at a time, setting the numeric variable `i` to point to element 0, then element 1, and so on until all have been processed:

```
for (i in examples)
{
```

Within this loop the string variable `text` is populated with the contents of each example, but with all the tags highlighted by placing them in a `<span>` section that has a CSS rule already applied to it to change the background color and other properties:

```
text = examples[i].replace(/>/gi,    "&gt;")
text =           text.replace(/</gi,    "<span class='tag'>&lt;")
text =           text.replace(/&gt;/gi, "&gt;</span><wbr>")
```

The code works by replacing all > characters with > HTML entities. Then all < characters are replaced with `<span class='tag'>` followed by the < entity. Finally, to close the `<span>` elements, the > tags that were just replaced have `</span>` appended to them.

Note Note the use of the `<wbr>` tag immediately following the closing `</span>` tags. This element is invisible in the browser but allows a line break to be added for formatting purposes if required, which helps the lines wrap neatly in the left-hand column of the table. Without this tag, the tag name and following word will be joined together and processed as a single nonbreakable word by the HTML layout engine. For example, `</i>in` in the fourth row will break before the <, whereas breaking after the > is also acceptable and leaves less ragged formatting (also in the fourth row `<span>span` will otherwise break only before the < and not after the > as it does now).

Next, the CSS rule of the current element in the `rules[]` array is slightly modified for displaying in the table, by placing the rule on the line below the selector (with a `<br>` tag), followed by putting the closing curly brace on the line below that, with the end result being placed in the string `css`:

```
css   =    rules[i].replace(/{/,      "{<br> ")
css   =         css.replace(/}/,      "<br>}")
```

Then the `output` string (which was previous assigned HTML to start creating a table) has a row appended to it containing the example HTML in the first column, the CSS rule in the second, the selector type in the third, and the result of applying the rule in the fourth:

```
output += "<tr valign='top'><td width='250'>"  + text       +
          "</td><td class='rule' width='260'>" + css        +
          "</td><td width='80' class='type'>" + types[i]    +
          "</td><td width='250'>"              + examples[i] +
          '</td></tr>\n'
```

Last, in the loop, the rule in the current element of the `styles[]` array is inserted into the first `<style>` section of the document, and the loop code ends with a closing curly brace:

```
styles.insertRule(rules[i], styles.length)
}
```

With the array now processed by the loop, the inner HTML of the `<body>` section of the document is filled with the contents of the `output` string, which is the HTML that the code has assembled for displaying the finished table, and finished off with a final `</table>` tag:

```
document.body.innerHTML = output + '</table>'
```

Points of Interest

What is particularly interesting to note from the point of view of integrating JavaScript and CSS is the way that this example inserts CSS rules into a document using the `insertRule()` function. This may be something you'll have use for in a future project.

Other things to note include replacing `<` and `>` with `&lt;` and `&gt;` when you actually want to display those characters in a document (and not have them interpreted as being part of an HTML tag), and the fact that it is possible to construct the entire body section of a document from JavaScript should you have reason for so doing.

Oh, and not forgetting that, using JavaScript programs (such as this one) that are integrated tightly with CSS and the DOM, you may need to place your code within an `onload` event handler to ensure that all the CSS and other things you wish to access from JavaScript are actually ready when you come to call on them.

Summary

You now know how to apply all the various CSS selectors to your web pages. Whether you need to uniquely reference them by ID, in groups by class, by their attributes, or by their descendancy, or in any other way, you now have the tools you need to precisely style any HTML document. In Lesson 5 I'll explain the term *Cascade* in Cascading Style Sheets, and how it applies to selectors.

Self-Test Questions

Using these questions, test how much you have learned in this lesson. If you don't know an answer, go back and reread the relevant section until your knowledge is complete. You can find the answers in the appendix.

1. What is the type selector?

2. What is the descendant selector?

3. What is the child selector?

4. What is the ID selector?

5. What is the class selector?

6. How can you narrow the scope of ID and class selectors?

7. What is the attribute selector?

8. What is the equivalent attribute selector to the class selector `.classname`?

9. What is the universal selector?

10. How can you select groups of elements at a time?

Working with the Cascade

 To view the accompanying video for this lesson, please visit mhprofessional.com/nixoncss/.

One of the most fundamental things about CSS properties is that they cascade, which is why they are called Cascading Style Sheets. But what does this mean?

Cascading is a method used to resolve potential conflicts between the various types of style sheet a browser supports, and apply them in order of precedence by who created them, the method used to create the style, and types of properties selected.

Web browsers use a predefined order to determine which style has precedence and will therefore be used. They first look for all declarations that apply to an element, and which style sheet it came from. Author style sheets have the highest precedence, then user style sheets, and then the browser's default style sheets.

The more specific a selector is, the more precedence (also called specificity) it will get. For example, a style applied to a `<p>` element within a `<div>` element (for example, `div p { ... }`) will have a higher precedence than one just applied to a `<p>` element (for example, `p { ... }`). Web browsers also apply these rules by the order in which they were defined, so that newer rules have higher precedence than older ones, and rules in the document are given higher precedence than those in an included style sheet.

Style Sheet Creators

There are three main types of style sheet supported by all modern browsers. In order of precedence from high to low, they are as follows:

1. Those created by a document's author
2. Those created by the user
3. Those created by the browser

These three sets of style sheets are processed in reverse order. First, the defaults in the web browser are applied to the document. Without these defaults, web pages that don't use style sheets would look terrible. They include the font face, size and color, element spacing, table borders and spacing, and all the other reasonable standards a user would expect.

Next, if the user has created any user styles to use in preference to the standard ones, these are applied, replacing any of the browser's default styles that may conflict.

Last, any styles created by the current document's author are then applied, replacing any that have been created either as browser defaults or by the user.

Style Sheet Methods

Style sheets can be created in three ways or methods. In high to low order of precedence, they are as follows:

1. As inline styles

2. In an embedded style sheet

3. As an external style sheet

Again, these methods of style sheet creation are applied in reverse order of precedence. Therefore, all external style sheets are processed first, and their styles are applied to the document.

Next, any embedded styles (within `<style>` ... `</style>` tags) are processed, and any that conflict with external rules are given precedence and will override them.

Last, any styles applied directly to an element as an inline style (such as `<div style='color:red;'>`) are given the highest precedence and will override all previously assigned properties.

Style Sheet Selectors

There are three ways of selecting elements to be styled. Going from highest to lowest order of precedence, they are as follows:

1. Referencing by individual ID

2. Referencing by class or attribute

3. Referencing by element tag types (such as `<p>` or `<b>`)

When you write CSS, you can assign your selectors in any order you like, but due to the many types of selector and selector combinations, this is not necessarily the order in which the styles will be applied. Therefore, the browser has to make sense of the CSS you supply to it, and decide which rules are more important than others before applying them. This is done by calculating the specificity of selectors by ordering each from the widest to narrowest scope of action.

Calculating Specificity

The specificity of a selector is calculated by creating three-part numbers based on the selector components in the numbered list in the previous section. These compound numbers start off looking like [0:0:0]. When a selector is processed, each selector that has an ID component increments the first number by 1, so that the compound number would become [1:0:0]. Let's say that there is one ID reference in a particular selector, so the compound number becomes [1:0:0].

Then the number of class and attribute components in the selector is placed in the second part of the compound number. Let's say there are two of them, and so the number becomes [1:2:0].

Finally, all selector components that reference element tags are counted, and this number is placed in the last part of the compound number. Let's say there is one, so the final compound number becomes [1:2:1], which is all that is needed to compare this selector's specificity with any another.

Let's examine an example rule that would fulfill this specificity:

```
#content .main .heading p { font-weight:bold; }
```

Here, this rule refers to a section in the current document referred to by the ID of content. Within this section any part that is in a <p> element, which is itself within an element that uses the class heading and which is inside an element that uses the class main, is referenced by the rule.

As you can imagine, there might be lots of <p> tags in a large article, and there could be many other descendant rules like this that reference <p> elements. Therefore, the cascade is applied to give precedence to any that conflict. For instance, consider this rule:

```
#content #section1 .main .heading p { font-weight:bold; }
```

Now the compound number looks like [2:2:1] (which is greater), and so this new rule must take precedence over the preceding one (because it has a higher specificity). In the same way, even though the following rule also contains five selector components, it will lose out to the selector with two IDs in it, because its compound number is [1:2:2] (and 122 is less than 221):

```
#content .main .heading p span { font-weight:bold; }
```

But, because 122 is greater than 121, it will have higher precedence than the first example rule in this section.

Also, the specificity isn't affected by the order in which the components appear in a selector; the compound number created from that selector will still be the same, so all of these have the same precedence (of [1:2:1]):

```
#content .main .heading p { font-weight:bold; }
.heading p #content .main { font-weight:bold; }
.main #content .heading p { font-weight:bold; }
p .heading .main #content { font-weight:bold; }
```

Note If this precedence calculation sounds rather complicated, you'll be pleased to know that in most cases you can usually get by with a rule of thumb that goes: "In general, the more selector components in a selector the more specific the selector is likely to be." But remember that this is only a very rough rule because, for instance, two ID components beat three class components, which beats four type components (a compound number of [2:0:0] versus one of [0:3:0] versus one of [0:0:4], in which the decimal equivalent of 200 is greater than 30, which is itself greater than 4).

When Rules Are Particularly Important

As I said, in a tie the most recently processed rules take precedence, but you can force an earlier rule to a higher precedence with the !important tag, like this:

```
p { font-weight:bold !important; }
```

When you do this, all previous settings to that property (including other !important rules) are overridden and any future settings will be ignored. For example, the second of the two following rules would normally take precedence, but the !important setting gives the first one priority:

```
h1 { font-style:italic !important; }
h1 { font-style:normal;          }
```

The following example (*important.htm* in the accompanying archive) illustrates this, as shown in Figure 5-1. If you load this example into a browser, the heading will display in italic (and not normal):

```
<!DOCTYPE html>
<html>
  <head>
    <title>The !important tag</title>
    <style>
      h1   { font-style :italic !important;      }
      h1   { font-style :normal;                 }
```

```
        body { font-size  :130%;                        }
        .tag { font-family:monospace; font-size:90%; }
    </style>
  </head>
  <body>
    <h1>This is a heading</h1>

    <p>Even though the second rule for the <span
      class='tag'>&lt;h1&gt;</span> tag in the following CSS
      rules sets the heading to normal and would normally take
      precedence due to be the newest rule...</p>

    <pre>
      h1 { font-style:italic !important; }
      h1 { font-style:normal;            }</pre>

    <p>...the preceding rule that sets it to italic uses the
      <span class='tag'>!important</span> tag, and so it
      overrides subsequent rules.</p>
  </body>
</html>
```

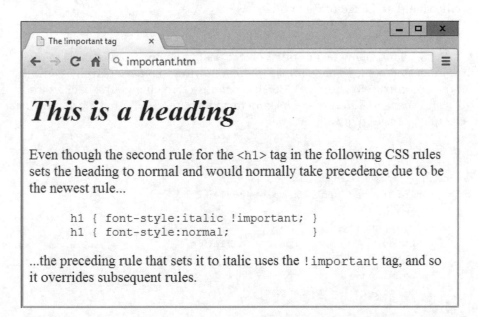

FIGURE 5-1   Using the `!important` keyword to enforce a rule's precedence

If at all possible, you should try to steer clear of this feature because it breaks the cascade and also makes it infuriatingly difficult to track down seemingly impossible bugs, until you find an !important lurking somewhere. Of course, you may not have a choice when maintaining legacy websites, but I have yet to be convinced there is ever a need to use this feature on a properly designed web page—take my advice and you'll avoid potential headaches in the future. That said, though, the !important keyword can be successfully employed locally on a browser's user style sheets, to specify default browser styles to assist visually impaired users, for example, by always ensuring the text is large enough for them to read.

So What Are Divs and Spans Anyway?

Divs and spans are types of containers used for organizing HTML content, and they have different qualities. By default, a div has infinite width (at least to the browser edge) that can be seen by applying a border to one, like this:

```
<div style='border:1px solid green;'>Hello</div>
```

A span, however, is only as wide as the text it contains. Therefore, the following line of HTML shows the border only around the word Hello, and it does not extend to the right-hand edge of the browser.

```
<span style='border:1px solid green;'>Hello</span>
```

Also, spans follow text or other objects as they wrap around and can therefore have a complicated border. For example, in the following web page (saved as *divandspan.htm* in the accompanying archive), CSS has been used to change the backgrounds of all divs and spans to different colors, and to add a border to both, before creating a few example spans and divs:

```
<!DOCTYPE html>
<html>
  <head>
    <title>Div and span example</title>
    <style>
      div, span {
        border          :1px solid black;
        color           :#ee0;
        padding         :5px;
        margin          :20px 0;
      }
      div {
        background-color:#fa8;
      }
```

```
      span {
        background-color:#8af;
      }
      body {
        font-family     :Arial;
        font-size       :18pt;
        font-weight     :bold;
      }
    </style>
  </head>
  <body>
    <p>Drag the left or right border of your browser inwards
    and watch the elements below as you do so</p>

    <div>A div element</div>
    Unstyled text
    <div>A div element</div>

    <span>A span element</span>
    Unstyled text
    <span>A span element</span>

    <div>A div element - A div element - A div element -
    A div element - A div element - A div element - </div>

    <span>A span element - A span element - A span element -
    A span element - A span element - A span element - </span>
  </body>
</html>
```

Figure 5-2 shows what this page looks like in a web browser. It clearly shows how divs extend to the right-hand edge of a browser and force following content to appear at the start of the first available position below them.

The figure also shows how spans keep themselves to themselves and only take up the space required to hold their contents, without forcing following content to appear below them.

For example, in the bottom two examples of the figure, you can also see that when divs wrap around the screen edge, they retain a rectangular shape, whereas spans simply follow the flow of the text (or other contents) within them.

 Because <div> tags can only be rectangular, they are better suited for containing objects such as images, boxouts, quotations, and so on, while <span> tags are best used for holding text or other types of content that should be placed one after another inline, and which should flow from one side to the other.

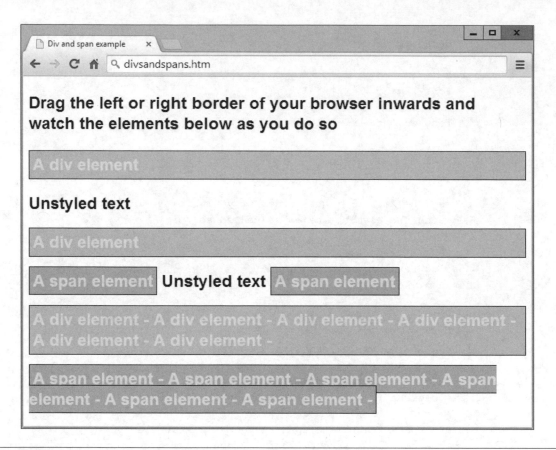

FIGURE 5-2 A variety of divs and spans of differing widths

Specifying Measurements

CSS supports an impressive range of different units of measurement, enabling you to tailor your web pages precisely to specific values, or by relative dimensions. The ones I generally use (and believe you will also find the most useful) are pixels, points, and percent.

Pixels

The size of a pixel varies according to the dimensions and resolution of the user's monitor. One pixel equals the width/height of a single dot on the screen, and so this measurement is best suited to monitors. For example:

```
.classname { margin:5px; }
```

Pixels are also the better-suited measurement for setting object dimensions and general layout of the elements of a web page.

Points

A point is equivalent in size to 1/72 of an inch. The measurement comes from a print design background and is best suited for that medium, but it is also commonly used on monitors. For example:

```
.classname { font-size:14pt; }
```

Points are best suited for setting the size of text and other related properties.

Inches

An inch is the equivalent of 72 points and is also a measurement type best suited for print. For example:

```
.classname { width:3in; }
```

Actually, I have never encountered any CSS that uses inches, but there must be websites somewhere that use them.

Centimeters

Centimeters are another unit of measurement best suited for print. One centimeter is a little over 28 points. For example:

```
.classname { height:2cm; }
```

I would be wary of using centimeters and millimeters because the result you see on the screen is entirely monitor-dependent. However, for print-only style sheets, they can be useful measurements.

Millimeters

A millimeter is 1/10th of a centimeter (or almost 3 points). Millimeters are another measure best suited to print. For example:

```
.classname { font-size:5mm; }
```

Picas

A pica is another print typographic measurement, which is equivalent to 12 points. For example:

```
.classname { font-size:1pc; }
```

Picas are best suited for extra large headline or other enlarged text.

Ems

One em is equal to the current font size and is therefore one of the more useful measurements for CSS because it is used to describe relative dimensions. For example:

```
.classname { font-size:2em; }
```

Ems are directly interchangeable with percent, in that one em is 100 percent.

Exs

An ex is also related to the current font size; it is equivalent to the height of a lowercase letter 'x.' This is a less popular unit of measurement that is most often used as a good approximation for helping to set the width of a box that will contain some text. Some designers think of the ex as being the height equivalent of using em units for width. For example:

```
.classname { width:20ex; }
```

Unless you have a clear reason for doing so, I recommend you generally avoid using this measurement because, when users enlarge or reduce the browser window contents (for example, by scrolling the mouse wheel while holding down the ALT key), any measurements set in values of ex will change at a greater rate—enlarged ex text gets much larger than the rest, while reduced ex text gets much smaller.

Percent

This unit is related to the em, in that 1 em is equivalent to 100 percent (when used on a font). When not relating to a font, this unit is relative to the size of the container of the property being accessed. For example:

```
.classname { height:120%; }
```

Once you have chosen your initial font and other element sizes, working in percent is often the best way to later modify these properties because all changes will be relative to the initial values.

Figure 5-3, created using the following (available as *measurements.htm* in the accompanying archive), shows each of these measurement types in turn being used to display text in almost identical sizes:

```
<!DOCTYPE html>
<html>
  <head>
    <title>Measurements</title>
    <style>
      p { margin:0; }
    </style>
```

```
  </head>
  <body>
    <p style='font-size:31px;'  >My size is 31 pixels       </p>
    <p style='font-size:24pt;'  >My size is 24 points       </p>
    <p style='font-size:0.33in;'>My size is 0.33 inches     </p>
    <p style='font-size:0.85cm;'>My size is 0.85 centimeters</p>
    <p style='font-size:8.5mm;'  >My size is 8.5 millimeters </p>
    <p style='font-size:2pc;'    >My size is 2 picas         </p>
    <p style='font-size:2em;'    >My size is 2 ems           </p>
    <p style='font-size:4.5ex;'  >My size is 4.5 exs         </p>
    <p style='font-size:200%;'   >My size is 200 percent     </p>
  </body>
</html>
```

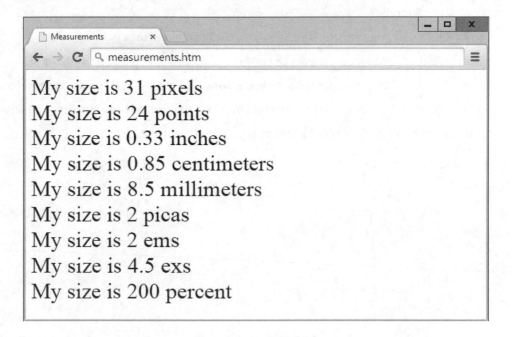

FIGURE 5-3 A selection of different measurements that display almost the same

Summary

In this lesson you have learned about the cascade, how to override the cascade when necessary using the !important keyword, and how to choose and specify exactly the measurements you need for the sizes and dimensions you require for the elements in your web pages. In Lesson 6, we'll move on to manipulating fonts with CSS, and handling typography in general.

Self-Test Questions

Using these questions, test how much you have learned in this lesson. If you don't know an answer, go back and reread the relevant section until your knowledge is complete. You can find the answers in the appendix.

1. What are the three types of style sheet?

2. What are the three methods of applying styles?

3. In what ways can elements be selected for styling?

4. What is a descendant selector?

5. In general, is a descendant selector more or less specific when it has more components?

6. How can you prevent later rules overriding the current one?

7. What is the biggest difference between a <div> and a <span> element?

8. Which is best suited for containing portions of text—a <div> or a <span> element?

9. Which measurement types are best suited for making relative property size changes?

10. Why is the CSS ex measurement type the odd-one out?

Selecting Fonts and Typography

 To view the accompanying video for this lesson, please visit mhprofessional.com/nixoncss/.

With CSS you can style fonts in a number of different ways using four main properties. These are the `font-family` property (previously known as the `face` attribute for the `font` HTML element), the `font-style` property, the `font-size` property, and the `font-weight` property.

You can also apply various types of decoration to fonts such as underlines, modify the spacing and alignment of text, the capitalization (or otherwise of text), and even the amount of indentation that should be applied.

Between these properties, you can use CSS to fine-tune the way text displays in your web pages, use different rules for different browsers or sizes (or types) of display, modify how a page looks when printed, enlarge and rearrange text for visually impaired users, and much more, all without having to change your source HTML—which is the whole point of CSS (the separation of content and layout).

Font Family

This property assigns the font family for use. It also lets you supply a list of font families in order of preference from left to right, so that styling can fall back gracefully when the browser doesn't have the preferred font family installed. For example, to set the default font for <p> elements you could use a CSS rule such as this:

```
p { font-family:Verdana, Arial, Helvetica, sans-serif; }
```

When a font family name is made up of two or more words, it is recommended that you enclose the name in quotation marks, as follows (Figure 6-1 shows both these sets of CSS rules being applied):

```
p { font-family:'Times New Roman', Georgia, serif; }
```

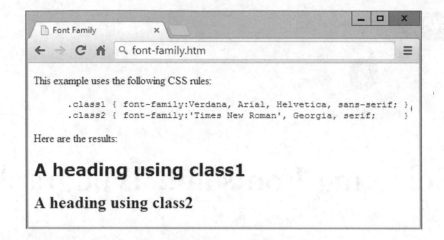

FIGURE 6-1 Selecting font families

 The idea behind recommending the use of quotes is to ensure that any punctuation or digits at the start of a word in a font family name will be properly processed by the browser. Without the quotes you would have to escape such characters, but if you use only alphabetic characters at the start of each word (almost always the case, anyway), then you can omit the quotes.

Generic Font Families

As you may have noticed in the final font family name supplied for the previous two examples, you can specify a generic name for a font family and let the browser choose the best font that matches from those it has available. For example, you can choose any of the following font family names, and a font such as (or similar to) the one listed by it in the comments will be applied:

```
p { font-family:serif;      } /* Times       */
p { font-family:sans-serif; } /* Arial       */
p { font-family:cursive;    } /* Comic Sans MS */
p { font-family:fantasy;    } /* Impact      */
p { font-family:monospace;  } /* Courier New  */
```

This lets you specify the font families you would prefer, and then supply a fallback for the browser to use if it doesn't have any of your preferred fonts available.

Actually, browsers will try to do this anyway, and if all fonts requested fail to match one the browser can display, it will try to find a similar one to those you have requested based on its knowledge of fonts. However, by assuming this task yourself, you make sure the browser will get it right.

Generic font family names are actually keywords and so they should never be placed in quotation marks.

The safest font families to use on a web page are those that should already be available to all web browsers and platforms, namely *Arial*, *Helvetica*, *Times New Roman*, *Times*, *Courier New*, and *Courier*. The *Verdana*, *Georgia*, *Comic Sans MS*, *Trebuchet MS*, *Arial Black*, and *Impact* fonts are safe for Mac and PC use, but may not be installed on other operating systems such as Linux.

There are also other less safe fonts such as *Palatino*, *Garamond*, *Bookman*, and *Avant Garde*, which are less widely available, so if you use any of these, make sure you offer a fallback to a safer font, to allow your web pages to degrade gracefully when a chosen font isn't available.

Font Style

With this property you can choose to display a font in one of three ways. The following rules create three classes (normal, italic, and oblique) that can be applied to elements to create these effects:

```css
.normal  { font-style:normal;  }
.italic  { font-style:italic;  }
.oblique { font-style:oblique; }
```

Here's an example that illustrates these rules in action:

```html
<!DOCTYPE html>
<html>
  <head>
    <title>Font Styles</title>
    <style>
      .italic  { font-style:italic;  }
      .oblique { font-style:oblique; }
      p { margin:0px; }
    </style>
  </head>
  <body>
    <p>Here are some CSS rules being applied to this page:</p>

    <pre>
      .italic  { font-style:italic;  }
      .oblique { font-style:oblique; }</pre>

    <p>Here is the result:</p><br>
```

```
    <p                 >Normal</p>
    <p class='italic' >Italic</p>
    <p class='oblique'>Oblique</p>
  </body>
</html>
```

When loaded into a browser, this example (saved as *font-style.htm* in the accompanying archive) displays as Figure 6-2.

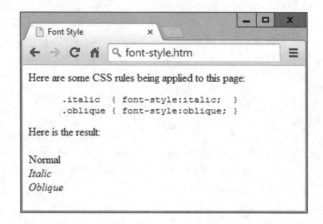

FIGURE 6-2   Changing font styles

 Have you noticed that the oblique setting seems to just display in italic? This is because italic fonts are usually extra fonts supplied as part of a family, and they are specially designed to look good when slanted. On the other hand, when you request an oblique font, you are asking the browser to slant a standard font in an oblique manner. The result will therefore often be the same (or very similar), but with the slight difference being that oblique fonts will not display any glyphs and may be a little less readable. The matter is further confused, though, in that fonts that do not come with an italic version, will display as oblique when you request italics.

Font Size

There are two ways you can change the size of text. These are by relative amounts, or by providing fixed values. A fixed setting looks like the following rule, which sets the default paragraph font size to 14 point:

```
p { font-size:14pt; }
```

Or, to work with the current default font size, and style various types of text such as headings relative to that size, you can work in percentages.

For example, to modify the six heading types, you might use CSS such as the following, in which the <h6> element starts off 10 percent bigger than the default, and then each greater size of heading element is set a further 20 percent larger than the previous one:

```
h6 { font-size:110%; }
h5 { font-size:130%; }
h4 { font-size:150%; }
h3 { font-size:170%; }
h2 { font-size:190%; }
h1 { font-size:210%; }
```

Figure 6-3 shows these font sizes as created using the following example (*font-size .htm* in the accompanying archive):

```
<!DOCTYPE html>
<html>
  <head>
    <title>Font Size</title>
    <style>
      h6 { font-size:110%; }
      h5 { font-size:130%; }
      h4 { font-size:150%; }
      h3 { font-size:170%; }
      h2 { font-size:190%; }
      h1 { font-size:210%; }
      p  { font-size:12pt; }
      p, h1, h2, h3, h4, h5, h6 { margin:0px; }
    </style>
  </head>
  <body>
    <p>Here are some CSS rules being applied to this page:</p>

    <pre>
      h6 { font-size:110%; }
      h5 { font-size:130%; }
      h4 { font-size:150%; }
      h3 { font-size:170%; }
      h2 { font-size:190%; }
      h1 { font-size:210%; }
      p  { font-size:12pt; }</pre>

    <p>Here is the result:</p><br>

    <h1>Heading 1</h1>
    <h2>Heading 2</h2>
    <h3>Heading 3</h3>
```

```
      <h4>Heading 4</h4>
      <h5>Heading 5</h5>
      <h6>Heading 6</h6>
      <p>Paragraph text</p>
   </body>
</html>
```

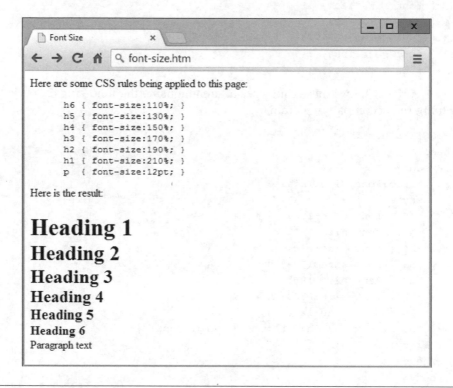

FIGURE 6-3   All heading sizes and the default paragraph size have been set.

Font Weight

This property specifies whether or not to display a font in bold by assigning values of either normal or bold, like this:

```
.bold { font-weight:bold; }
```

Here are the contents of *font-weight.htm*, which display as Figure 6-4:

```
<!DOCTYPE html>
<html>
  <head>
    <title>Font Weight</title>
    <style>
      .bold { font-weight:bold; }
```

```
          p { margin:0px; }
      </style>
   </head>
   <body>
      <p>Here is a CSS rule being applied to this page:</p>

      <pre>
        .bold { font-weight:bold; }</pre>

      <p>Here is the result:</p><br>

      <p            >Normal</p>
      <p class='bold'>Bold</p>
   </body>
</html>
```

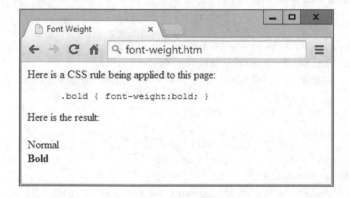

FIGURE 6-4   Applying a value to the **font-weight** property

Changing Text Styles

Whichever font you use, you can change the decoration, spacing, and alignment of text displayed with it. For example, to display in italics or bold, you use the font-style and font-weight properties, and to underline, you use the text-decoration property.

Text Decoration

You can use the text-decoration property to apply underline, line-through, overline, and blink effects to text. For example, the following rule creates a new class called overline that applies overlines to text. The weight of these lines will be the same as that of the font:

```
.overline { text-decoration:overline; }
```

In Figure 6-5 you can see a selection of font decorations as created using this example (*text-decoration.htm*):

```
<!DOCTYPE html>
<html>
  <head>
    <title>Text Decoration</title>
    <style>
      .overline  { text-decoration:overline;      }
      .underline { text-decoration:underline;     }
      .strikeout { text-decoration:line-through; }
      p { margin:0px; }
    </style>
  </head>
  <body>
    <p>Here are some CSS rules being applied to this page:</p>

    <pre>
      .overline  { text-decoration:overline;      }
      .underline { text-decoration:underline;     }
      .strikeout { text-decoration:line-through; }</pre>

    <p>Here is the result:</p><br>

    <p                  >Normal</p>
    <p class='overline' >Overline</p>
    <p class='underline'>Underline</p>
    <p class='strikeout'>Strikeout</p>
  </body>
</html>
```

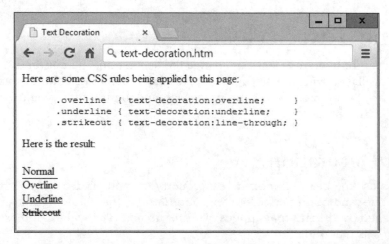

FIGURE 6-5 The decoration rules in use

Line, Word, and Letter Spacing

You can modify line, word, and letter spacing with properties available for each. For example, the following rule changes the line spacing for paragraphs by modifying the line-height property to be 50 percent larger, the word-spacing property is set to 10 pixels, and letter-spacing is set to 1 pixel:

```
p {
  line-height    :150%;
  word-spacing   :10px;
  letter-spacing:1px;
}
```

In Figure 6-6 you can see the result of enhancing the spacing of a quotation, created with the following example (*font-spacing.htm*):

```
<!DOCTYPE html>
<html>
  <head>
    <title>Font Spacing</title>
    <style>
      p            { line-height    :150%;
                     word-spacing   :10px;
                     letter-spacing:1px;          }
      .justify   { text-align     :justify;    }
      .uppercase { text-transform:uppercase;  }
      .indent    { text-indent    :20px;        }
    </style>
  </head>
  <body>
  Here are some CSS rules being applied to this page:<br>

    <pre>
      p            { line-height    :150%;
                     word-spacing   :10px;
                     letter-spacing:1px;          }
      .justify   { text-align     :justify;    }
      .uppercase { text-transform:uppercase;  }
      .indent    { text-indent    :20px;        }</pre>

  Here's the result:<br><br>

    <p class='justify indent'>
      <span class='uppercase'>I've missed more than</span> 9000 shots in
      my career. I've lost almost 300 games. 26 times I've been trusted
      to take the game winning shot and missed. I've failed over and
      over and over again in my life. And that is why I succeed.
```

```
        - Michael Jordan
     </p>
   </body>
</html>
```

FIGURE 6-6   Changing word and letter spacing and a variety of other text properties

 The `<p>` element in this example makes use of both the `justify` and the `indent` classes within a single `class` attribute assignment. Try loading this example into a browser and noting how the quote neatly reformats itself as you resize the width of the browser.

Horizontal Alignment

There are four types of text alignment available in CSS: `left`, `right`, `center`, and `justify`. In the following rule, default paragraph text is set to full justification:

```
p { text-align:justify; }
```

In Figure 6-6 the quotation has been set to fully right-justify with the `justify` value.

Managing Uppercase and Lowercase

The properties available for transforming the case of text include none, `capitalize`, `uppercase`, and `lowercase`. For example, the following rule creates a class called `toupper` that will ensure all text is displayed in upper case when it is used:

```
.toupper { text-transform:uppercase; }
```

In Figure 6-6 the first few words have been transformed into uppercase using this property.

Text Indenting

With the `text-indent` property, you can indent the first line of a block of text by an amount of your choosing. For example, the following rule indents the first line of every paragraph by 30 pixels, although a different unit of measurement (perhaps a percent increase) could also be applied:

```
p { text-indent:30px; }
```

In Figure 6-6 the quoted paragraph has also been indented using this property.

Summary

Having learned about basic font families, styles, spacing, alignment, and so on, you will now be fully proficient in making text display in the best possible way for the designs you are working to. In Lesson 7, we'll continue our exploration by looking at coloring and positioning text.

Self-Test Questions

Using these questions, test how much you have learned in this lesson. If you don't know an answer, go back and reread the relevant section until your knowledge is complete. You can find the answers in the appendix.

1. With which property can you change the family of font to display?
2. How can you set a font to display in italic?
3. How can you change the size a font displays at?
4. How can you make a font display in bold face?
5. What CSS would you use to choose the Helvetica font with a fallback of sans serif?
6. How can you underline text with CSS?

7. With which property can you change the vertical spacing of lines?

8. With which properties can you change word and letter spacing of a font?

9. How can you specify an indent for text?

10. What CSS declaration might you use to capitalize a section of text?

Manipulating Color and Position

 To view the accompanying video for this lesson, please visit mhprofessional.com/ nixoncss/.

Having mastered the styling of fonts and typography in general, in this lesson we'll take a look at what else can be done with text, such as changing its color, applying background gradient fills, and specifying where and how text should be positioned. Along the way, you'll also learn how to style other elements with color and positioning too, because many of the rules covered apply not just to text but to many other types of element as well.

You'll also learn how you can completely lift an element off the page (out of its in-line position) and locate it anywhere you like in its parent object, or even anywhere on (or off) the current browser window. This will show you the basics of how you can go about constructing dynamic effects using CSS—with nary a hint of JavaScript in sight.

Colors

Colors can be applied to the foreground and background of text and objects using the `color` and `background-color` properties (or by simply using the `background` property). These colors can be named colors (such as `black` or `white`), colors created from hexadecimal RGB strings (such as `#ffff00` or `#446688`), or colors created with the `rgb()` and `rgba()` CSS functions.

The main 16 color names defined by the W3C (*w3.org*) standards organization in HTML 4.01 include *aqua, black, blue, fuchsia, gray, green, lime, maroon, navy, olive, purple, red, silver, teal, white,* and *yellow.*

The following example uses a color name to set the text color for an object with the ID of `intro` to the color navy:

```
#intro { color:navy; }
```

You can also apply a color value to the background property, like this:

```
#intro { background:teal; }
```

Using long six hex digit color strings (#RRGGBB) now, in the following example, the foreground color of text in all divs is set to yellow (because on a computer display, hexadecimal levels of ff red, plus ff green, plus 00 blue creates the color yellow), by assigning a value to the color property:

```
div { color:#ffff00; }
```

In Figure 7-1, the top band shows the following background and color rules being applied to a div element, using a class with the name blueonyellow:

```
.blueonyellow { background:yellow; color:blue; }
```

FIGURE 7-1   A range of text and background colors, fills, and gradients

Using `rgb()`

If you don't wish to work in hexadecimal (base 16), you can specify your colors using numbers from 0 to 255 with the `rgb()` function, as in the following rule, which changes the background color of the current document to aqua (maximum green, plus maximum blue):

```
body { background:rgb(0, 255, 255); }
```

And you're not limited to just working in ranges of 256 levels per color, because you can also use percentages instead, with values from the lowest amount of each primary color through to the highest (from 0 to 100), like this (remembering to use the % sign for percentages):

```
body { background:rgb(58%, 95%, 74%); }
```

You can even use floating point values for much finer color control, like this:

```
body { background:rgb(23.4%, 67.6%, 15.5%); }
```

Short Color Strings

In CSS there is also a short form of the six digit hex string, in which only the first of each two byte pair of digits is used for each color. For example, instead of assigning the color #123456, you use the value #135, omitting the second hex digit from each pair.

This results in roughly the same color (#113355) and is most useful where exact color matches are not required. The difference between a six-digit and a three-digit color strings is that the former supports over 16 million different colors, while the latter supports just over 4,000 (in fact, one 4,096th the colors of the former).

Also, without losing color accuracy, wherever you intend to use a color such as #112233 (where each digit is repeated), it is the direct equivalent of, for example, #123 (because the repeated digits are implied by the shorter version) and, while you can use either string to create the exact same color, the shorter string saves memory and bandwidth and makes your CSS rules easier to read. In this book I use either type of color string according to the color required at the time, but prefer shorter strings if possible.

Gradients

As well as filling in backgrounds in a solid color, you can also apply a gradient, which will then automatically flow smoothly from one color to another (or more).

For example, here's a rule to display an orange gradient on the background of an element called object:

```
#object {
  background:linear-gradient(#fb0, #f50);
}
```

If you must cater to older browsers, you might choose to include a simple background color rule too, to display the average color across the gradient, making a pair of rules such as this:

```
#object {
  background:#f80;
  background:linear-gradient(#fb0, #f50);
}
```

The first declaration will be applied and then, if the browser understands gradients, it will swiftly be overwritten by the second one, which will replace it. If the browser doesn't understand gradients, then it will consider the second declaration invalid and will ignore it.

Linear Gradients

In its simplest form, a linear gradient requires only a start and end color, which it will then use to fill the element from top to bottom, graduating smoothly from the first to the last color, as shown at the top right of Figure 7-1.

 Please load the accompanying examples at *20lessons.com* into a browser to see the all the colors described in this book.

But you can actually have a lot more input into the appearance of a gradient by applying more colors. Each of these colors is called a color stop and by default all the colors you specify will be spaced equidistantly from each other. Therefore, you can create a sort of rainbow effect with CSS such as this:

```
#object {
  background:linear-gradient(
    red, orange, yellow, green, blue, indigo, violet);
}
```

The result is the second box down on the left of Figure 7-1, where all the colors have smoothly graduated from top to bottom and from red to violet.

But you don't have to just use vertical gradients because you can specify the direction of the gradient with an extra direction argument, such as the following (with the value to use highlighted in bold), which causes the gradient to flow from left to right, as shown in the second box down on the right of Figure 7-1.

```
#object {
  background:linear-gradient(
    90deg, red, orange, yellow, green, blue, indigo, violet);
}
```

The way to understand the direction argument is to think of it like a clock, with the 12 o'clock position being 0deg. The position of a number on the imaginary clock represents the destination of a gradient, which therefore *starts* at the opposite time location which, in the case of 0deg, is 6 o'clock. The value of 90deg therefore represents a position at 3 o'clock, which causes a left to right direction of gradient (starting at 9 o'clock).

Likewise 180deg represents the default direction of top to bottom (12 o'clock to 6 o'clock), and 270deg sets the direction to go from right to left (3 o'clock to 9 o'clock). You can also, of course, use all the other values in between for diagonal linear gradients.

Radial Gradients

In a similar manner to linear gradients, you can also create them radially, so that they flow out from a given point. For example, the following rule creates a green radial gradient, as shown in the third box down on the left of Figure 7-1:

```
#object {
  background:radial-gradient(#0a0, #0f0);
}
```

The gradient starts in the center of the element and then radiates outward, slowly changing from the first to the last color stop.

As with linear gradients, you may also use as many colors as you like, so the following creates a rainbow effect radial gradient, as shown in the third box down on the right of Figure 7-1.

```
#object {
  background:radial-gradient(
    red, orange, yellow, green, blue, indigo, violet);
}
```

The default type of radial fill is an ellipse, but you can change this to a circle by prepending to the list of color stop values like this (with the gradient type highlighted in bold):

```
#object { background:radial-gradient(
  circle, red, orange, yellow, green, blue, indigo, violet);
}
```

If you wish to define the width and height of the outer edge of a radial gradient, you can prepend a further argument containing two percentage values. The first sets the outer width and the second the outer height, like this:

```
#object { background:radial-gradient(
  80% 20%, circle, red, orange, yellow, green, blue, indigo, violet);
}
```

Controlling Color Stops

The way gradients have been implemented also allows you to change the position along the gradient at which each color should be placed. Therefore, for example, if you want to modify the rainbow effect so that the outer colors occupy less of the fill and the inner ones more, you could use a rule such as this (with the percentage positions highlighted in bold):

```
#object {
  background:linear-gradient(
    red 0%, orange 5%, yellow 25%, green 50%,
    blue 75%, indigo 95%, violet 100%);
}
```

In this example, red will quickly graduate to orange (at locations 0% and 5% from the start) and the same for indigo to violet (at 95% and 100% from the start). From orange to yellow, though, is a distance of 20 percent, as is blue to indigo. While, in the middle, green is 25 percent from both yellow and blue.

You can achieve a similar result with radial gradients, and because the first and last color stops are assumed to be at 0 and 100 percent, you can omit those position values if that is where you want these colors to sit in the gradient, like this:

```
#object {
  background:radial-gradient(
    red, orange 5%, yellow 25%, green 50%,
    blue 75%, indigo 95%, violet);
}
```

Repeating Gradients

When you want a gradient effect to repeat, it is not necessary to provide several elements alongside each other, each with its own gradient. Instead you can make a gradient repeat multiple times in a single element. To do this, you use the repeating- prefix on either type of gradient property name, like this (as shown in the top two segments of the image in Figure 7-2):

```
#object1 {
  background:repeating-linear-gradient(yellow, lime 20%);
}
#object2 {
  background:repeating-radial-gradient(blue, violet 20%);
}
```

When using the repeating versions of these gradients, the repetition starts at the end of the last color stop in a sequence. Therefore, in the preceding example, the gradient ends at 20 percent, and so it repeats further four times (because 100 ÷ 20 is 5).

Or, if your final color stop is at 50 percent, then only one repeat will apply (for a total of two instances of the gradient), and if it is greater than 50 percent, there will only be a partial repeat.

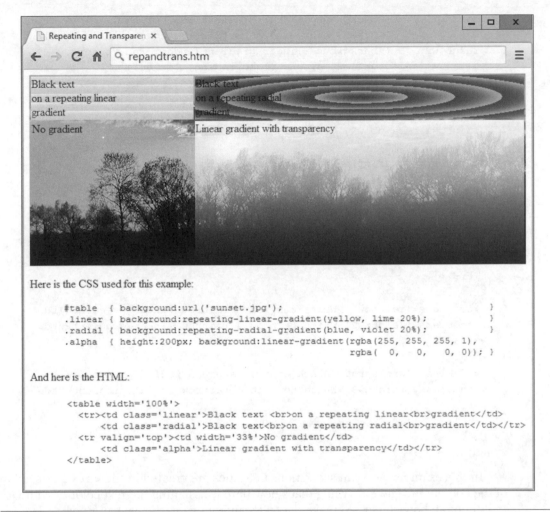

FIGURE 7-2   Repeating linear and radial gradients

An Example Document

The core CSS and HTML used to create Figure 7-1 are very similar to the following web document, which is extracted from the *colors.htm* file in the accompanying archive.

```
<!DOCTYPE html>
<html>
 <head>
  <title>Colors and Gradients</title>
  <style>
   .blueonyellow { background:yellow; color:blue;              }
   .orangegrad   { background:linear-gradient(#fb0, #f50);     }
```

```
      .rainbow1      { background:linear-gradient(red, orange, yellow,
                       green, blue, indigo, violet);                      }
      .rainbow2      { background:linear-gradient(90deg, red, orange,
                       yellow, green, blue, indigo, violet);              }
      .rainbow3      { background:radial-gradient(red, orange, yellow,
                       green, blue, indigo, violet);                      }
      .greengrad     { background:radial-gradient(#0a0, #0f0);            }
      .rainbow1, .rainbow2, .rainbow3 { color:white;                      }
    </style>
    <script src='prefixfree.js'></script>
  </head>
  <body>
  <table style='width:100%;'>
   <tr>
    <td class='blueonyellow'>Blue text on a yellow background</td>
    <td class='orangegrad'>Black text on an orange linear gradient</td>
   </tr>
   <tr>
    <td class='rainbow1'>White text on a rainbow linear gradient</td>
    <td class='rainbow2'>White text on a rainbow linear gradient</td>
   </tr>
   <tr>
    <td class='greengrad'>Black text on a green radial gradient</td>
    <td class='rainbow3'>White text on a rainbow radial gradient</td>
   </tr>
  </table>
  </body>
</html>
```

In this example, you can see various CSS rules are created in the <style> section of the document. The only thing that's new here is assigning the text color of white to the three rainbow classes, to make the text stand out from the backgrounds.

Underneath the style section, the inclusion of the *prefixfree.js* file in the <script> section confers CSS compatibility across all browsers, obviating the need to list any additional browser-specific versions of CSS rules (see the section a little later entitled "The *preefixfree.js* Utility").

In the <body> of the document, the CSS rules are then applied to <td> elements within a simple <table>, although they could equally have been applied to spans, divs, or any other elements that support a background property.

Note The file in the accompanying archive also includes some extra CSS and HTML, which is purely there to enable the displaying of both the rules and the results of applying the rules at the same time, without the need for you to use view source or refer back to the code in this book to compare the two.

Alpha Transparency

Gradients have one more little trick up their sleeve, which is the ability to support transparency, leading to an ever greater (and more subtle) variety of effects. For example, suppose you would like to fade a color in over an image. One way to do this is to fade from a transparent to a non-transparent color, which is where the `rgba()` function (standing for red, green, blue, and alpha transparency) comes into its own, as shown here:

```
#object {
  background:linear-gradient(
    rgba(255, 255, 255, 1), rgba(0, 0, 0, 0));
}
```

In this rule the `rgba()` function has been used to create two color stops. The first color is set to white with an alpha value of 1 (fully opaque), and the second color is black with an alpha value of 0 (fully transparent).

The gradient therefore acts to lighten the image at the top and let more of it through at the bottom. Because of the transparency gradient, the lightening at the top starts off very strong because the white being applied is opaque, while the darkening at the bottom is weaker because there is a large amount of transparency being applied.

The bottom two segments of the image in Figure 7-2 show an unmodified image of a sunset in the left-hand part, while the right-hand part of the image has the gradient overlaid.

An Example Document

In the following example (extracted from *repandtrans.htm* in the accompanying archive), looking at the `<style>` section you can see that the value `url('sunset .jpg')` is applied to the background property of the element with the ID of `table`. This sets the background of that element to the image supplied (more on this in Lesson 12). This is followed by rules for a linear, and then a radial gradient (applied to the classes `linear` and `radial`), and a rule for a linear gradient with alpha transparency (plus the height of the class is set to 200px), applied to the class `alpha`:

```
<!DOCTYPE html>
<html>
 <head>
  <title>Repeating and Transparency</title>
  <style>
   #table  { background:url('sunset.jpg');                         }
   .linear { background:repeating-linear-gradient(yellow, lime 20%); }
   .radial { background:repeating-radial-gradient(blue, violet 20%); }
   .alpha  { height:200px; background:linear-gradient(
             rgba(255, 255, 255, 1), rgba(0, 0, 0, 0));            }
```

```
   </style>
   <script src='prefixfree.js'></script>
 </head>
<body>
 <table id='table' style='width:100%;'>
  <tr>
   <td class='linear'>Black text on a repeating linear gradient</td>
   <td class='radial'>Black text on a repeating radial gradient</td>
  </tr>
  <tr style='vertical-align:top'>
   <td width='33%'>No gradient</td>
   <td class='alpha'>Linear gradient with transparency</td>
  </tr>
 </table>
 </body>
</html>
```

As in the previous example document, the rules are applied to <td> table cell elements, and in this example the image is being applied to the background of the entire table.

Gradients and Browser Compatibility

There is one odd browser out in the gradients department. Namely Safari, which, instead of using linear-gradient and radial-gradient property names (and their associated repeating versions), requires you to preface each of these with the keyword -webkit-, like this (highlighted in bold):

```
#obj { background:-webkit-linear-gradient(#fb0, #f50);                    }
#obj { background:-webkit-radial-gradient(red, purple);                   }
#obj { background:-webkit-repeating-linear-gradient(#fb0, #f50 33%);   }
#obj { background:-webkit-repeating-radial-gradient(red, purple 33%); }
```

However, see the section entitled "The *prefixfree.js* Utility" a little later on for a handy alternative.

CSS3 Browser Incompatibilities

A few years ago, when CSS3 was still being rolled out, each browser implemented things slightly differently, and applied its own vendor-specific names for many new CSS3 features. For example, Apple led the development of a lot of the CSS3 transitions, and so used the prefix -webkit- for these properties. Then other browsers implemented their own features, or copied others, each with their own property prefixes until, at one point, this meant that for many rules you had to supply separate CSS for each of the Opera, Chrome, Firefox, Safari, Internet Explorer browsers, and more!

However, when Apple chose the Webkit engine for its browser it became more compatible with Chrome (which had also chosen Webkit), and when Opera chose to use Chrome as the base for its browser there was no longer any need to consider modern versions of Opera as different from Chrome.

Over time, many of the proprietary properties became standardized, as browser developers implemented the W3C standard names, operation, and syntax of their versions of CSS, and so the list of browsers needed to take into account for any particular rule has, thankfully, decreased.

Nevertheless differences remain because not all properties have been standardized yet, even though many of them haven't changed for years, while developers like you and me have had to continue writing overly inflated web documents to cover all inconsistencies, as we wait for finalization of these standards into commonly used property names.

Therefore, in this book I always make a note when you should supply alternative rules for particular browsers, based on the situation as it stood at the time of publication.

Older Browsers

If you need to allow for browsers older than a year or two (or thereabouts), then you will have to supply the following browser-specific prefixes for many CSS properties:

- Apple Safari: `-webkit-`
- Google Chrome: `-webkit-`
- Microsoft Internet Explorer: `-ms-`
- Mozilla Firefox: `-moz-`
- Opera: `-o-`
- Konqueror: `-khtml-`

For a complete analysis of all the vendor prefix properties and when and where you might need to employ them, check out *tinyurl.com/cssvendorprefixes*. Another very useful website for keeping up-to-date on what browsers support which features is *caniuse.com*. Just browse the lists or enter a search term, and you'll be presented with full compatibility details for all known versions of each browser. And to ensure compatibility, I recommend you also have copies of all the main browsers your target users will have access to, in order to test your web pages on each and every one of them.

Fortunately, though, as you'll discover in the following section, there is a simple alternative to including additional rules for browsers that insist on doing things their own way.

Let George Do It

When I was learning to program, the first principle that was drummed into me was to "Let George do it." By this my teacher meant that I should write code in which for every feature or function I needed, I should assume that some unknown person named George would write it for me, so that I could concentrate on formulating the core of my code. When you follow this approach while programming, you're able to continue building the main framework of a feature by leaving all the little intricacies and fiddly bits to George.

Of course, once the code is finished, you must then take the place of George and actually write all those missing parts, but you can still leave anything else you uncover for another George to do. And so you proceed until as many levels of Georgeness as are required have been traversed, and there's nothing left for George to do—and thus your code is complete.

This is a good way to write your web documents too. Whenever you feel the need for something to be styled, give it a class or ID name and leave the styling up to George. Later on you can become George and implement the styling required. Or you may be lucky enough to work in a team where a real George will help out.

And you can also hand off parts of your CSS to George too. You see, when you are assembling your CSS rules and know that various browsers may require different prefixes to the rule names, or use slightly different arguments, you can leave handling all that to George—just get on with completing your style sheet first using the standard property names, and don't bother yourself about dealing with all the possible incompatibilities. That way you'll finish the style sheet much more quickly

Then, with your style sheet completed, you now have a couple of options. You can become George and work through all the incompatibilities, adding alternate rules and property names wherever required (rather a tiresome task). Or you can take advantage of the fact that your web surfers will all be using computers to view your web pages, and let George (their computer) do the hard work.

The *prefixfree.js* Utility

Therefore, let's take a look at the *prefixfree.js* utility (see Figure 7-3), which aims to automate the process of properly prefixing property names for you. You can find it at *tinyurl.com/prefixfree*, where you can click the large circular icon at the top left of the screen to download a JavaScript file to be your George.

The program is less than 2 KB in size and can be easily added to your web pages by loading it in with the following instruction (assuming you saved the file in the current folder), which should ideally be located in the <head> section right after the style sheet(s):

```
<script src='prefixfree.js'></script>
```

And that's all there is to it. Once loaded, this program will check your style sheets and update them to the required property names according to the browser in which it finds itself running, out of the following browser versions (and higher): Internet Explorer 9, Opera 10, Firefox 3.5, Safari 4, all versions of Chrome, and all mobile versions of Safari, Android browser, Chrome, and Opera. In tests I have found it to be highly reliable, with only a few niggling issues that I easily overcame by slightly reformatting the rules I was using in a different way.

FIGURE 7-3   With *prefixfree.js*, you can forget about CSS3 browser incompatibilities.

And so I believe that this is the best approach to take. Let's leave all those irritating inconsistencies for George to deal with, while we get on with the task at hand, which is developing great web documents. Therefore, although I point out where a property has incompatibilities with certain browsers (and what the alternative property names or arguments are), I don't include all those alternative CSS rules within the examples for this book, as it only complicates things. Instead I concentrate on the standard versions of properties and rules and avoid being side-tracked. Because, after all, in a few years all the properties covered will have finally become standardized anyway—we're just ahead of the curve...

...all thanks to George!—a.k.a. programmer Lea Verou (see *lea.verou.me*) and her wonderful *prefixfree.js* utility—a copy of which is included in the accompanying archive of files (although you should always get hold of the latest version directly from her website).

Note There's another George you can use, called *Express Prefixr*, that doesn't require the user to have JavaScript enabled. Instead it accepts a section of CSS that you copy into an input field, and processes it into fully prefixed CSS, suitable for use in all major browsers. You can then paste the result back into your code and voilà! Just visit the program's website at *tinyurl.com/expressprefixr* to try it out (as shown in Figure 7-4). And there's another similar utility to this called *Auto Prefixer*, which you can access at *tinyurl.com/autoprefixer*.

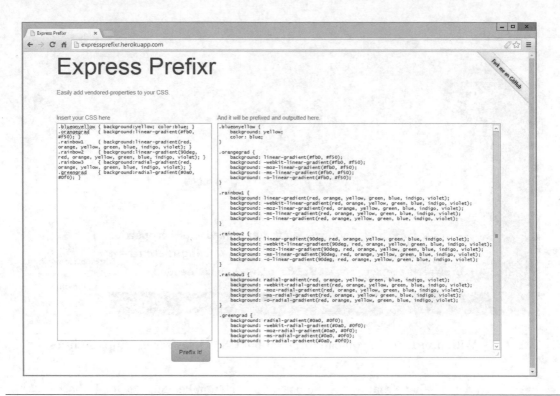

FIGURE 7-4   The CSS on the left has been prefixed for all major browsers by Express Prefixr.

Positioning Elements

By default all elements in the web page rest in the exact position in which they have been placed within the document, and as a result of how any other impacting elements may have moved it about.

But they don't have to stay there because elements can be moved about by changing their `position` property, from the default of `static` to one of `absolute`, `relative`, or `fixed`.

When an element is set to have `absolute` positioning, it is removed from the document, and any other elements that can will reflow themselves into the newly released space. With the element now removed from the body of the document, you can then position it anywhere you like using the `top`, `right`, `bottom`, and `left` properties. The element will then reside either on top of or behind other elements.

Absolute Positioning

Therefore, for example, to move an object with the ID of `elem` to an absolute location (by assigning the value `absolute` to the `position` property) that is 200 pixels down from the document top and 200 pixels in from the left, you can apply the following rules to it:

```
#elem {
  position:absolute;
  top     :200px;
  left    :200px;
}
```

As well as pixels, you can specify the location in any other valid CSS measurement, and values can be offscreen too, even through the use of negative values.

Relative Positioning

Instead of moving an object to an absolute location, you can move it relative to the location it would normally occupy in the normal document, by setting the position property to relative.

Therefore, for example, to move elem 25 pixels down and 25 pixels to the left of its normal location, you would use the following rules:

```
#object {
  position:relative;
  top     : 25px;
  left    :-25px;
}
```

Fixed Positioning

There is one further type of position you can use by assigning the value fixed to the position property. This moves the element to an absolute location, but only within the current browser viewport, and there it stays.

If the document is scrolled, the element will remain exactly where it was placed, with the scrolling occurring beneath it. For example, to fix the object to the top-right corner of the browser window, you could use the following rules:

```
#object {
  position:fixed;
  top     :0px;
  right   :0px;
}
```

In Figure 7-5 the following set of rules (with the important differences between them highlighted in bold) has been applied to three objects, and the browser has been reduced so that it is necessary to scroll down to see the remainder of the web page. When you do so, it is immediately obvious that the element with fixed positioning remains in place even when the page is scrolled.

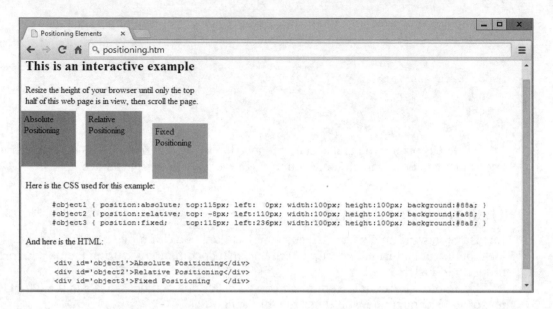

FIGURE 7-5   Using different positioning values

```
#object1 {
  position   :absolute;
  top        :115px;
  left       :0px;
  width      :100px;
  height     :100px;
  background:#88a;
}
#object2 {
  position   :relative;
  top        :-8px;
  left       :110px;
  width      :100px;
  height     :100px;
  background:#a88;
}
#object3 {
  position   :fixed;
  top        :115px;
  left       :236px;
  width      :100px;
  height     :100px;
  background:#8a8;
}
```

Looking at these rules, the element with absolute positioning is located at exactly 115 pixels down, with zero horizontal offset, while the element with relative positioning is actually moved up by 8 pixels and then indented from the left margin by 110 pixels in order to line up alongside the first element.

In Figure 7-5 the element with fixed positioning initially lines up with the other two elements, but has stayed put in a static location while the others have been scrolled up the page, and now appears offset below them. Here is the HTML for the three elements to which the rules are applied:

```
<div id='object1'>Absolute Positioning</div>
<div id='object2'>Relative Positioning</div>
<div id='object3'>Fixed Positioning   </div>
```

Illustrating a handy use for this feature, Figure 7-6 shows a simple dock bar created using a value of `fixed` for the `position` property to align all the icons at the screen bottom, in a similar way to the OS X Dock. Using a little JavaScript or proprietary CSS transforms, the icons can be made to resize as the mouse passes over them, as is happening to the second one.

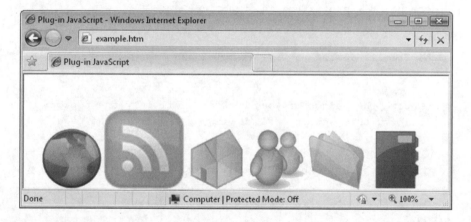

FIGURE 7-6   Creating a simple dock bar using the **position** property

 See my book *The Web Developer's Cookbook* (McGraw-Hill Education, 2012) for ready-to-use CSS and JavaScript code you can use to help with creating dock bars and many other interactive features.

An Example Document

The following example (extracted from *positioning.htm* in the accompanying archive) is how the preceding code comes together into an HTML document. It should all be quite straightforward, with the exception of the rule applied to div elements. What is happening here is that I have assigned a rule to change the `padding` property of all <div> elements to 5 pixels, so that there is a small gap between the edges and the contents.

I also chose not to add these 5 pixels to the existing dimensions of each <div> (which would make them bigger), and instead opted to take those 5 pixels from their inner dimensions by applying the border-box value to the box-sizing property (more of which in Lesson 12):

```
<!DOCTYPE html>
<html>
  <head>
    <title>Positioning Elements</title>
    <style>
      #object1 { position:absolute; top:115px; left:  0px;
                 width:100px; height:100px; background:#88a; }
      #object2 { position:relative; top: -8px; left:110px;
                 width:100px; height:100px; background:#a88; }
      #object3 { position:fixed;    top:115px; left:236px;
                 width:100px; height:100px; background:#8a8; }
      div      { padding:5px; box-sizing:border-box;          }
    </style>
    <script src='prefixfree.js'></script>
  </head>
<body>
    <h2>This is an interactive example</h2>

    <p>
      Resize the height of your browser until only the top<br>
      half of this web page is in view, then scroll the page.
    </p>

    <div id='object1'>Absolute Positioning</div>
    <div id='object2'>Relative Positioning</div>
    <div id='object3'>Fixed Positioning   </div>
  </body>
</html>
```

Summary

In this lesson you have learned how to apply foreground and background colors to elements, how to use linear and radial gradients instead of solid colors, the use of repeating gradients and alpha transparency, and how to precisely position elements in the browser. In Lesson 8, we'll move on to examining pseudo-classes and the shorthand CSS rules.

Self-Test Questions

Using these questions, test how much you have learned in this lesson. If you don't know an answer, go back and reread the relevant section until your knowledge is complete. You can find the answers in the appendix.

1. What are three ways you can supply a color to a CSS property without using a CSS function?

2. How would you assign the color yellow to a property using the CSS rgb() function and decimal numbers (remembering that on computer monitors red plus green equals yellow)?

3. How can you assign the color blue to a property using the CSS rgb() function and percentage values?

4. What rule might you use to assign a linear vertical gradient to graduate smoothly from white to black, to the background of an object?

5. What rule might you use to assign a linear horizontal gradient to graduate from red to green to blue smoothly, to the background of an object?

6. What rule might you use to create a radial background gradient from color #345 to color #678?

7. What values does the position property support?

8. What rules might you use to place an element in a set location at the top left of the browser such that it is not subject to scrolling?

9. What is one way to remove an element from view without altering its opacity, dimensions, or other visibility properties?

10. How can you give a color alpha transparency when assigning it to a property?

Handling Pseudo-Selectors and Using Shorthand Properties

To view the accompanying video for this lesson, please visit mhprofessional.com/nixoncss/.

CSS is actually a lot more powerful and subtle language than it may at first glance seem. It's not just a method for applying styles to IDs, classes, and elements because it can do much more than that. For example, with pseudo-classes and elements it can transform the capitalization of letters, change elements dynamically when they are interacted with (for example, by hovering over or clicking them), or simply by giving them focus (selecting them).

In fact you can even color alternate rows in a table differently, insert content before and/or after elements, or simply select the first line of a paragraph to be manipulated. All these things are achieved using what are called pseudo-classes and pseudo-elements, and this lesson will show you them and how to use them.

Then we'll take a look at how to write CSS more quickly and keep file size down at the same time, by combining properties together into single shorthand properties.

Introducing the Pseudo-Selectors

The job of pseudo-selectors is to classify elements using characteristics other than their name, attributes, or other content that cannot be deduced from the document tree. They include the pseudo-selectors `first-line`, `first-child`, and `first-letter`.

All pseudo-selectors are added to other selectors with a : (colon) character, with the exception of the new CSS3 pseudo-elements, for which a :: (double colon) is intended to be used instead.

However, the *w3.org* website (*tinyurl.com/w3colons*) states: "The new CSS3 way of writing pseudo-elements is to use a double colon to set them apart from pseudo-classes [but] CSS3 still allows for single colon pseudo-elements, for the sake of backwards compatibility, and we would advise that you stick with this syntax for the time being."

Therefore, because the W3 recommends keeping the old styling at the moment, that's what I do in this book until they say otherwise, and so I use only the single colon form throughout (but you should at least be prepared that this might change in the future).

There is one exception to this though (otherwise it wouldn't be a good rule, would it?), and that's the new `selection` pseudo-element (see "Miscellaneous Pseudo-selectors" later in this lesson), which won't work unless you use the double colon. So my new rule in this book is to only use double colons where they are strictly necessary—there... fixed.

Anyway, for example, to create a class called `cap` for emphasizing the size of the first letter of an element, you would use a rule such as the following:

```
.cap:first-letter {
  font-size:500%;
}
```

 When you apply the `cap` class to an element, the first letter of any text in the element will be displayed according to the declarations listed following the selector. In this instance, an increase of five times text size will occur. Actually, if you want the remaining text to neatly flow around it, you also need to make the first letter float to the left too, as follows:

```
.cap:first-letter {
  font-size:500%;
  float     :left;
}
```

This works in the same way as if the first letter were an image or any other object. Figure 8-1 shows the following two sets of rules (saved as *first-letter.htm* in the accompanying archive) being applied to a paragraph of text:

```
#example {
  border       :1px dotted #888;
  background   :#eee;
  width        :400px;
  padding      :10px;
  text-align   :justify;
}
.cap:first-letter {
  line-height  :75px;
  font-size    :600%;
  float        :left;
  margin-right:5px;
}
```

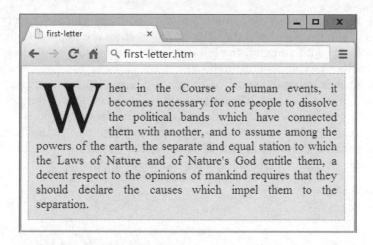

FIGURE 8-1   The first letter of the paragraph has been directly referenced.

In this example, the paragraph has the ID of example and applies a few rules to create a border, set the background color, restrict the width, and apply padding and justification to the element. The cap class sets the font to six times larger than the current size, and applies a value to line-height that will ensure it is just the right height to accommodate the letter to allow the remaining text to flow smoothly around it. Without the line-height rule there could be too small or too large a gap underneath the letter.

Then, as well as floating the element to the left, a little more space is placed to the right of the letter by applying a 5-pixel right-side margin. The paragraph these rules are applied to looks like this (and the full example is saved in the companion archive as *first-letter.htm*):

```
<div id='example' class='cap'>
  When in the Course of human events, it becomes necessary for one
  people to dissolve the political bands which have connected them
  with another, and to assume among the powers of the earth, the
  separate and equal station to which the Laws of Nature and of
  Nature's God entitle them, a decent respect to the opinions of
  mankind requires that they should declare the causes which impel
  them to the separation.
</div>
```

Note   Unlike colons used to separate properties from values, the colons in a pseudo-selector may not be preceded with or followed by any spaces.

Let's look at the first-line pseudo-element now, which works in the same way but applies only to the first line of a paragraph. How is the first line detected?

Well, the rules of the pseudo-element are applied to the element until the text has to move on to the next line, and then the standard rules are applied to it. This means that whatever width you give an element, only as much of the element contents that will fit on the first line will be modified.

Here's an example in action (as shown in Figure 8-2 and saved as *first-line.htm* in the companion archive). It's similar to the previous one, but doesn't increase the text size by anywhere near as much. In fact, all that has changed is the `font-size` rule (oh, and the `line-height`, `margin-right`, and `float` declarations have been removed because they would now be superfluous), so I only need to show you the new pseudo-element (the paragraph, of course, being unchanged):

```
.cap:first-line {
  font-size:160%;
}
```

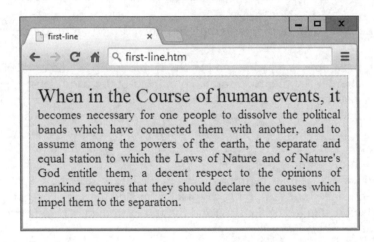

FIGURE 8-2   The entire first line of the paragraph has been directly referenced.

Link-Related Pseudo-Classes

CSS2 pseudo-classes include `hover`, `link`, `active`, and `visited`, all of which are mostly useful for applying to anchor elements, as in the following rules, which set the default color of all links to blue, links that have already been visited to navy, links that are in the process of being clicked to red, and links that are being hovered over by the mouse to cyan:

```
a:link    { color:blue; }
a:visited { color:navy; }
a:active  { color:red;  }
a:hover   { color:cyan; }
```

Looking in more detail at the `hover` pseudo-class, for example, you can do a lot more than just change a link's color with a pseudo-class. For example, you can change its background color, font size, or any other CSS properties you like, as follows:

```
a:hover {
  color       :green;
  background :blue;
  font-size   :12pt;
  font-weight:bold;
}
```

Here I have used the `background` property with a single argument, instead of the longer `background-color` property.

The `active` pseudo-class is also dynamic in that it effects a change to a link during the time between the mouse button being clicked and released, as with this rule, which changes the link color to olive:

```
a:active { color:olive; }
```

Another interesting dynamic pseudo-class is `focus`, which is applied only when an element is given focus by the user selecting it with the keyboard or mouse, as with the following rule, which uses the universal selector to always place a dark gray, dashed, 1-pixel border around the currently focused object:

```
*:focus { border:1px dashed #444; }
```

Using the following CSS rules (from *linkandfocus.htm* in the companion archive), Figure 8-3 lists two links and an input field. The first link shows up as navy because it has already been visited in this browser, but the second link has not and displays in blue. The TAB key has been pressed and the focus of input is the first link, so its background has changed color. When either of the links is clicked, it will display in purple, and when hovered over with the mouse, it will show in red:

```
a:link     { color     :blue;   }
a:visited { color     :navy;   }
a:hover    { color     :red;    }
a:active   { color     :purple; }
*:focus    { background:#8cf;   }
```

Internet Explorer takes an unfocused document as actually having focus applied to the entire web page, and this can completely mess up styling of the focus pseudo-element. Therefore, you should never apply focus to the universal selector. Instead you can narrow down the scope to get the same or similar results, by prefacing the universal selector with a parent element, like this:

```
body *:focus { border:1px solid #888; }
```

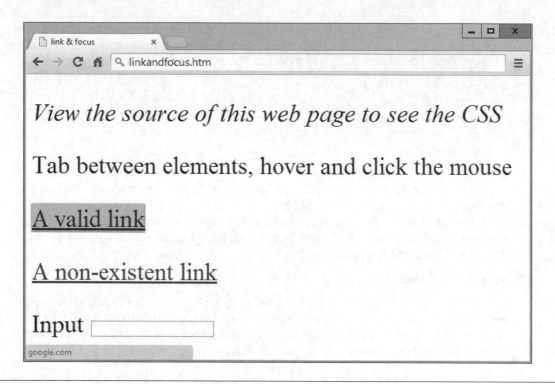

FIGURE 8-3   Link and focus pseudo-classes

Accessing Elements Numerically

Now we get to really start having some fun with CSS by accessing elements by their numerical position within a parent element using a range of position-related pseudo-classes, starting with `first-child` which, as you would expect, simply accesses the first child element of a parent, whatever type of element it may be.

For example, if you are displaying text in such a way that all paragraphs should be indented except for the first one, you can achieve this as follows (which also shows the CSS rules to format the example text in general):

```
#example {
  border      :1px dotted #888;
  background :#eee;
  width       :400px;
  padding     :10px;
  text-align :justify;
}
p {
  text-indent:30px;
  margin      :0;
```

```
}
p:first-child {
  text-indent:0;
}
```

The first p rule sets all paragraphs to have a text indent of 30 pixels, and removes all margins around paragraphs. The second applies the `first-child` pseudo-class in which the `text-indent` value is set to 0. The result is that all paragraphs will have a 30-pixel indent applied except the first one.

Here is the example text that, when the preceding rules are applied to it, results in Figure 8-4. As you can see, there is nothing in the example that indicates this type of formatting should occur, so we have total separation of content and styling—always the goal when using CSS to its best advantages:

```
<div id='example'>
  <p>When in the Course of human events, it becomes necessary for one
  people to dissolve the political bands which have connected them
  with another, and to assume among the powers of the earth, the
  separate and equal station to which the Laws of Nature and of
  Nature's God entitle them, a decent respect to the opinions of
  mankind requires that they should declare the causes which impel
  them to the separation.</p>
  <p>We hold these truths to be self-evident, that all men are
  created equal, that they are endowed by their Creator with
  certain unalienable Rights, that among these are Life, Liberty
  and the pursuit of Happiness.</p>
  <p>That to secure these rights, Governments are instituted among
  Men, deriving their just powers from the consent of the governed.</p>
  <p>That whenever any Form of Government becomes destructive of
  these ends, it is the Right of the People to alter or to abolish
  it, and to institute new Government, laying its foundation on such
  principles and organizing its powers in such form, as to them shall
  seem most likely to effect their Safety and Happiness.</p>
</div>
```

There is, however, a potential problem in that `first-child` doesn't discriminate between types of elements, and therefore it may not necessarily result in the effect you require. For example, in Figure 8-5 a heading has been supplied to the example and consequently the first paragraph is no longer the first child, and so it has become indented.

So, where you need to style only elements of a certain type, you should use the `first-of-type` pseudo-class, like this example, which simply replaces the previous one:

```
p:first-of-type { text-indent:0; }
```

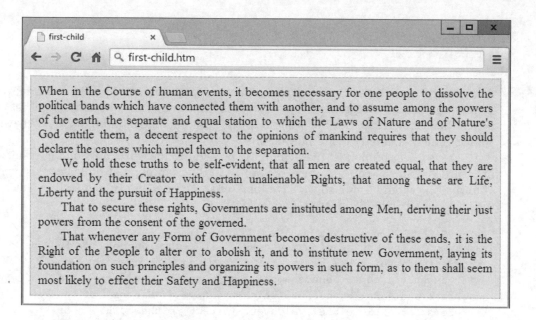

FIGURE 8-4   Unlike the rest, the first paragraph is not indented.

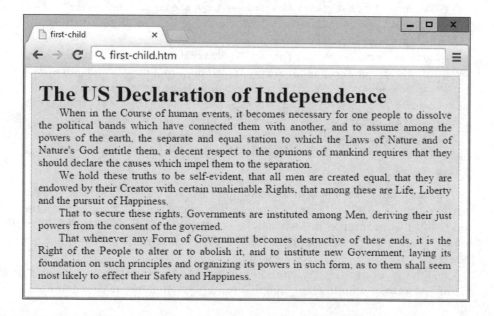

FIGURE 8-5.   After adding a heading, the first paragraph has become indented.

Now, if you look at Figure 8-6 (created with *first-of-type.htm* in the companion archive), you can see that the first paragraph is no longer indented because only elements of type p are accessed by this `first-of-type` pseudo-class, and so it is once again the first of these.

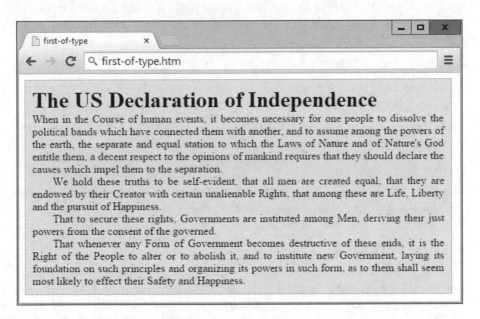

FIGURE 8-6 By using `first-of-type`, the first paragraph is no longer indented.

Using `last-child` and `last-of-type`

In the same way that you can access the first child or first child element of a type, you can also apply CSS rules to the last child or last child element of a type with the `last-child` and `last-of-type` pseudo-classes. You use them in exactly the same manner and only the last child element will be styled.

Selecting Elements by Numeric Location

If the element you need to access is neither the first nor the last child, then you can still use CSS to modify its styling using the `nth-child()` pseudo-class. With this type of class you must supply an expression that will uniquely refer to the element in question. At its simplest you supply a number, and that will represent the element number to access, like the following, which will style the 5th element (*multipass*!) in the list:

```
ul li:nth-child(5) { color:blue; }
```

You can also select numerically by type in the following manner, which will uniquely reference only the 5th paragraph in a div (and not just the 5th element):

```
div p:nth-of-type(5) { color:red; }
```

You can even go a little deeper into this by starting at the end and working backward, using the `nth-last-child()` pseudo-class as follows, which references the 5th element from the end:

```
ul li:nth-last-child(5) { color:blue; }
```

Or, you can get even more precise by choosing exactly the element type to reference, as in this example, which accesses only the 5th paragraph from the end of the div:

```
div p:nth-last-of-type(5) { color:red; }
```

Using Expressions

As well as giving single numeric values to these types of pseudo-class, you can provide an expression to give even more interesting control, by supplying the n part of nth. For example, to reference all the odd items in a list, you could use a rule such as this:

```
ul li:nth-child(2n+1) { color:red; }
```

The way n works is like a programming language variable. It begins with a value of 0 and then adds 1 with each additional child that is processed. The number 2 next to it is used the same way as in an algebraic equation—it is multiplied by the value in n.

Therefore, for a list of nine items, the values of 2n will be 2×0, 2×1, 2×2, 2×3, 2×4, 2×5, 2×6, 2×7, and 2×8. Thus the elements in the list that will get styled will be at locations 0, 2, 4, 6, and 8. Now the +1 part of the expression comes into play, turning the final results into the values 1, 3, 5, 7, and 9, so all the odd items will be styled.

In the same way, the following rule will style all the even elements in the same list, by simply changing the +1 to +2:

```
ul li:nth-child(2n+2) { color:red; }
```

Actually the +2 is unnecessary because it is okay to reference the 0th element, because it will be ignored by the browser. Therefore, you can more simply just use the declaration:

```
ul li:nth-child(2n) { color:red; }
```

In fact the designers of CSS made it even easier for you to access odd and even elements by supporting the values odd and even, like this (as shown in Figure 8-7, saved as *nth-child.htm* in the accompanying archive):

```
ul li:nth-child(odd)  { color:red;  }
ul li:nth-child(even) { color:pink; }
```

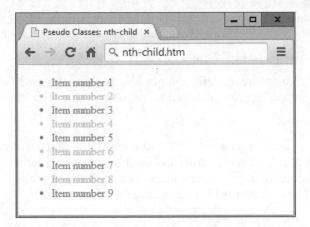

FIGURE 8-7   The odd and even list items have been separately styled.

But when you need to get more complicated than simply accessing odd or even elements, you have to use the equation format. For example, to style every third element, you can use this rule:

```
ul li:nth-child(3n) { color:red; }
```

This equates to the values 3×0, 3×1, 3×2, and 3×3, which are locations 0, 3, 6, and 9 (with the 0th element simply being ignored). Or you could also style every third item, but start instead from the first (not 0th) item, like this (to style items 1, 4, and 7):

```
ul li:nth-child(3n+1) { color:red; }
```

Or you could style every third item starting from the second one, like this (to style items 2, 5, and 8):

```
ul li:nth-child(3n+2) { color:red; }
```

 You can also supply equations to all the other nth rules, and even a negative value to n (to select only a range of elements at the start of a list), or you can use negative values in the second term of the equation too. However, to avoid overcomplicating matters, I won't take this any further, and will leave it up to you to invent any weird and wonderful selections you may need.

Relational Selectors

A couple of pseudo-classes let you select either according to whether an element is empty or whether it doesn't contain another class or ID. For example, you can style a `<div>` with the ID of `mydiv` when it is empty like this (which in this instance makes it half invisible):

```
#mydiv:empty { opacity:0.5; }
```

Or, you can, for example, style all elements except for those that you specify, as with this rule which targets anything that is not an image element:

```
:not(img) { margin-left:20px; }
```

Or, you can be more specific and preface this selector with another so that, for example, the preceding rule attached to the ID `myid` results in the following:

```
#myid:not(img) { margin-left:20px; }
```

Here this selector will affect only those elements that are descendants of the element with the ID of `myid`. You can also apply `not` to another element and/or supply to it values that are not elements, as with the following example, which styles only those `<div>` elements that do not use the class `info`:

```
div:not(.info) { margin-left:20px; }
```

Figure 8-8 (created with *not.htm* in the accompanying archive) shows this rule being used on a range of different elements. In it you can clearly see how the two `<div>` elements that do not use the class `info` have been styled with a border and background color.

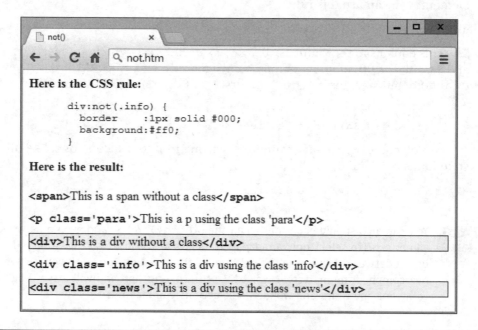

FIGURE 8-8   Only `<div>`s *not* using the `info` class have been styled.

Miscellaneous Pseudo-Selectors

You can also style elements in a range of miscellaneous ways. For example, there are the enabled and disabled pseudo-classes that will reference an element such as an input field either if it has been enabled, or disabled, like this:

```
#myinput:enabled  { background:white; }
#myinput:disabled { background:gray;  }
```

You can style a checkbox if it has been checked like this:

```
#mycheckbox:checked { border:1px dotted gray; }
```

Or, you can style radio buttons of indeterminate (neither chosen or unchosen) state, like this:

```
#myradio:indeterminate { border:1px solid black; }
```

There's also a somewhat esoteric selector you can use in the case of document URLs that point to a subsection of a target web page using the # symbol (for example, http://mywebsite.com/news.htm#latest), and an element in the document *also* uses the same ID (in this instance latest). When both of these occur, you can style the relevant element accordingly, as follows:

```
#latest:target { font-weight:bold; }
```

Finally, there's the pseudo-selector out I mentioned near the start that requires a double colon in front of it, namely the selection pseudo-element. Using this selector, you can modify the color, background, background-color, and text-shadow properties of text selected by dragging the mouse, or using SHIFT with the cursor keys.

For example, because of the * universal selector, the following rule changes the default white-on-blue of all selections in a document to yellow-on-red:

```
*::selection {
  color     :yellow
  background:red;
}
```

Note Sometimes when you use the selection pseudo-element, you can end up with the standard selection (which may extend to the right-hand edge of the current element), and also the newly defined selection colors, both active at the same time, because only the element's content properties have been changed. This is most often seen in and around input and textarea elements, and in the bullet points of lists.

You may, of course, apply this pseudo-element to just single elements, classes or IDs, or groups of them as required. Also, I didn't mention it before, but in the accompanying archive I added the preceding rule to the *nth-child.htm* file, so that you can try it out for yourself by dragging the mouse pointer across the content. The result should look like Figure 8-9.

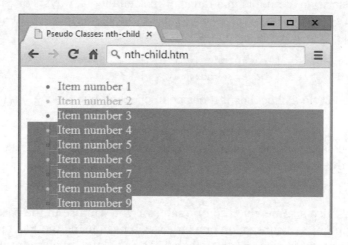

FIGURE 8-9   The selection text and background colors have been modified.

Pseudo-Elements That Add Content

Finally, in the collection of CSS things that are pseudo, come the pseudo-elements that actually insert new content into a document, rather than just styling, namely `before` and `after`. What they do is simply add content before and/or after an element. For example, you can preface a quotation with a quotation mark like this:

```
.quote:before {
  content:open-quote;
}
```

So, let's use this to create some rules to style blockquotes, like this:

```
blockquote {
  border-left  :10px solid #ccc;
  background   :#eee;
  padding      :10px;
  text-align   :justify;
  quotes       :'\201C''\201D''\2018''\2019';
}
blockquote:before {
  line-height  :60px;
  content      :open-quote;
  font-size    :500%;
  float        :left;
  margin-right :10px;
  color        :#ccc;
}
```

Here all `blockquote` elements have been styled such that they have a thick left-hand border, a light gray background, 10 pixels padding, and justified text. The types of quotation marks to use are also specified.

Then in the `before` pseudo-element section, the `content` property has the value `open-quote` assigned to prepend that symbol to the element, line height is adjusted, along with font size, the symbol is floated to the left, given some space to its right, and set to a light gray color. The result of applying these rules to the element below can be seen in Figure 8-10 (created using *beforeandafter.htm* in the accompanying archive).

```
<blockquote>
  When in the Course of human events, it becomes necessary for one
  people to dissolve the political bands which have connected them
  with another, and to assume among the powers of the earth, the
  separate and equal station to which the Laws of Nature and of
  Nature's God entitle them, a decent respect to the opinions of
  mankind requires that they should declare the causes which impel
  them to the separation.
</blockquote>
```

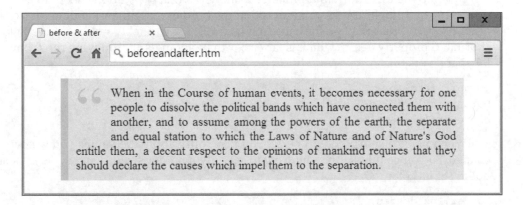

FIGURE 8-10   The quotation has been styled and prepended with a quotation mark.

Notice that there is nothing at all in this HTML element to suggest its styling (not even a class name)—everything is handled purely with CSS. You can also use the `after` pseudo-element in much the same manner.

Shorthand Properties

Related CSS properties can be concatenated into shorthand properties to save your time and make your CSS easier to follow, but this does come with a caveat. Whenever you supply a shorthand property, you are, by implication, assigning default values for any properties you do not assign. So if you, for example, set only three of five possible properties, then the remaining two properties will have the default values selected, rather than having undefined values.

As long as you are aware of this caveat, though, you can use shorthand properties liberally. Just replace any such shorthand properties you have problems with by a set of non-shorthand properties if you encounter problems.

 The order in which font properties should be applied to a shorthand rule is sometimes important. Even though you may often get away with moving the values around with some shorthand properties, with others it can break the rule. Therefore, to avoid any problems, I recommend you get used to applying the values in the recommended orders listed in this section.

Border and Outline Shorthand

When I'm styling with CSS, there's a shorthand property I frequently use to keep track of element boundaries, as follows:

```
border:1px solid #888;
```

By applying this shorthand property to any element(s) that don't seem to be displaying quite right, I can sometimes find the border, margin, or padding (or other property) that may be the cause. Once fixed, I can quickly remove this single shorthand property again, which is far easier than adding and removing the following longhand version:

```
border-width:1px;
border-style:solid;
border-color:#888;
```

When using a shorthand property, you need only apply the values you wish to change. So you could use the following to set only a border's width and style, choosing not to set its color too:

```
border:2px dotted;
```

So, the three longhand border properties that can be combined into a shorthand rule are as follows:

- `border-width`
- `border-style`
- `border-color`

And you might combine them in this way (as shown around the quotation in Figure 8-11, created using *shorthand.htm* from the accompanying archive):

```
#example { border:1px dotted gray; }
```

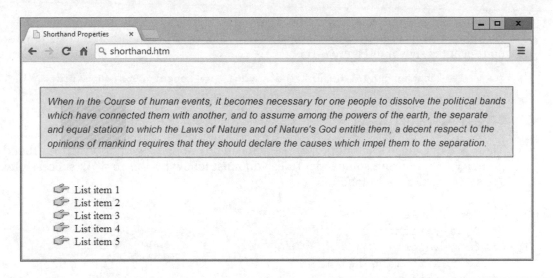

FIGURE 8-11   All this styling was created using shorthand CSS rules.

Outlines work the same way. They have the following possible longhand properties that can be assigned using shorthand:

- `outline-width`
- `outline-style`
- `outline-color`

And they can be applied like this (as shown immediately surrounding the dotted border in Figure 8-11):

```
#example { outline:1px solid green; }
```

Background Shorthand

Backgrounds have five main longhand properties that can be concatenated into a shorthand property:

- `background-color`
- `background-image`
- `background-repeat`
- `background-position`
- `background-attachment`

For example, this rule sets the background to light gray, loads in the image *back.png*, placing it in a fixed position 60 pixels in and down from the top-left corner, with no repeat (as shown in Figure 8-11):

```
#example { background:#eee url('back.png') no-repeat 60px 60px fixed; }
```

Font Shorthand

There are five longhand font properties that can be brought together into a shorthand property, but there are some strict rules you must follow for this to work successfully. These properties are as follows:

- `font-style`
- `font-variant`
- `font-weight`
- `font-size/line-height`
- `font-family`

When the `font` shorthand property is used, the `font-style`, `font-variant`, and `font-weight` properties must come before the `font-size` and `font-family` properties, both of which must exist or the rule will be ignored. If you need to specify a line height, you must run the `font-size` and `line-height` properties together with a / character.

For example, this rule sets an italic, sans-serif font, with a size of 15 pixels, and a line height of 150 percent (as shown in Figure 8-11):

```
#example { font:italic 15px/150% sans-serif; }
```

Margin and Padding Shorthand

Margins and padding have the following longhand properties that can be combined into shorthand:

- `margin-top`
- `margin-right`
- `margin-bottom`
- `margin-left`

Or for padding:

- `padding-top`
- `padding-right`
- `padding-bottom`
- `padding-left`

Unlike the preceding properties, though, providing fewer than four values doesn't simply assume defaults for the unassigned properties. Instead the number of values supplied has meaning, as follows:

- **One value**   Set all sides
- **Two values**   First sets top and bottom, second sets left and right
- **Three values**   First sets top, second sets left and right, third sets bottom
- **Four values**   First sets top, second sets right, third sets bottom, fourth sets left

So, to set all the padding values to the same, you could use a shorthand property such as this:

```
#example { padding:10px; }
```

And, for example, to set the left and right margins to 20 pixels and the top and bottom margins to 40 pixels, you would use a rule like this (both these padding and margin shorthand properties were used in Figure 8-11):

```
#example { margin:40px 20px; }
```

 Margins and padding are explained in greater detail in Lesson 9.

List Shorthand

Finally there's shorthand available for lists, which take the following longhand properties:

- list-style-type
- list-style-position
- list-style-image

These can be combined in the following way, for example, the result of which is shown in Figure 8-11:

```
ul li { list-style:square inside url(hand.png) }
```

Summary

Even though many of the properties in this lesson are not fully explained until later on, it has given you a good grounding in some very subtle (yet powerful) ways of using CSS, and has also shown how you can save time and make your CSS code easier to follow by using shorthand properties.

In Lesson 9 we'll move on to examining the box model, which is the way CSS looks at HTML web pages when it decides how to apply the rules you give it.

Self-Test Questions

Using these questions, test how much you have learned in this lesson. If you don't know an answer, go back and reread the relevant section until your knowledge is complete. You can find the answers in the appendix.

1. With which pseudo-element can you modify only the first letter of an element?

2. With which pseudo-element can you modify only the first line of an element?

3. What rule would you use to make all previously visited links display in navy?

4. How can you style only the first child of an element?

5. How can you select (a) just the third child of a parent, and (b) every odd-numbered child?

6. How can you add content before and after an element using CSS?

7. Give a shorthand declaration to create a 2-pixel dotted red border.

8. Provide a shorthand declaration to create a nonrepeating background from the image *picture.jpg,* with a default background color of yellow.

9. What shorthand declaration would you use to set an italic Courier New font in 14 point?

10. What two shorthand declarations could you use to set the top and bottom margins of an element to 10 pixels, its left and right margins to 20 pixels, its top padding to 5 pixels, its left and right padding to 10 pixels, and its bottom padding to 15 pixels?

LESSON 9

Understanding the Box Model

To view the accompanying video for this lesson, please visit mhprofessional.com/nixoncss/.

When designing the CSS system, its developers needed to come up with a method of taking into account not just the elements being styled, but also their relationship to other elements, mainly with regard to spacing.

It was decided that there were three main areas to cover, which were padding, borders, and margins, with everything else applying to the contents of an element. Because HTML documents appear like boxes within boxes when looked at this way, the system of nested sets of properties surrounding an element was called the *Box Model*.

To allow for fine tuning of layout, the four edges of each part of the box model were made uniquely modifiable, as well as in pairs (left/right and top/bottom) or all together, and you are given the option of these types of spacing either being added to the dimensions of an element, or being taken from its existing width and height.

Visualizing the Box Model

When working with CSS, it helps to have a clear visual understanding of how the box model will apply to your styling, so take a look at Figure 9-1, which shows a standard example of the nested levels of the CSS box model.

Virtually all elements have (or can have) the box model properties of padding, border, and margin, including the document body, whose margin you can, for example, remove with the following rule:

```
body { margin:0px; }
```

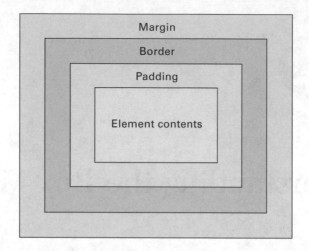

FIGURE 9-1   The nested levels of the CSS box model

Actually, when supplying 0 values in CSS, it's recommended to omit any measurement type (unit), because 0 is zero in all measurements. So the preceding rule is better applied as follows:

```
body { margin:0; }
```

Anyway, once you have the hang of the box model, you will be well on your way to creating professionally laid out pages, because these properties alone will make up much of your page styling.

Setting Margins

The margin is the outermost level of the box model. It separates elements from each other and its use is quite smart. For example, assume you have chosen to give a number of elements a default margin of 10 pixels around each. When placed on top of each other, this would create a gap of 20 pixels due to adding the widths together.

However, to overcome this potential issue, when two elements with margins are directly one above the other, only the larger of the two margins is used to separate them. If both margins are the same size, just one of the sizes is used. This is called margin collapse, and it results in layout looking more natural than if there were no collapsing. However, you should note that the margins of absolutely positioned or inline elements do not collapse.

The margins of an element can be changed en masse with the margin shorthand property, or individually with margin-top, margin-right, margin-bottom, and margin-left. As described in Lesson 8, when setting the margin property, you can supply between one and four arguments, which have the effects commented in the following declarations (and which apply in clockwise order from the top when four values are supplied):

```
margin:1px;              /* top / right / bottom / left */
margin:1px 2px;          /* top/bottom        right/left */
margin:1px 2px 3px;      /* top      right/left     bottom */
margin:1px 2px 3px 4px;  /* top      right    bottom    left */
```

I like to think of shorthand edge (or side) rules as working like this:

- **1 value**   Think of a square (□)—applies to all edges.
- **2 values**   Think of a plus sign (+)—apply top/bottom, then left/right.
- **3 values**   Think of a division sign (÷)—apply top, then left/right, then bottom.
- **4 values**   Think of a diamond (◇)—apply top, then right, then bottom, then left.

In Figure 9-2, images of nine children's building bricks have been laid out next to each other, with eight of them blue and the central one red. All bricks share the same margins and are therefore neatly butted up against each other.

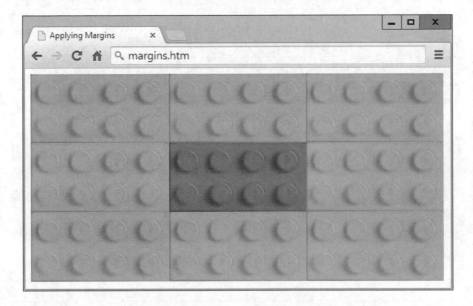

FIGURE 9-2   Nine children's building bricks butted up against each other.

This is the HTML and CSS used to create Figure 9-2 (saved as *margins.htm* in the accompanying archive), with the HTML for the central brick highlighted in bold:

```
<!DOCTYPE html>
<html>
  <head>
    <title>Applying Margins</title>
```

```
<style>
  body {line-height:0; }
</style>
</head>
<body>
  <img src='b.png'><img src='b.png'><img src='b.png'><br>
  <img src='b.png'><img class='r' src='r.png'><img src='b.png'><br>
  <img src='b.png'><img src='b.png'><img src='b.png'>
</body>
</html>
```

Note that the only thing different about the central brick is that it has the class r applied to it, although there is no class r defined. Now take a look at Figure 9-3 to see what happens when we create the class by adding it into the <style> section, as follows:

```
.r { margin:10px 20px 30px 40px; }
```

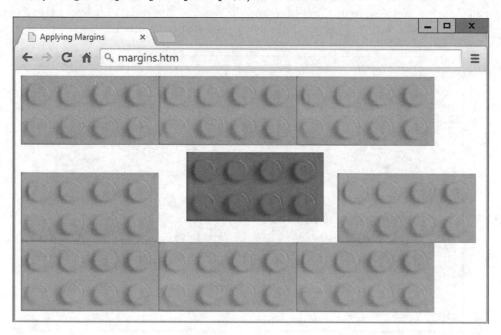

FIGURE 9-3   The central brick's margin settings have pushed the other bricks about.

In this figure you can see that the shorthand rule has set a top margin of 10 pixels, a right margin of 20 pixels, a bottom margin of 30 pixels, and a left margin of 40 pixels. You can clearly see these gaps around the central brick, and the effect that these margins have had on the surrounding objects, in that both rows two and three are now pushed down by a total of 40 pixels (10 pixels plus 30 pixels top and bottom margins), and the right-hand brick in the middle row has been pushed to the right by 60 pixels (20 pixels plus 40 pixels right and left margins).

Using Borders

The border level of the box model is similar to the margin except that there is no collapsing. It is the next level as we move from the outside of the box in toward the content area. The main properties used to modify borders are border, border-top, border-right, border-bottom, and border-left, and each of these can have other sub-properties added as suffixes, such as -color, -style, and -width. So, for example, border-left-width sets only the width of the left border.

The four shorthand ways of accessing individual property settings used for the margin property also apply with the border-width property, so all the following are valid declarations:

```
border-width:1px;              /* top / right / bottom / left */
border-width:1px 2px;          /* top/bottom        right/left */
border-width:1px 2px 3px;      /* top      right/left      bottom */
border-width:1px 2px 3px 4px;  /* top      right     bottom     left */
```

Figure 9-4 (created from the file *borders.htm* in the accompanying archive) shows the result of the following addition to the <style> section of the previous example, the result being very similar except that an orange border now takes the place of the margin:

```
.r {
  border-style:solid;
  border-color:orange;
  border-width:10px 20px 30px 40px;
}
```

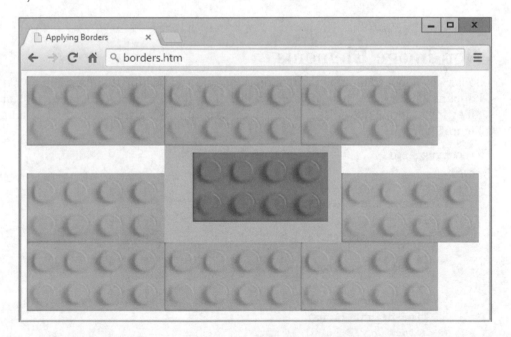

FIGURE 9-4   The border now occupies the same space that the margin did previously.

Applying Padding

The deepest of the box model levels (other than the contents of an element) is the padding, which is applied inside any borders and/or margins. The main properties used to modify padding are padding, padding-top, padding-right, padding-bottom, and padding-left.

The four ways of accessing individual property settings used for the margin and border properties also apply with the padding property, so all of the following are valid declarations:

```
padding:1px;              /* top / right / bottom / left */
padding:1px 2px;          /* top/bottom       right/left */
padding:1px 2px 3px;      /* top      right/left    bottom */
padding:1px 2px 3px 4px;  /* top      right     bottom    left */
```

If I tried to illustrate a comparable padding rule to the previous margin and border rules, all you would see is a similar result to Figure 9-3, so in Figure 9-5 I have applied settings to all of the margin, border, and padding properties of the central brick, so that you can see the result of each nested inside the other, using this CSS rule:

```
.r {
  border-style:solid;
  border-color:orange;
  margin       :10px 20px 30px 40px;
  border-width:10px 20px 30px 40px;
  padding      :10px 20px 30px 40px;
}
```

Non-image Elements

So far we've looked at applying margins, borders, and padding to images, but what happens when we do this with a <div> element, for example? Well, take a look at the following example (saved as *div1.htm* in the accompanying archive), which results in Figure 9-6:

```
<!DOCTYPE html>
<html>
  <head>
    <title>Box model with Divs</title>
    <style>
      body {line-height:0; }
      .r {
        width        :200px;
        height       :100px;
        background   :green;
        line-height  :12px;
        border-style:solid;
```

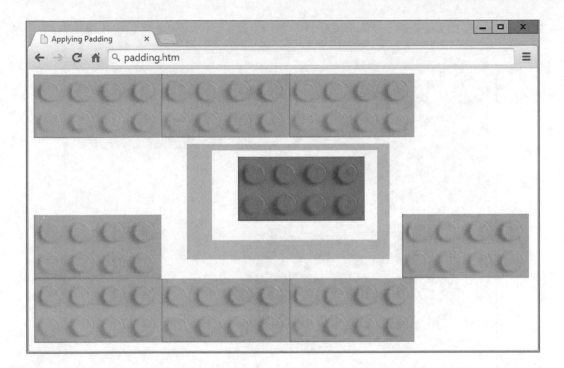

FIGURE 9-5 A margin, border, and padding have all been applied to the central brick.

```
         border-color:orange;
         margin      :10px 20px 30px 40px;
         padding     :10px 20px 30px 40px;
         border-width:10px 20px 30px 40px;
      }
   </style>
</head>
<body>
  <img src='b.png'><img src='b.png'><img src='b.png'><br>
  <img src='b.png'><div class='r'>Some Text</div><img src='b.png'><br>
  <img src='b.png'><img src='b.png'><img src='b.png'>
</body>
</html>
```

Note Note how the padding applied to the inner element also takes on the green background color, giving the effect that the element has enlarged.

To make this <div> similar to the bricks, four new declarations have been added and the central image is replaced with a <div> (all highlighted in bold), but the effect is not great because the <div> has forced a new line above and below it. So let's fix

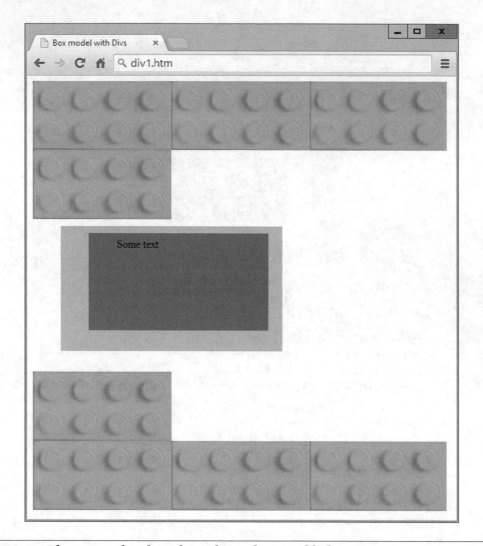

FIGURE 9-6   The **<div>** has forced new lines above and below it.

that by changing its `display` property to `inline-block`, so that it will flow inline like a `<span>` element, by adding this declaration:

```
display:inline-block;
```

Actually, the difference is more subtle than that because there are three types of elements with different inline (or otherwise) properties, as follows:

- **Inline elements**   Respect left and right margins and padding (but not top and bottom margins), allow other elements to sit to their left and right, and may not have their width and height set.

- **Block elements** Have the same width as their parent element, can have their width and height set, and force a line break following the block element.
- **Inline-block elements** Allow other elements to sit to their left and right, can have their width and height set, and respect top and bottom margins and padding, and width and height.

So, you see, when I previously said that `inline-block` elements behave like `<span>`s, this is only half true—they are both `<span>`- and `<div>`-like at the same time.

Looking at Figure 9-7 the result is a little better, but there's still a lot of extra, unwanted space around the element. This is because images happily line up with the top of each other, but other elements line up with their bottom-right-hand corners.

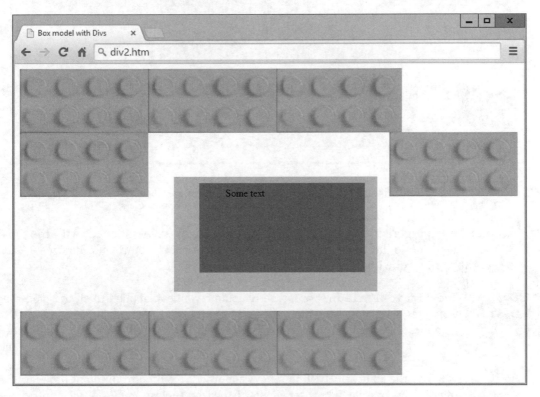

FIGURE 9-7 The elements are now inline, but not as close to each other as they could be.

To deal with this, we'll need to adjust the `vertical-align` properties of the images, as follows, resulting in Figure 9-8:

```
img { vertical-align:top; }
```

Finally we have made the `<div>` act almost like an image. Not that this is always desirable, but I felt it was necessary to show you the steps you need to take that are different between images and other elements when you want to align them precisely with each other.

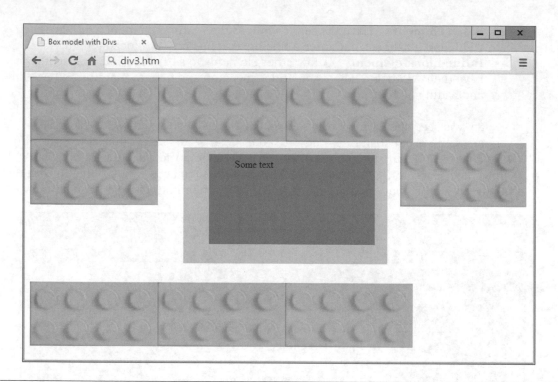

FIGURE 9-8   The **<div>** is now behaving almost like an image.

The left and right bricks in the middle row are now level (aligned) with the top of the <div> due to the vertical-align property of top, whereas in Figures 9-2 to 9-5 they are level with the bottom of the central image.

 The vertical-align:top property could have been applied to all the preceding examples and then all the figures would have looked the same, but I didn't want to complicate things by including this property earlier on. You can also use absolute positioning for your elements if you prefer, and never worry about margins pushing each other about (or how they may or may not collapse). But if you do so, you will lose the ability of HTML to reflow smoothly according to different browser dimensions, or when a browser window is resized (unless you use JavaScript to directly control a reflow according to your design).

The Object Contents

Deep within the box model levels, at its very heart, lies the basic element that can be styled in all the ways discussed in this book, and which can (and often will) contain further sub-elements, which in turn may contain sub–sub-elements, and so on, each with their own styling and box model settings.

However, as you'll learn in the following section, even this part of an element is not quite as immutable as you might think.

Changing the Box Model

So far we've looked at the box model from the point of view that the inner dimensions of an object are unchangeable, and that any modifications such as adding padding and borders will *increase* the object's size.

However, sometimes you need to have very precisely dimensioned elements where it is preferable for padding and borders (but not margins) to be *subtracted* from an element's dimensions. To support this requirement, you can specify the form of the box model you require, using the box-sizing property, like this:

```
* { box-sizing:content-box; }
* { box-sizing:border-box;  }
```

The first of these rules is the default, in which padding and borders extend the dimensions of an element, while the second rule tells the browser to apply both the border and padding properties (but not the margin) into the existing dimensions of all elements.

Figure 9-9 (created using *box-sizing.htm* in the companion archive) shows how that single rule (plus removing the rule to add margins) changes the preceding example to make the <div> fit in the same space as the bricks, although resulting in a substantially reduced area for the text to squeeze into.

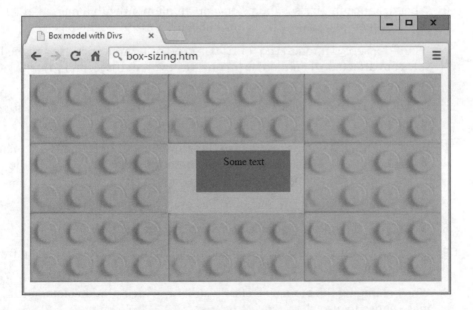

FIGURE 9-9   The **<div>** now has identical dimensions to the images.

When you change box sizing this way, you may also want to modify the pseudo-elements `before` and `after` to ensure they also fit within the existing bounds of an element, using the following rule: `*, *:before, *:after { box-sizing:border-box; }`.

Summary

This lesson marks the end of your introduction to the basics of CSS. You can now style your HTML documents in an incredible variety of ways, and have learned how to precisely control colors, location, dimensions, and much more. Starting with Lesson 10, we'll be looking at the more advanced and exciting features that CSS3 offers, including transitions, animations, and transformations.

Self-Test Questions

Using these questions, test how much you have learned in this lesson. If you don't know an answer, go back and reread the relevant section until your knowledge is complete. You can find the answers in the appendix.

1. What is meant by the term CSS box model?

2. What are the four levels of the box model?

3. What distance in pixels is there between an element with a margin of 40 pixels, that has been placed directly below one with a margin of 20 pixels?

4. When the `margin`, `padding`, or `border-width` properties are assigned, which sides are affected when there is (a) one, (b) two, (c) three, and (d) four values supplied?

5. How can you make a block element such as a `<div>` display inline with other elements?

6. When aligning elements together so that they flow inline, what is the main difference between assigning a `<div>` element's `display` property the value `inline-block`, compared with simply assigning it the value `inline`?

7. What is one way to ensure the top edges of inline elements align?

8. What is the default value of the `box-sizing` property?

9. How can you make an element's padding and border widths get taken from (rather than added to) its width and height?

10. When changing the box sizing of a document, which pseudo-elements does it make sense to also alter?

PART II

CSS3

Introduction to CSS3

To view the accompanying video for this lesson, please visit mhprofessional.com/nixoncss/.

The first implementation of CSS was initially drawn up in 1996 and then released in 1999. By 2001 all new browser releases had supported it, but even so the standard was once again revised in 2008. At the same time (beginning in 1998) CSS2 was already being drawn up, and the standard was eventually completed in 2007, but revised again in 2009.

Then there's CSS3, which commenced development in 2001, and of which some features were proposed only as recently as 2012. Therefore, the development process will likely continue for some time before a final recommendation for CSS3 is agreed upon, if ever. And even though CSS3 isn't yet complete, people are already beginning to put forward suggestions for what is sometimes termed CSS4 (and even ideas for the related HTML6 too).

So, as you will gather, the development of web standards is in a constant state of flux, and therefore a book such as this can only give a summary of the state of play at a given point in time. Therefore, I recommend that you regularly check in with the following websites to keep current with the latest developments:

- *css3.info* for the latest news on CSS3
- *quirksmode.org* for the latest browser compatibility issues

This lesson, however, gives an overview of what CSS3 has to offer right now (although some features still require browser-specific prefixes, or a JavaScript program to add the prefixes for you). Explanations of how all these examples work (and how the effects are achieved) are in the following lessons.

Attribute Selectors

As well as the standard selector types already covered in this book, there are three enhancements in CSS3 that enable you to more easily match elements based on the contents of their attributes using the three new operators: ^, $, and *. As you will see in Lesson 11, these let you select from the start or end of a matching element, and use wildcards in your matches.

Improved Backgrounds

New properties have been added to backgrounds in CSS3, for clipping, changing the origin of a background image, and specifying how borders are to be displayed relative to background images. Additionally CSS3 now supports multiple background images, as shown in Figure 10-1, and created with the following HTML (saved as *multiplebackgrounds.htm* in the accompanying archive):

```
<!DOCTYPE html>
<html>
  <head>
    <title>Multiple Backgrounds</title>
    <style>
      .frame {
        font-family:'Times New Roman';
        font-style :italic;
        font-size  :170%;
        text-align :center;
        padding    :60px;
        width      :500px;
        height     :300px;
        background :url('b1.gif') top     left  no-repeat,
                    url('b2.gif') top     right no-repeat,
                    url('b3.gif') bottom left  no-repeat,
                    url('b4.gif') bottom right no-repeat,
                    url('ba.gif') top           repeat-x,
                    url('bb.gif') left          repeat-y,
                    url('bc.gif') right         repeat-y,
                    url('bd.gif') bottom        repeat-x;
      }
      .frame h1, .frame p { margin:0; }
    </style>
  </head>
  <body>
    <div class='frame'>
      <h1>Certificate</h1>
      <p>This is to certify that</p>
      <br><hr style='width:50%'><br>
```

```
      <p>Has successfully completed the<br>
      20 Lessons CSS & CSS3 Course</p>
    </div>
  </body>
</html>
```

FIGURE 10-1   This certificate employs eight background images.

Lesson 12 explains these features in detail.

Enhanced Borders

In CSS3 there are many new ways of applying colors to borders, and using images as borders, and you can also specify a border radius to create rounded borders too, as shown in Figure 10-2 (and explained in full detail in Lesson 13), using the following HTML (saved as *roundedborders.htm* in the accompanying archive):

```
<!DOCTYPE html>
<html>
  <head>
    <title>Rounded Borders</title>
    <style>
      .circle {
        background     :lime;
```

```
      color          :navy;
      width          :300px;
      height         :300px;
      font-family    :sans-serif;
      font-size      :18pt;
      font-style     :italic;
      line-height    :22pt;
      border         :5px solid green;
      border-radius  :150px;
      text-align     :center;
      display        :table-cell;
      vertical-align:middle;
    }
  </style>
</head>
<body>
  <div class='circle'>
    Learn from<br>
    yesterday, live<br>
    for today, hope for<br>
    tomorrow. The important<br>
    thing is not to stop<br>
    questioning.<br><br>
    - Albert Einstein
  </div>
</body>
</html>
```

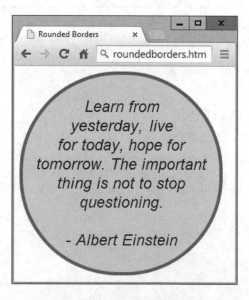

FIGURE 10-2   Yes, you can even have round elements in CSS3.

Box Shadows

Shadows can now be placed behind elements in CSS3, as shown in Figure 10-3, in which an image of a clock is shown without any extra styling, and then is repeated but with a box shadow added, using this HTML (saved as *box-shadow.htm* in the accompanying archive):

```
<!DOCTYPE html>
<html>
  <head>
    <title>Adding Box Shadows</title>
    <style>
      .shadow { box-shadow:10px 10px 15px #aaa; }
    </style>
  </head>
  <body>
    <img style='margin-right:30px' src='clock.png'>
    <img class='shadow'            src='clock.png'>
  </body>
</html>
```

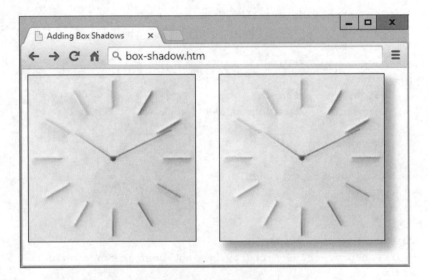

FIGURE 10-3   The second instance of the image has been given a box shadow.

Element Overflow

Overflow is where text is too large to fit within an element, and the way overflowing of element contents is handled is vastly improved in CSS3 with numerous options now available. For example, Figure 10-4 shows an element without any overflow control,

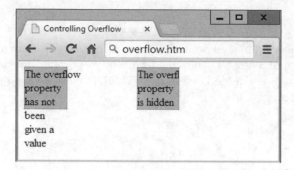

FIGURE 10-4   The right-hand element has all overflowing content hidden.

and then with the `overflow` property set to `hidden`, using this HTML (saved as *overflow.htm* in the accompanying archive):

```
<!DOCTYPE html>
<html>
  <head>
    <title>Controlling Overflow</title>
    <style>
      .box1, .box2 {
        background  :#fa8;
        width       :60px;
        height      :60px;
        border      :1px dotted #888;
        float       :left;
        margin-right:100px;
      }
      .box2 { overflow:hidden; }
    </style>
  </head>
  <body>
    <div class='box1'>
      The overflow property has not been given a value
    </div>
    <div class='box2'>
      The overflow property is hidden in this div
    </div>
  </body>
</html>
```

There is also a new `opacity` property in CSS3 for choosing how opaque (and consequently how see-through) an element should appear, and this can also be accessed as alpha transparency when specifying colors.

Multicolumn Layout

Compatible browsers supporting the new CSS3 column properties will neatly flow contents across columns, as shown in Figure 10-5, in which the first few paragraphs of this lesson have been flowed across four columns using the following HTML (saved as *multiplecolumns.htm* in the accompanying archive):

```
<!DOCTYPE html>
<html>
  <head>
  <title>Multiple Columns</title>
    <style>
      .columns {
        text-align  :justify;
        font-size   :16pt;
        column-count:4;
        column-gap  :1em;
        column-rule :1px solid black;
      }
    </style>
    <script src='../prefixfree.js'></script>
  </head>
  <body>
    <div class='columns'>
      The first implementation of CSS was initially drawn up in 1996
      and then released in 1999. By 2001 all new browser releases
      supported it, but even so the standard was once again revised
      in 2008. At the same time (beginning in 1998) CSS2 was already
      being drawn up, and the standard was eventually completed in
      2007 - but revised again in 2009. Then there's CSS3, which
      commenced development in 2001, and of which some features were
      proposed only as recently as 2012. Therefore the development
      process will likely continue for some time before a final
      recommendation for CSS3 is agreed. And even though CSS3 isn't
      yet complete, people are already beginning to put forward
      suggestions for CSS4 (and even ideas for HTML6 too).
    </div>
  </body>
</html>
```

Box shadows, overflow, and columns are explained in Lesson 14.

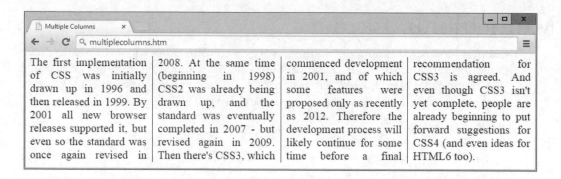

The first implementation of CSS was initially drawn up in 1996 and then released in 1999. By 2001 all new browser releases supported it, but even so the standard was once again revised in 2008. At the same time (beginning in 1998) CSS2 was already being drawn up, and the standard was eventually completed in 2007 - but revised again in 2009. Then there's CSS3, which commenced development in 2001, and of which some features were proposed only as recently as 2012. Therefore the development process will likely continue for some time before a final recommendation for CSS3 is agreed. And even though CSS3 isn't yet complete, people are already beginning to put forward suggestions for CSS4 (and even ideas for HTML6 too).

FIGURE 10-5   Flowing text across columns

Extended Color Handling and Opacity

CSS3 brings several new ways of defining colors using primary colors, or hue, saturation, and luminance, as well as supporting the use of alpha transparency, which is fully detailed in Lesson 15. Figure 10-6 shows the range of possible colors available using these techniques, in the form of a color circle. Even though monochrome versions of this book do not do it justice, you can just make out the light 'Y' shape that separates the three primary colors, and also see how the luminance gradually increases from the center to the rim.

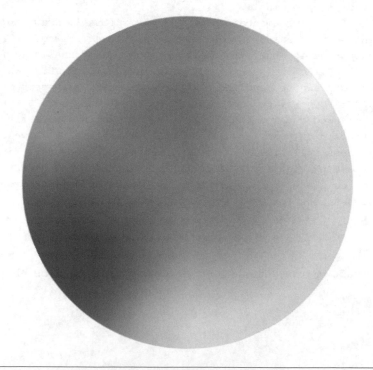

FIGURE 10-6   A color wheel displaying both hue and saturation

Additional Text Effects

New text effects are available in CSS3, including shadows (as shown in Figure 10-7, which uses the HTML below—*text-shadow.htm* in the accompanying archive), plus overflow handling (as previously described), and more precise control over word wrapping:

```
<!DOCTYPE html>
<html>
  <head>
  <title>Text Shadows</title>
    <style>
      .shadow { text-shadow:4px 4px 4px #aaa; }
    </style>
  </head>
  <body>
    <h1 class='shadow'>Shadows help text jump off the page</h1>
  </body>
</html>
```

FIGURE 10-7   Adding a shadow to text

Box Sizing

You saw this new property briefly described in the previous lesson. It allows you to decide whether the attributes you apply to an element such as padding should appear outside the dimensions of a specified element, or if the padding or other attribute should be applied inside, thus reducing the space available for the content.

Resizing and Outlines

Using CSS3 you can add resizing tabs to elements such as iframes and textareas so that users can resize them to their liking. You can also choose the offset in pixels to apply to an element when it gains focus.

Text effects, box-sizing, resizing, and outlines are all covered in Lesson 16.

Web Fonts

With CSS3 you can now have your own fonts display on your web pages or, far more conveniently, you can use those supplied by a third party, as with the vast collection of over 600 Google fonts shown in Figure 10-8, and explained in Lesson 17.

FIGURE 10-8   Accessing the several hundred freely available Google fonts

Transitions and Transformations

You can also use CSS3 to resize HTML elements, rotate them in all three dimensions, and even animate these transformations into smooth transitions. Figure 10-9 shows an image of an iPad in its original form, and then rotated by 75 degrees in three dimensions, using the following HTML (saved as *3drotation.htm* in the accompanying archive):

```
<!DOCTYPE html>
<html>
  <head>
```

FIGURE 10-9   An element is rotated by 75 degrees in 3D space around the X, Y, and Z axes.

```
    <title>3D Rotation</title>
    <style>
     .rotate {
       position :absolute;
       transform:rotate3d(1, 1, 1, 75deg);
     }
    </style>
    <script src='../prefixfree.js'></script>
  </head>
  <body>
    <img style='margin-right:100px' src='ipad.png'>
    <img class='rotate'            src='ipad.png'>
  </body>
</html>
```

Lessons 18 to 20 cover all aspects of transitions, transformations, and other 3D effects.

Summary

CSS3 comprises a huge number of powerful and flexible additions and improvements to CSS, bringing features previously not even possible using JavaScript, but now directly controllable with just a few lines of CSS. In Lesson 11, I will begin explaining them in detail.

Self-Test Questions

Using these questions, test how much you have learned in this lesson. If you don't know an answer, go back and reread the relevant section until your knowledge is complete. You can find the answers in the appendix.

1. How recently were features still being proposed for CSS3?

2. How can multiple background images be added to an element?

3. What is the major new enhancement to CSS borders?

4. Which property supports creating rounded borders?

5. Which property lets you add box shadows to elements?

6. Which property lets you add shadows to text?

7. With which property can you control how overflowing content is handled?

8. Which three properties are concerned with supporting multiple columns?

9. How many free web fonts does the Google Fonts service currently offer?

10. Which function is used to rotate elements in three dimensions?

Using Selectors and Attribute Selectors

 To view the accompanying video for this lesson, please visit mhprofessional.com/nixoncss/.

Selectors are used in CSS to match HTML elements. They are the means by which you target elements of a web page for styling. There are a number of types of selectors now available in CSS3, and there are also some new operators you can use to zone your rules in even more precisely.

This relatively short lesson provides a complete summary of the CSS selectors by supplying a recap of the selectors you've already learned (mainly in Lesson 8), before moving on to introducing what's new with attribute selectors that gives you even greater choice when applying CSS rules.

Summary of Selector Types

There are several types of selectors in CSS, enabling you to approach styling elements from a variety of different standpoints. Some of these selectors you have already learned about, and some you haven't, but as they are the cornerstone of CSS, I have summarized them here.

The Universal Selector

This selector makes use of the * (asterisk) wildcard symbol and can be used to apply a rule to any element of a document, or simply to whole subsections or parts. At its simplest you can assign a rule such as the following, which will set the text color of absolutely everything (unless otherwise styled) to a gray color:

```
* { color:#555; }
```

Of course, this is a rather drastic thing to do, and you'd be more likely to limit the impact of this all-encompassing selector by making it a descendant (or child) of another such as the document body, like this:

```
body * { color:#555; }
```

Type Selectors

Type selectors refer to types of HTML elements such as `<b>` elements, or a `<div>` or `<span>`, and so on, like this:

```
b { color:red; }
```

In this example all `<b>` elements will now use the color red. Any HTML element name can be used as a type selector, including `<html>`, `<body>`, `<iframe>`, and so on.

Class Selectors

When you want to apply sets of rules to many different elements that may or may not be of different types, you can create a class. The rules for the class are then applied to any element to which you add the class.

Class names commence with a period, as in the following example, which will set the color of text to blue for all elements that use the class `headlines`:

```
.headlines { color:blue; }
```

A class is then applied to an element using its `class` attribute, like this:

```
<div class='headlines'>This is the main section</div>
```

ID Selectors

To uniquely target single elements, you can give them an ID name and create rules just for that element, as in the following example, which uses the # (known as the hash or pound symbol) to identify the target as being an ID, setting the font weight of the target with the ID of `username` to bold:

```
#username { font-weight:bold; }
```

To apply an ID to an element, assign its name to the element's `id` attribute, like this:

```
Welcome: <span id='username'>FlorenceNightingale123</span>.
```

Descendant Selectors

Moving on in complexity (or maybe I should say flexibility), you can select the descendant elements of a parent element by separating their names with a space character. These selectors can include type selectors such as <span>s or <div>s, classes, IDs, or the universal selector.

In the following example, all <em> elements that occur anywhere within <span> elements will have their text color set to green:

```
span em { color:green; }
```

Child Selectors

If necessary, you can be more precise with your descendant selectors by turning them into child selectors, such that only direct children of the parent that fit the rule will be styled. In this example, only direct <em> children of <div> elements will have their background color set to lime because of the use of the > (greater than) symbol between them:

```
div > em { background:lime; }
```

Any grandchildren or lower descendant elements will not be targeted by this selector.

Adjacent Sibling Selectors

Sometimes you need to style elements (or selectors) because of their sibling relationship to others (rather than the more typically seen descendant relationships). In which case you can achieve this by using the + (plus) symbol between the two affected selectors. For example, this styles any <b> element that is immediately preceded by an <i> element:

```
i + b { color:gray; }
```

Another allowed rule of this type might be the following, in which any <span> that immediately follows a <div> will be styled:

```
div + span { margin-left:20px; }
```

You can even select types that are the same. For example, the following will style all <p> elements that immediately follow another <p> element:

```
p + p {text-indent:1.5em; }
```

General Sibling Selectors

New to CSS3, you can now generalize your styling of siblings by allowing them to occur anywhere within the same parent element (as long as the second element comes after the first), and still have them counted as adjacent. To do this, use the

~ (tilde) symbol to separate the two, as in the following rule, which styles all <b> elements that are general siblings of (and preceded by) <i> elements:

```
i ~ b { color:olive; }
```

 I make interesting use of general sibling selectors in some of the transform examples in Lessons 18–20, where they provide the mechanism for the mouse passing over one element to actually change the properties of a different (but adjacent) element.

Attribute Selectors

Using attribute selectors, you can target elements according to the attributes they have been given. For example, the following rule will set any elements whose href attribute value contains exactly info.htm. I explain attribute selectors in greater detail following this summary of selectors, including how to search within attribute strings too, using CSS3 enhancements:

```
a[href='info.htm'] { color:red; }
```

Pseudo-Classes

With pseudo-classes you can apply dynamic interactivity to your web pages. They are selectors that often interact dynamically with user input, as with the following example, which sets the hover state of all links to display the link in bold text:

```
a:hover { font-weight:bold; }
```

Pseudo-Elements

Using pseudo-elements, you can even modify elements to an extent by adding content before and after them, for example, or, as in the following case, by changing the size of the first letter of all <p> elements to 300 percent larger than the current setting:

```
p::first-letter { font-size:300%; }
```

Pseudo-selectors also include the more complex numeric selectors such as nth-child and nth-of-type, as explained in Lesson 8, as well as other powerful selectors like not, empty, first-line, and more.

Figure 11-1, created with *css2selectors.htm* from the companion archive, shows examples of all these selector types in action.

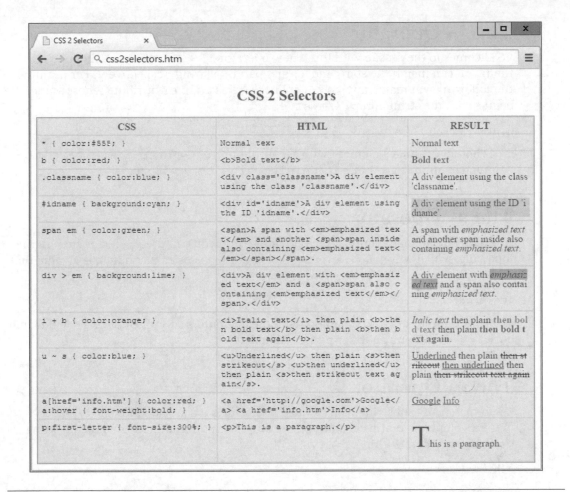

FIGURE 11-1   The CSS2 selectors

Attribute Selectors

With CSS3 it has been decided that most of these selectors work just fine the way they are, but three enhancements in particular have been made to attribute selectors so that you can more easily match elements based on the contents of their attributes.

For example, as previously explained, in CSS2 you can use a selector such as a[href='info.htm'] to match the exact value info.htm when found in an href attribute, but there's no way to match only a portion of a string, which is where the following enhancements come into play.

The ^= Operator

CSS3 comes to the rescue with three new operators: ^=, $=, and *=. Using one of them you can match the start, end, or any part of a string, respectively. For example, the following will match any <a> element that has an href attribute whose value begins with the string http://mysite:

```
a[href^='http://mysite']
```

Therefore, an <a> element with the attribute href='http://mysite.com' will match, but href='http://thisismysite.com' will not.

The $= Operator

Alternatively, to match only at the end of a string, you can use a selector such as the following, which will match any <img> element whose src attribute has a value that ends with .png:

```
img[src$='.png']
```

For example, an <img> element with the attribute src='photo.png' will match, but <img src='snapshot.jpg'> will not.

The *= Operator

Or, to match any substring, you can use a selector such as the following to select any <a> elements that have an href attribute with a value that contains the string google anywhere within it:

```
a[href*='google']
```

For example, the element <a href='http://google.com'> will match, while <a href='http://gmail.com'> will not.

Figure 11-2 shows these three new operators in use, with example CSS, HTML, and the results displayed.

In the first row only the mysite.com link is shown in red, because it matches the rule in the CSS column, while the first one doesn't. In the second row, only the smiley face matches the CSS rule because it has a .png file extension. And in the third row, only the first URL matches because it has the text google in its href value.

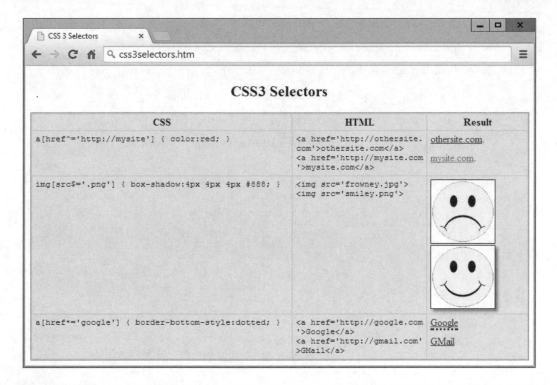

FIGURE 11-2 The CSS3 attribute selectors

Summary

Now that you are armed with all the tools you could ever want to select and style elements in every conceivable way, in the following lessons we'll move on to using these selectors to apply CSS rules, starting with the new background capabilities of CSS3.

Self-Test Questions

Using these questions, test how much you have learned in this lesson. If you don't know an answer, go back and reread the relevant section until your knowledge is complete. You can find the answers in the appendix.

1. What does the universal selector enable you to style, and what is a potential disadvantage to using it?

2. What is a type selector?

3. What is the difference between ID and class selectors?

4. What is a descendant selector?

5. What is a child selector, and which symbol does it use?

6. What is an adjacent sibling selector, and which symbol does it use?

7. What is a general sibling selector, and which symbol does it use?

8. What does an attribute selector do?

9. Using an attribute selector, how can you search (a) from the start of a string, and (b) at the end of a string?

10. Using an attribute selector, how can you search for a match anywhere in a string?

Setting Backgrounds

 To view the accompanying video for this lesson, please visit mhprofessional.com/nixoncss/.

CSS2 provides a lot of support for backgrounds, but there were still areas connected with the CSS box model that needed improvement, and which have now been addressed in CSS3, with two new properties: `background-clip` and `background-origin`.

Between them you can specify where a background should start within an element, and also how to clip the background so that it doesn't appear in parts of the box model where you don't want it to.

To accomplish this, both properties support the following attributes:

- **border-box**   Refers to the outer edge of the border
- **padding-box**   Refers to the outer edge of the padding area
- **content-box**   Refers to the outer edge of the content area

These properties are used by the latest versions of all major browsers. Also there's a new `background-size` property, and multiple backgrounds are now supported too.

The `background-clip` Property

This property specifies whether the background should be ignored (clipped) if it appears within either the border or padding area of an element. For example, the following declaration states that the background may display in all parts of an element, all the way to the outer edge of the border:

```
background-clip:border-box;
```

To restrict the background from appearing within the border area of an element, you can restrict it to only the section of an element inside the outer edge of its padding area, like this:

```
background-clip:padding-box;
```

Or, to restrict the background to display only within the content area of an element, you would use this declaration:

```
background-clip:content-box;
```

Figure 12-1, created using *backgroundclip.htm* from the accompanying archive (and listed here), shows three rows of elements in which the first row uses `border-box` for the `background-clip` property; the second uses `padding-box`; and the third uses `content-box`.

```
<!DOCTYPE html>
<html>
 <head>
  <title>CSS3 Background Clip</title>
  <style>
   .outer {
    border           :1px solid #000;
    float            :left;
    margin           :10px;
   }
   .inner {
    position         :relative;
    font-family      :'courier new', monospace;
    font-size        :12px;
    border           :1px solid #000;
    width            :100%;
    height           :100%;
   }
   .box {
    background       :url('marble.png');
    background-position:top left;
    background-repeat :no-repeat;
    font-weight      :bold;
    border           :20px dashed #00f;
    padding          :20px;
    background-color :#0cc;
    width            :140px;
    height           :140px;
   }
   .info {
    position         :absolute;
    bottom           :0;
```

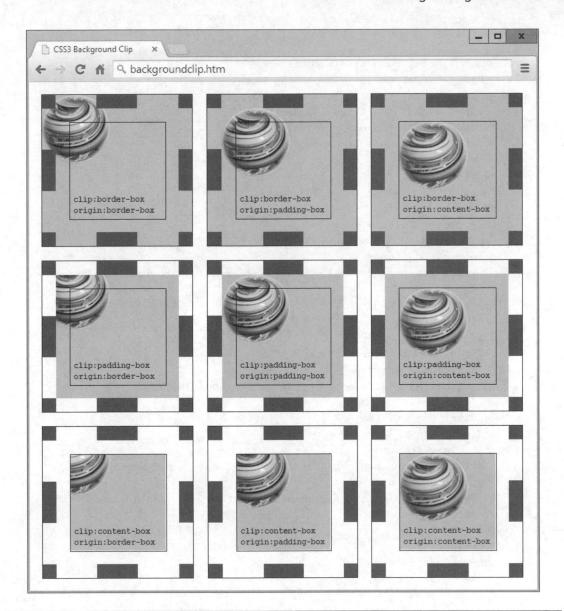

FIGURE 12-1   Different ways of combining the new CSS3 background properties

```
  padding              :5px;
  }
  .obb { background-origin:border-box;   }
  .opb { background-origin:padding-box;  }
  .ocb { background-origin:content-box;  }
  .cbb { background-clip   :border-box;  }
  .cpb { background-clip   :padding-box; }
  .ccb { background-clip   :content-box; }
 </style>
 <script src='../prefixfree.js'></script>
</head>
<body>
 <div class='outer'>
  <div class='box obb cbb'>
   <div class='inner'>
    <span class='info'>clip:border-box<br>origin:border-box</span>
   </div>
  </div>
 </div>
 <div class='outer'>
  <div class='box opb cbb'>
   <div class='inner'>
    <span class='info'>clip:border-box<br>origin:padding-box</span>
   </div>
  </div>
 </div>
 <div class='outer'>
  <div class='box ocb cbb'>
   <div class='inner'>
    <span class='info'>clip:border-box<br>origin:content-box</span>
   </div>
  </div>
 </div>
 <div class='outer'>
  <div class='box obb cpb'>
   <div class='inner'>
    <span class='info'>clip:padding-box<br>origin:border-box</span>
   </div>
  </div>
 </div>
 <div class='outer'>
  <div class='box opb cpb'>
   <div class='inner'>
    <span class='info'>clip:padding-box<br>origin:padding-box</span>
   </div>
```

```
    </div>
   </div>
   <div class='outer'>
    <div class='box ocb cpb'>
     <div class='inner'>
      <span class='info'>clip:padding-box<br>origin:content-box</span>
     </div>
    </div>
   </div>
   <div class='outer'>
    <div class='box obb ccb'>
     <div class='inner'>
      <span class='info'>clip:content-box<br>origin:border-box</span>
     </div>
    </div>
   </div>
   <div class='outer'>
    <div class='box opb ccb'>
     <div class='inner'>
      <span class='info'>clip:content-box<br>origin:padding-box</span>
     </div>
    </div>
   </div>
   <div class='outer'>
    <div class='box ocb ccb'>
     <div class='inner'>
      <span class='info'>clip:content-box<br>origin:content-box</span>
     </div>
    </div>
   </div>
  </body>
</html>
```

In the first row, the inner box (an image of a marble that has been loaded into the top-left of the element, with repeating disabled) is allowed to display anywhere in the element. You can also clearly see it displayed in the border area of the first box because the border has been set to dashed.

Note   In the second column the marble has been forced to move out of the border area and into the padding area, and in the third column it has been moved even deeper inside, into the content area. This is done using the `background-origin` property, explained in the following section.

In the second row, neither the background image nor the background color displays in the border area, because they have been clipped to the padding area with a `background-clip` property value of `padding-box`.

Then, in the third row, both the background color and the image have been clipped to display only within the content area of each element, using a `background-clip` property of `content-box`.

The `background-origin` Property

With this property you can also specify where you would like a background image to be located by specifying where the top left of the image should start. For example, the following declaration states that the background image's origin is to be the top-left corner of the outer edge of the border:

```
background-origin:border-box;
```

To set the origin of an image to the top-left outer corner of the padding area, you would use this declaration:

```
background-origin:padding-box;
```

Or to set the origin of an image to the top-left corner of an element's inner content section, you would use this declaration:

```
background-origin:content-box;
```

Looking again at Figure 12-1, the first column uses a `background-origin` property of `border-box`, the second column uses `padding-box`, and the third column uses `content-box`. Consequently, in each row the background image displays at the top left of the border in the first box, the top left of the padding in the second, and the top left of the content in the third box.

 The only differences to note between the rows, with regard to the origins of the background in Figure 12-1, are that in rows two and three the background is clipped to the padding and content areas respectively, and therefore outside these areas no portion of the background is displayed.

Compatibility Issues

As is often the case in the ever-evolving field of web development, some browsers handle things differently. For example, older versions of the Firefox and Safari browsers have their own property names.

The standard property names are `background-clip` and `background-origin`, but on older Firefox (and other Gecko-based browsers) they are called `-moz-background-clip` and `-moz-background-origin`. While on older Safari browsers (and others based on the Webkit rendering engine), their names are `-webkit-background-clip` and `-webkit-background-origin`.

Therefore, when you use the `background-clip` property, if you wish your CSS rules to apply on as wide a range of browsers as possible, you may choose to also use the alternate property names to ensure that they recognize what you want to achieve.

You should also take into account that older versions of Firefox and Safari use the nonstandard values of `border`, `padding`, and `content` for these properties, instead of `border-box`, `padding-box`, and `content-box`.

 Of course, the *prefixfree.js* program supplied in the accompanying archive (downloadable for free from *20lessons.com*), will take care of all these issues for you—just include it in any web pages you create that use these features, and you won't have to worry about the proprietary prefixes for any browsers.

The `background-size` Property

In the same way that you can specify the width and height of an image when used in an `<img>` tag, you can now also do the same for background images on the latest versions of all major browsers.

Because each browser works differently, you will need the following set of declarations to change the size of a background on all browsers (where *ww* is the width and *hh* is the height), or use the *prefixfree.js* utility in the accompanying archive to do this for you:

```
-moz-background-size    :wwpx hhpx;
-webkit-background-size:wwpx hhpx;
-o-background-size      :wwpx hhpx;
background-size         :wwpx hhpx;
```

If you prefer, you can use only one argument, and then the second value will be assumed to be `auto`. You can also specify the width and/or height as a percentage, instead of a fixed value, and the size will then be relative to the background positioning area.

Using the `auto` Value

If you wish to scale only one dimension of a background image, and then have the other one scale automatically to retain the same proportions, you can use the value `auto` for the other dimension, like this:

```
background-size:100px auto;
```

This sets the width to 100 pixels and the height to a value proportionate to the increase or decrease in width.

Multiple Backgrounds

With CSS3 you can now attach multiple backgrounds to an element, each of which can use the previously discussed CSS3 background properties. Figure 12-2 shows an example of a certificate, in which eight different images have been assigned to the background, to create the four corners and four edges of the certificate border.

FIGURE 12-2 This framed photo comprises a `div` with eight different background images.

To display multiple background images in a single CSS declaration, you separate them with a comma. For example, here is the CSS that was used to create the border in Figure 12-2, with plenty of white space and formatting added to make it clear what is happening.

```
background:
  url('b1.gif') top    left  no-repeat,
  url('b2.gif') top    right no-repeat,
  url('b3.gif') bottom left  no-repeat,
  url('b4.gif') bottom right no-repeat,
  url('ba.gif') top    repeat-x,
  url('bb.gif') left   repeat-y,
  url('bc.gif') right  repeat-y,
  url('bd.gif') bottom repeat-x;
```

The first four lines place the corner images into the four corners of the element, and the final four place the edge images, which are handled last because the order of priority for background images goes from high to low. Where they overlap, additional background images will appear *behind* already placed images. If they weren't in this order, then the repeating edge images would display on top of the corners, which would be incorrect.

Then the photo is also placed into the frame by adding it after the border images, and taking advantage of the fact that previously added images appear in front of newer ones:

```
url('image.jpg') top left no-repeat;
```

Also, to make the photo frame work as a true border, the inner white portions of the corner images have been set to transparent to allow the photo to appear there, while the outer corners were kept opaque, preventing the photo from displaying.

Using this CSS you can resize the containing element to any dimensions and the border will correctly resize to fit, allowing photos (or other content) of any dimensions, which is a lot easier than using tables or multiple elements to achieve the same effect. What's more, this feature is supported by the latest versions of all major browsers on all platforms.

The HTML and CSS used to create this figure (listed here) is saved in the accompanying archive as *backgroundimages.htm*. The images used by the document are in Figure 12-3.

```
<!DOCTYPE html>
<html>
  <head>
    <title>Multiple Backgrounds</title>
    <style>
      .frame {
        width       :632px;
        height      :455px;
        background :url('b1.gif')    top     left   no-repeat,
                    url('b2.gif')    top     right  no-repeat,
                    url('b3.gif')    bottom  left   no-repeat,
                    url('b4.gif')    bottom  right  no-repeat,
                    url('ba.gif')    top            repeat-x,
                    url('bb.gif')    left           repeat-y,
                    url('bc.gif')    right          repeat-y,
                    url('bd.gif')    bottom         repeat-x,
                    url('image.jpg') top     left   no-repeat;
      }
    </style>
    <script src='../prefixfree.js'></script>
  </head>
  <body>
    <div class='frame'></div>
  </body>
</html>
```

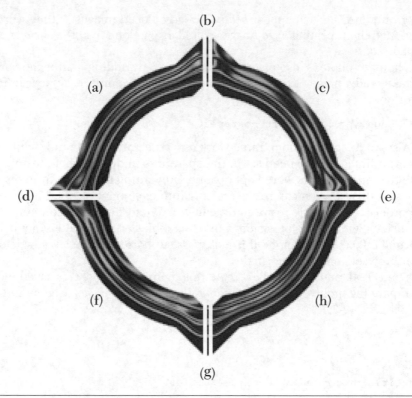

FIGURE 12-3   (a) Top left corner: *b1.gif.* (b) Top center edge: *ba.gif.* (c) Top right corner: *b2.gif.* (d) Left center edge: *bb.gif.* (e) Right center edge: *bc.gif.* (f) Bottom left corner: *b3.gif.* (g) Bottom center edge: *bd.gif.* (h) Bottom right corner: *b4.gif.*

Summary

You will now be able to create almost any background you need for your web pages using single or multiple images, scale them to your exact requirements, and support dynamic resizing of browsers and elements in which the backgrounds will always look good.

If you ever produce any animations in your web pages, you can create a great 3D effect by moving the background(s) about in relation to the foreground movement, and even enlarging and reducing their width and height to simulate zooming in and out.

In Lesson 13 we'll take a detailed look into the world of CSS3 borders.

Self-Test Questions

Using these questions, test how much you have learned in this lesson. If you don't know an answer, go back and reread the relevant section until your knowledge is complete. You can find the answers in the appendix.

1. What does the `border-box` value refer to?

2. What does the `padding-box` value refer to?

3. What does the `content-box` value refer to?

4. What is the purpose of the `background-clip` property?

5. What values can you supply to the `background-clip` property?

6. What is the purpose of the `background-origin` property?

7. What values can you supply to the `background-origin` property?

8. How can you alter the size of a background image?

9. How can you scale one background image dimension and have the other scale automatically to match?

10. What CSS declaration might you use to load the background image *corner.gif* into the top right-hand corner of an element, with no repetition?

Attaching Borders

 To view the accompanying video for this lesson, please visit mhprofessional.com/ nixoncss/.

CSS3 brings a lot more flexibility to the way borders can be presented, by allowing you to independently change the colors of all four border edges, to display images for the edges and corners, to provide a radius value for applying rounded corners to borders, and to place box shadows underneath elements.

Used singly or in combination these features let you style elements in such a way that you would never realize they were crafted with just HTML and CSS. As you will see in one of the examples in this chapter, the power and flexibility of these new features goes beyond the Web, as you can use them to create borders for posters and documents too (just use your browser's Print function).

The `border-color` Properties

There are two ways you can apply colors to a border. First, you can assign a single color to the property, as follows:

```
border-color:#888;
```

This declaration sets all the borders of an element to mid-gray. You can also set border colors individually, like this (which sets the border colors to various shades of gray):

```
border-top-color   :#000;
border-left-color  :#444;
border-right-color :#888;
border-bottom-color:#ccc;
```

You can also set all the colors individually with a single declaration, as follows:

```
border-color:#f00 #0f0 #880 #00f;
```

This declaration sets the top border color to #f00, the right one to #0f0, the bottom one to #880, and the left one to #00f (red, green, orange, and blue, respectively). You can also use color names (or six-digit hexadecimal strings) for these arguments.

The `border-style` Properties

It is possible to apply a wide variety of border styles, either to the entire border of an element or to individual edges. To do this, you can assign values to the border-style property, like this:

```
border-style:dotted;
```

The visible styles available include dotted, dashed, solid, double, groove, ridge, inset, and outset. Figure 13-1 shows eight images using each of these values in turn, using the following HTML (saved as *borderstyles.htm* in the accompanying archive):

```
<!DOCTYPE html>
<html>
  <head>
    <title>Border Styles</title>
    <style>
      img {
        padding      :10px;
        margin       :10px;
        border-color:#8ac;
        border-width:10px;
      }
      .dotted { border-style:dotted; }
      .dashed { border-style:dashed; }
      .solid  { border-style:solid;  }
      .double { border-style:double; }
      .groove { border-style:groove; }
      .ridge  { border-style:ridge;  }
      .inset  { border-style:inset;  }
      .outset { border-style:outset; }
    </style>
    <script src='../prefixfree.js'></script>
  </head>
<body>
  <img class='dotted' src='photo.jpg'>
  <img class='dashed' src='photo.jpg'>
  <img class='solid'  src='photo.jpg'>
  <img class='double' src='photo.jpg'>
  <img class='groove' src='photo.jpg'>
```

```
    <img class='ridge'  src='photo.jpg'>
    <img class='inset'  src='photo.jpg'>
    <img class='outset' src='photo.jpg'>
  </body>
</html>
```

FIGURE 13-1   The eight types of border styles available in CSS

You can also address each of the edges of an element individually, like this:

`border-top-style:double;`

In Figure 13-2, the following modified CSS from the previous example (the entire HTML is saved as *moreborderstyles.htm* in the accompanying archive) applies border styles in a similar way to the previous example but only to one of the top, left, right, or bottom borders of each picture:

```
.dotted { border-top-style    :dotted; }
.dashed { border-left-style   :dashed; }
.solid  { border-right-style  :solid;  }
.double { border-bottom-style :double; }
.groove { border-top-style    :groove; }
.ridge  { border-right-style  :ridge;  }
.inset  { border-left-style   :inset;  }
.outset { border-bottom-style :outset; }
```

FIGURE 13-2 The border styles are applied only to single edges.

 See how when a single border is applied without a matching opposite border, the image is displaced away from that border.

You can also set all the edges of an element to different border styles in a clockwise direction from top to left, using a single declaration, like this:

```
border-style:dotted groove inset dashed;
```

The `border-image` Properties

On the latest versions of all major browsers, it is possible to display images for the four edges and four corners of an element. Using this feature, you can achieve similar results to those in the section "Multiple Backgrounds" (see Lesson 12), but you use only a single image comprising all eight elements, such as the one in Figure 13-3.

In this image there are four corners, each separated from the others by a single pixel edge. Your edges may have more detail than a single pixel's width or height, and your corners can also be smaller or larger.

To attach this image to an element as its border, you use declarations such as these:

```
border-image-source:url('border.png');
border-image-width :130px 208px 130px 208px;
border-image-slice :130 208 130 208;
```

FIGURE 13-3   A compound image (*border.png*) used for creating borders

The first CSS declaration loads in the border image. The second sets the width of the borders, which can be a single value if all the images are of the same dimensions, or it can list the dimensions in clockwise order from the top to the left. If the fourth, or third and fourth values are omitted, then the second, or first and second values are reused.

The last declaration has four values that represent the top, right, bottom, and left number of pixels to use for each of the corners. Like `border-image-width`, this may be a single value that applies to all edges, or four values, with one for each edge. If the fourth, or third and fourth values are omitted, then the second, or first and second values are reused.

Whatever space remains is used for the edges, and therefore you should not use any more than 50 percent of an image's dimensions on any corner, as shown in Figure 13-4, in which light-colored lines have been added to divide the eight elements to make them more clearly visible. The tiny area in the central ninth portion of an image is ignored.

In the case of the *border.png* example, it is 417 × 261 pixels, with each of the corners being 208 × 130 pixels, leaving a single pixel width or height for the edge parts. You can also use percent values in place of pixels by adding a % character to them, like this (although pixels can be more precise):

```
border-image-source:url('border.png');
border-image-width :130px 208px 130px 208px;
border-image-slice :49.99% 49.99% 49.99% 49.99%;
```

In this instance the 49.99 percent value is the largest value that makes sense for most image sizes, and which will also work in all browsers. In this instance, due to repetition, the second and third declarations can be shortened to:

```
border-image-width :130px 208px;
border-image-slice :49.99%;
```

FIGURE 13-4 The *border.png* image divided into its constituent parts and enlarged

Figure 13-5 shows this image being used to create an opening-hours sign for a tea room, similar to the photo example in Lesson 12, only here a single image is used rather than several. The HTML for this figure is as follows, and is saved in the accompanying file archive as *borderimage.htm*.

```
<!DOCTYPE html>
<html>
  <head>
    <title>CSS3 Border Image Example</title>
    <style>
      .border {
        font-family         :'Times New Roman';
        font-style          :italic;
        font-size           :175%;
        text-align          :center;
        width               :800px;
        height              :600px;
        display             :table-cell;
        vertical-align      :middle;
        border-image-source:url('border.png');
```

```
        border-image-width :130px 208px;
        border-image-slice :49.99%;
      }
    </style>
    <script src='../prefixfree.js'></script>
  </head>
  <body>
    <div class='border'>
      <h1>TEA ROOM</h1>
      <h2>Open Daily</h2>
      <h3>9am to 5pm</h3>
    </div>
  </body>
</html>
```

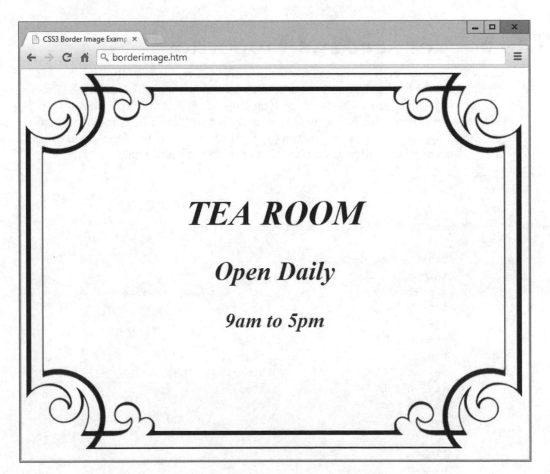

FIGURE 13-5   A sign for a tea room created using a single-border image

If you load this example into a browser, try resizing the browser width and watch how the borders are "elastic" and collapse as they reduce in size. When you reduce the browser to a very small width (such that the corners touch each other), the border images will even begin to be scaled down in size automatically to keep everything looking good.

By the way, Internet Explorer sometimes seems to use slightly different math when calculating dimensions of border images, and occasionally grabs a few pixels where it shouldn't, which can then get stretched across the background (generally this happens when using single pixel edges). If you experience this problem, create an image with larger edge parts.

 To obtain the vertical centering of the text in this example, I used a sneaky trick, which is to set the `display` property of the element to `table-cell` so that I could then apply the value `middle` to its `vertical-align` property.

The `border-radius` Properties

Prior to CSS3 talented web developers came up with numerous different tweaks and fixes in order to achieve rounded borders, generally using <table> or <div> tags.

But now adding rounded borders to an element is really simple, and it works on the latest versions of all major browsers, as shown in Figure 13-6, in which a 20-pixel border is displayed in a variety of ways. The HTML for this figure is saved in the accompanying file archive as *borderradius.htm*, and is listed next.

```
<!DOCTYPE html>
<html>
  <head>
    <title>CSS3 Border Radius Examples</title>
    <style>
      .border1, .border2, .border3, .border4 {
        margin-bottom          :10px;
        font-family            :'Courier New', monospace;
        font-size              :9pt;
        text-align             :center;
        padding                :10px;
        width                  :200px;
        height                 :200px;
        line-height            :15px;
        background             :#04a;
        border                 :20px solid #080;
        color                  :#fff;
        float                  :left;
        margin                 :10px;
      }
```

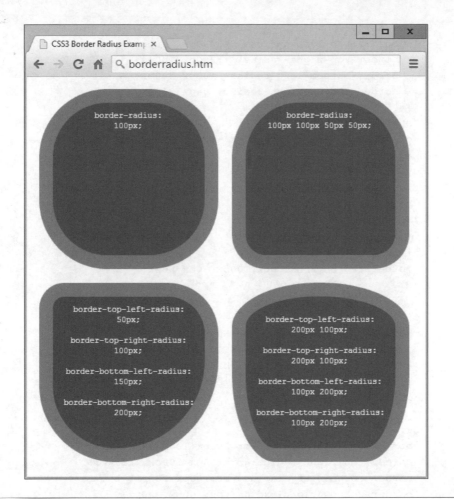

FIGURE 13-6   A selection of different **border-radius** styles

```
.border1 {
  border-radius              :100px;
 }
.border2 {
  border-radius              :100px 100px 50px 50px;
}
.border3 {
  border-top-left-radius     :50px;
  border-top-right-radius    :100px;
  border-bottom-left-radius :150px;
  border-bottom-right-radius:200px;
}
```

```
        .border4 {
          border-top-left-radius      :200px 100px;
          border-top-right-radius     :200px 100px;
          border-bottom-left-radius :100px 200px;
          border-bottom-right-radius:100px 200px;
        }
    </style>
    <script src='../prefixfree.js'></script>
  </head>
<body>
  <div class='border1'>
    border-radius:<br>100px;
  </div>

  <div class='border2'>
    border-radius:<br>100px 100px 50px 50px;
  </div>

  <div class='border3'>
    border-top-left-radius:<br>50px;<br><br>
    border-top-right-radius:<br>100px;<br><br>
    border-bottom-left-radius:<br>150px;<br><br>
    border-bottom-right-radius:<br>200px;
  </div>

  <div class='border4'><br>
    border-top-left-radius:<br>200px 100px;<br><br>
    border-top-right-radius:<br>200px 100px;<br><br>
    border-bottom-left-radius:<br>100px 200px;<br><br>
    border-bottom-right-radius:<br>100px 200px;
  </div>
  </body>
</html>
```

To create a rounded border with a radius of 20 pixels, you could simply use the following declaration, which sets all the corners to 20 pixels:

```
border-radius:20px;
```

Note   It's not quite as easy as that, however, because although most browsers will work fine with `border-radius` and other similar properties, some older versions of the major browsers use different property names, and if you wish to support them, you will need to also use `-moz-` and `-webkit-` prefixes. But, as with this example, if you include the *prefixfree.js* utility in a `<script>` section, you won't have to worry about these browser inconsistencies.

If you prefer, you can specify a separate radius for each of the four corners, like this (applied in a clockwise direction starting from the top-left corner):

```
border-radius:10px 20px 30px 40px;
```

Or you can also address each corner of an element individually, like this:

```
border-top-left-radius     :20px;
border-top-right-radius    :40px;
border-bottom-left-radius  :60px;
border-bottom-right-radius:80px;
```

And, when referencing individual corners, you can supply two arguments to choose a different vertical and horizontal radius—giving more interesting and subtle borders—like this:

```
border-top-left-radius     :40px 20px;
border-top-right-radius    :40px 20px;
border-bottom-left-radius  :20px 40px;
border-bottom-right-radius:20px 40px;
```

The first argument is the horizontal radius, and the second is the vertical radius.

Summary

In Lesson 12 we examined creating backgrounds, some of which emulated borders, while in this one we've looked at advanced border techniques. In Lesson 14 we'll complete our study of styling behind and around elements, by learning how to add shadows to them, handle content that may overflow from them, and even move our focus back inside HTML elements, to see how to use CSS3 for flowing text across multiple columns.

Self-Test Questions

Using these questions, test how much you have learned in this lesson. If you don't know an answer, go back and reread the relevant section until your knowledge is complete. You can find the answers in the appendix.

1. What are the three ways you can change all the borders of an element to the same color?

2. How can you set all four borders of an element to different colors with a single declaration?

3. How can you change the color of just one border of an element?

4. How can you set all four borders of an element to different styles with a single declaration?

5. Which three properties are often used together to assemble multiple border images to make up an element's border?

6. What is the purpose of the `border-image-width` property?

7. What is the purpose of the `border-image-slice` property?

8. How can you give all four corners of an element the same border radius?

9. How can you assign a radius to just a single corner of an element?

10. How can you apply a different radius to each corner of an element using a single CSS declaration?

Controlling Box Shadows, Overflow, and Columns

 To view the accompanying video for this lesson, please visit mhprofessional.com/nixoncss/.

Having looked in detail at backgrounds and borders, in this lesson we examine other means of making your web pages look outstanding, including adding shadows, specifying what should happen to text that's too large to fit in an element, and flowing text over two or more columns, newspaper-style.

With the three features in this lesson, you'll be able to apply styles to your web pages that will really make the difference between them being just so-so and simply outstanding.

Adding Box Shadows

A great way to emphasize an object is to give it a box shadow. To do this, you specify a horizontal and vertical offset from the object, the blur radius (amount of blurring to add to the shadow), (optionally) a value representing the distance over which to spread the shadow, and the color to use, like this:

```
box-shadow:15px 15px 10px #888;
```

The two instances of 15px specify the vertical and horizontal offset from the element, and these values can be negative, 0, or positive. The 10px specifies the blur radius (amount of blurring), with smaller values resulting in a sharper blue. And the #888 is the color for the shadow, which can be any valid color value. The result of this

rule can be seen applied to two different elements in Figure 14-1, using the HTML
here (and saved as *boxshadow.htm* in the accompanying archive at *20lessons.com*):

```html
<!DOCTYPE html>
<html>
  <head>
  <title>Box Shadow Example</title>
    <style>
      .box {
        width          :300px;
        height         :140px;
        font-size      :190%;
        color          :yellow;
        text-align     :center;
        background     :#e88;
        line-height    :27px;
        border         :10px solid #008;
        float          :left;
        margin         :70px 30px 0 20px;
      }
      .circle {
        background     :lime;
        color          :navy;
        width          :300px;
        height         :300px;
        font-family    :sans-serif;
        font-size      :200%;
        font-style     :italic;
        line-height    :22pt;
        border         :10px solid green;
        border-radius  :160px;
        margin         :60px;
        text-align     :center;
        display        :table-cell;
        vertical-align :middle;
      }
      .shadow {
        box-shadow     :15px 15px 10px #888;
      }
    </style>
    <script src='../prefixfree.js'></script>
  </head>
  <body>
    <div class='box shadow'>
      <br>Most HTML elements are rectangular,
      to fit easily in a layout, but...
    </div>
```

```
<div class='circle shadow'>
    ...making<br>
    Elements in<br>
    CSS turn circular<br>
    is easy if you<br>
    use border-<br>
    radius<br>
  </div>
</body>
</html>
```

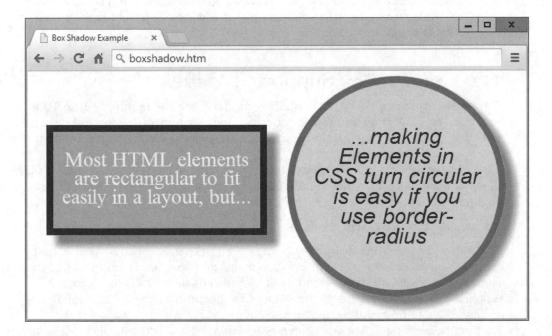

FIGURE 14-1 Box shadows are displayed under two different shapes of element.

As you can see, although the property name is called box-shadow, rounded borders are also taken into account, even to the extent that when an element is made circular, the shadow will follow that curve, so you are not restricted to simple, rectangular box shadows. Incidentally, if you resize the browser's width, you'll see that the circle will squash into an oval shape to keep it on-screen.

When setting up box shadows, it's often a good idea to test a variety of horizontal and vertical offset values to determine the best location for the shadow. Remember that shadows need not only fall below an element and may, indeed, appear at any edge or corner. Or you can set no offset at all if you plan on simply having a blur effect completely surround an element.

And while you are at it, it's also worthwhile testing a range of different blur settings to achieve exactly the right effect. At the same time, either matching the shadow color to the background or contrasting it can obtain some eye-catching results.

All recent versions of the major browsers support this property, but older ones may require the browser-specific prefixes such as -moz-, so it can be worth including the *prefixfree.js* utility when using box shadows to handle these prefixes for you.

 Even though images with alpha transparency may appear to have a rounded or other nonrectangular border, the box-shadow property will only ever display in rectangular form unless you apply a rounded border to the image. So, if you need shadows around or under images to take alpha transparency into account, this is achievable using the HTML5 canvas element and JavaScript (but that's a topic for another book).

The box-shadow Supported Values

The values supported by the box-shadow property are the required vertical and horizontal offset of the shadow, the optional values for blur radius, spread distance, and color, and a value for specifying whether the shadow should be inset, rather than appear outside the element.

So far we've seen the two offsets, blur radius, and color being used, but let's take a look at what happens when we also bring the spread argument into play, like this (highlighted in bold):

```
box-shadow:0 0 10px 10px #888;
```

In this instance the offsets have been set to 0 so that the shadow is directly behind the element, and the blur radius remains at 10px, but is only just discernable. Therefore, to make the shadow stand out, a spread distance value of 10px is also supplied which clearly displays the shadow, as shown in Figure 14-2 (created with *boxshadow2.htm* from the accompanying archive).

Finally, after the color, you can choose to make the shadow display inside, rather than outside, an element by supplying the value inset, like this:

```
box-shadow:0 0 20px 10px #444 inset;
```

The result of using the inset value is shown in Figure 14-3 (created with *boxshadow3.htm* in the accompanying archive).

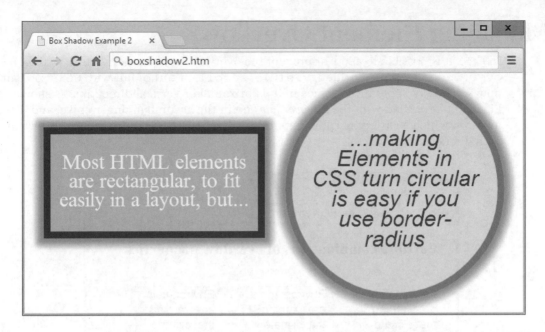

FIGURE 14-2   The shadow has been centered and given a spread of 10 pixels.

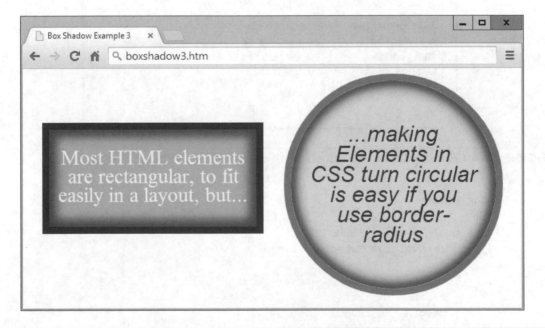

FIGURE 14-3   The shadow now displays on the elements' insides.

Managing Element Overflow

In CSS2 it is possible to allow or prevent the overflow from an element by setting the overflow property to hidden, visible, scroll, or auto. But with CSS3 you can now separately apply these values in the horizontal or vertical directions, as shown in Figure 14-4 (created with the file *overflow.htm* in the accompanying archive, and listed next), in which a variety of combinations are displayed for content that overflows in both directions.

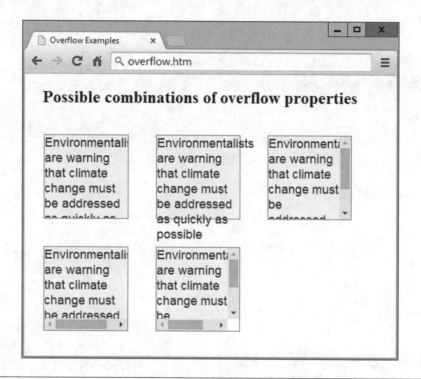

FIGURE 14-4   Some possible combinations of the various overflow properties

```
<!DOCTYPE html>
<html>
  <head>
    <title>Overflow Examples</title>
    <style>
      .box1, .box2, .box3, .box4, .box5 {
        float     :left;
        margin    :20px;
        font-family:Arial;
```

```
        font-size  :18px;
        border     :1px solid #f00;
        width      :120px;
        height     :120px;
        background :#ff6;
        color      :#00a;
      }
      .box1 {
        overflow-x :hidden;
        overflow-y :hidden;
      }
      .box2 {
        overflow-x :visible;
        overflow-y :visible;
      }
      .box3 {
        overflow-x :hidden;
        overflow-y :visible;
      }
      .box4 {
        overflow-x :visible;
        overflow-y :hidden;
      }
      .box5 {
        overflow-x :scroll;
        overflow-y :scroll;
      }
    </style>
    <script src='../prefixfree.js'></script>
  </head>
<body>
  <h2>   Possible combinations of overflow properties</h2>
  <div class='box1'>
    Environmentalists are warning that climate change
    must be addressed as quickly as possible
  </div>
  <div class='box2'>
    Environmentalists are warning that climate change
    must be addressed as quickly as possible
  </div>
  <div class='box3'>
    Environmentalists are warning that climate change
```

```
      must be addressed as quickly as possible
    </div>
    <div class='box4'>
      Environmentalists are warning that climate change
      must be addressed as quickly as possible
    </div>
    <div class='box5'>
      Environmentalists are warning that climate change
      must be addressed as quickly as possible
    </div>
  </body>
</html>
```

You must be careful with how you assign these values, because sometimes when you set the `overflow-x` or `overflow-y` properties to `visible`, the contents of the element don't actually display outside of it. According to the W3C specifications, the reason for this is that some combinations with the `visible` argument are not possible and that if one is specified as `visible`, while the other is either `scroll` or `auto`, then the `visible` value should be changed to `auto`.

There are also few differences in how these properties are implemented, though, because as well as this rule, in Internet Explorer versions 6 through 9, any `visible` property, when combined with a `hidden`, is also changed to `hidden`.

Here are some examples of using the properties:

```
overflow-x:hidden;
overflow-x:visible;
overflow-y:auto;
overflow-y:scroll;
```

Flowing Text over Multiple Columns

One of the most requested features by web developers was multiple columns, and this has finally been realized with CSS3—with even Internet Explorer having caught up in its recent versions.

Flowing text over multiple columns is as easy as specifying the number of columns, and then (optionally) choosing the spacing between them, and the type of dividing line (if any), as shown in Figure 14-5, which was created using the file *multiplecolumns.htm* in the accompanying archive.

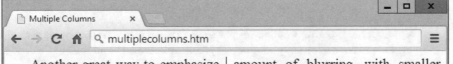

Another great way to emphasize an object is to give it a box shadow. To do this you specify a horizontal and vertical offset from the object, the amount of blurring to add to the shadow, and the color to use, like this: `box-shadow:15px 15px 10px #888;`

The two instances of `15px` specify the vertical and horizontal offset from the element, and these values can be negative, 0 or positive. The `10px` specifies the amount of blurring, with smaller values resulting in less blurring. And the `#888` is the color for the shadow, which can be any valid color value.

Although the property name is called `box-shadow`, rounded borders are also taken into account, even to the extent that when an element is made circular, the shadow will follow that curve, so you are not restricted to simple, rectangular box shadows.

FIGURE 14-5   A two-column layout displaying the start of this lesson

The HTML and CSS used to create the figure is as follows:

```
<!DOCTYPE html>
<html>
  <head>
  <title>Multiple Columns</title>
  <style>
    .columns {
      text-align  :justify;
      font-size   :16pt;
      column-count:2;
      column-gap  :1em;
      column-rule :1px solid black;
    }
    .columns p {
      margin      :0;
      text-indent :30px;
    }
    .mono {
      font-family :monospace;
    }
  </style>
  <script src='../prefixfree.js'></script>
  </head>
```

```
<body>
  <div class='columns'>
    <p>Another great way to emphasize an object is to give it a box
    shadow. To do this you specify a horizontal and vertical offset
    from the object, the amount of blurring to add to the shadow,
    and the color to use, like this: <span class='mono'>box-shadow:
    15px 15px 10px #888;</span></p>
    <p>The two instances of <span class='mono'>15px</span> specify
    the vertical and horizontal offset from the element, and these
    values can be negative, 0 or positive. The <span class='mono'>
    10px</span> specifies the amount of blurring, with smaller
    values resulting in less blurring. And the <span class='mono'>
    #888</span> is the color for the shadow, which can be any valid
    color value.</p>
    <p>Although the property name is called <span class='mono'>
    box-shadow</span>, rounded borders are also taken into account,
    even to the extent that when an element is made circular, the
    shadow will follow that curve, so you are not restricted to
    simple, rectangular box shadows.</p>
  </div>
</body>
</html>
```

The first two lines of the CSS section simply tell the browser to right-justify the text, and to set it to a font size of 16 point. These declarations aren't needed for multiple columns, but they improve the text display in this example. The remaining lines set up the element so that in it the text will flow over two columns, with a gap of one em between the columns, and with a single pixel black border down the middle of each gap:

```
column-count:2;
column-gap   :1em;
column-rule :1px solid black;
```

The value assigned to the column count should be an integer number, the column gap value can be any legal CSS measurement, and the column rule values can be the same as you would supply to the border property.

For iOS, Android, Safari, Chrome, Opera, and Internet Explorer, this is all you need to do. But if you would like to support old versions of Firefox (and old versions of some other browsers) as well, you'll need to also add browser-specific prefixes to the rules, such as in the following lines (or use the *prefixfree.js* utility):

```
-moz-column-count:3;
-moz-column-gap   :1em;
-moz-column-rule :1px solid black;
```

Summary

In this lesson you have learned how to apply a wide range of box shadowing effects to your elements, how to control the way content overflows, scrolls, or is truncated when it is too large to fully fit within an element, and how to flow the content across multiple columns, which is arguably the most useful of the new features in the world of digital publishing.

In Lesson 15 we'll examine how to enhance your use of color and transparency using the range of new CSS3 features provided to support these features.

Self-Test Questions

Using these questions, test how much you have learned in this lesson. If you don't know an answer, go back and reread the relevant section until your knowledge is complete. You can find the answers in the appendix.

1. With which property can you add a shadow to an element?

2. Which two values are required by the box-shadow property?

3. Which two values change the blur radius and spread distance of a box shadow?

4. How can you change the color of a box shadow?

5. How can you make a box shadow display within an element instead of outside?

6. What new additions are there to the overflow property in CSS3?

7. What are the four values the overflow properties accept?

8. With which property can you cause text to flow over multiple columns?

9. How can you change the gap between multiple columns?

10. How can you place a vertical rule between multiple columns?

Adding Colors and Opacity

 To view the accompanying video for this lesson, please visit mhprofessional.com/ nixoncss/.

The ways you can define colors have been greatly expanded with CSS3, and you can now also use CSS functions to apply RGB (red, green, and blue), RGBA (red, green, blue, and alpha), HSL (hue, saturation, and luminance), and HSLA (hue, saturation, luminance, and alpha) colors—the alpha value allowing you to specify a color's transparency.

You can also use the global `opacity` property to change the opacity (or transparency) of entire objects, separately from applying colors.

HSL Colors

To define a color with the `hsl()` function, you must first choose a value for the hue of between 0 and 359 from a color wheel. Any higher color numbers simply wrap around to the beginning again, so the value of 0 is red, and so are the values 360 and 720.

In a color wheel, the primary colors of red, green, and blue are separated by 120 degrees, so that green therefore has the value 120, blue 240, and the numbers between these values represent shades comprising different proportions of the primary colors on either side.

Next you need the saturation level, which is a value between 0 and 100 percent. This specifies how washed out or vibrant a color will appear. Figure 15-1 shows a color wheel displaying both hue and saturation, forming a sort of Y shape, which you can even make out when viewed in monochrome. Red is at the top, green is at the 4 o'clock position, and blue is at 8 o'clock, with the arms and leg of the Y (at 10 o'clock, 2 o'clock, and 6 o'clock), being the colors magenta, yellow, and cyan.

FIGURE 15-1 A color wheel displaying both hue and saturation

The saturation values commence in the center of the wheel with a mid-gray color (a saturation of 0 percent) and then become more and more vivid as they progress to the outer edge (a saturation of 100 percent). All that's then left is for you to decide how bright you want the color to be by choosing a luminance value of between 0 and 100 percent.

A value of 50 percent for the luminance gives the fullest, brightest color, and decreasing the value (down to a minimum of 0 percent) results in making it darker until it displays as black. Increasing the value (up to a maximum of 100 percent) results in it getting lighter until it shows as white. You can visualize this as if you are mixing levels of either black or white into the color.

Therefore, for example, to choose a fully saturated yellow color with standard brightness (of 50 percent), you would use a declaration such as this:

```
color:hsl(60, 100%, 50%);
```

Or, for a darker blue color, you might use a declaration such as:

```
color:hsl(240, 100%, 40%);
```

You can also use this (and all other CSS color functions) with any property that accepts a color, such as `background-color`, `box-shadow`, and so on.

Figure 15-2 shows a selection of colors displayed using this function, created with the accompanying example file *hslcolors.htm*, listed next.

FIGURE 15-2   Using the **hsl()** function to display different colors

```
<!DOCTYPE html>
<html>
  <head>
    <title>HSL Colors</title>
    <style>
      div {
        width :400px;
        height:4px;
      }
    </style>
    <script src='../prefixfree.js'></script>
  </head>
  <body>
    <div style='background:hsl(  0, 100%, 50%)'></div>
    <div style='background:hsl( 12, 100%, 50%)'></div>
    <div style='background:hsl( 24, 100%, 50%)'></div>
    <div style='background:hsl( 36, 100%, 50%)'></div>
    <div style='background:hsl( 48, 100%, 50%)'></div>
    <div style='background:hsl( 60, 100%, 50%)'></div>
    <div style='background:hsl( 72, 100%, 50%)'></div>
    <div style='background:hsl( 84, 100%, 50%)'></div>
```

```
<div style='background:hsl( 96, 100%, 50%)'></div>
<div style='background:hsl(108, 100%, 50%)'></div>
<div style='background:hsl(120, 100%, 50%)'></div>
<div style='background:hsl(132, 100%, 50%)'></div>
<div style='background:hsl(144, 100%, 50%)'></div>
<div style='background:hsl(156, 100%, 50%)'></div>
<div style='background:hsl(168, 100%, 50%)'></div>
<div style='background:hsl(180, 100%, 50%)'></div>
<div style='background:hsl(192, 100%, 50%)'></div>
<div style='background:hsl(204, 100%, 50%)'></div>
<div style='background:hsl(216, 100%, 50%)'></div>
<div style='background:hsl(228, 100%, 50%)'></div>
<div style='background:hsl(240, 100%, 50%)'></div>
<div style='background:hsl(252, 100%, 50%)'></div>
<div style='background:hsl(264, 100%, 50%)'></div>
<div style='background:hsl(276, 100%, 50%)'></div>
<div style='background:hsl(288, 100%, 50%)'></div>
<div style='background:hsl(300, 100%, 50%)'></div>
<div style='background:hsl(312, 100%, 50%)'></div>
<div style='background:hsl(324, 100%, 50%)'></div>
<div style='background:hsl(336, 100%, 50%)'></div>
<div style='background:hsl(348, 100%, 50%)'></div>
<div style='background:hsl(360, 100%, 50%)'></div>

<div style='background:hsl(360, 100%, 50%)'></div>
<div style='background:hsl(348,  97%, 50%)'></div>
<div style='background:hsl(336,  94%, 50%)'></div>
<div style='background:hsl(324,  91%, 50%)'></div>
<div style='background:hsl(312,  87%, 50%)'></div>
<div style='background:hsl(300,  84%, 50%)'></div>
<div style='background:hsl(288,  81%, 50%)'></div>
<div style='background:hsl(276,  78%, 50%)'></div>
<div style='background:hsl(264,  74%, 50%)'></div>
<div style='background:hsl(252,  71%, 50%)'></div>
<div style='background:hsl(240,  68%, 50%)'></div>
<div style='background:hsl(228,  65%, 50%)'></div>
<div style='background:hsl(216,  61%, 50%)'></div>
<div style='background:hsl(204,  58%, 50%)'></div>
<div style='background:hsl(192,  55%, 50%)'></div>
<div style='background:hsl(180,  52%, 50%)'></div>
<div style='background:hsl(168,  48%, 50%)'></div>
<div style='background:hsl(156,  45%, 50%)'></div>
<div style='background:hsl(144,  42%, 50%)'></div>
<div style='background:hsl(132,  39%, 50%)'></div>
<div style='background:hsl(120,  35%, 50%)'></div>
```

```
      <div style='background:hsl(108,   32%,  50%)'></div>
      <div style='background:hsl( 96,   29%,  50%)'></div>
      <div style='background:hsl( 84,   26%,  50%)'></div>
      <div style='background:hsl( 72,   22%,  50%)'></div>
      <div style='background:hsl( 60,   19%,  50%)'></div>
      <div style='background:hsl( 48,   16%,  50%)'></div>
      <div style='background:hsl( 36,   13%,  50%)'></div>
      <div style='background:hsl( 24,    9%,  50%)'></div>
      <div style='background:hsl( 12,    6%,  50%)'></div>
      <div style='background:hsl(  0,    3%,  50%)'></div>

      <div style='background:hsl(  0,    3%,   3%)'></div>
      <div style='background:hsl( 12,    6%,   6%)'></div>
      <div style='background:hsl( 24,    9%,   9%)'></div>
      <div style='background:hsl( 36,   13%,  13%)'></div>
      <div style='background:hsl( 48,   16%,  16%)'></div>
      <div style='background:hsl( 60,   19%,  19%)'></div>
      <div style='background:hsl( 72,   22%,  22%)'></div>
      <div style='background:hsl( 84,   26%,  26%)'></div>
      <div style='background:hsl( 96,   29%,  29%)'></div>
      <div style='background:hsl(108,   32%,  32%)'></div>
      <div style='background:hsl(120,   35%,  35%)'></div>
      <div style='background:hsl(132,   39%,  39%)'></div>
      <div style='background:hsl(144,   42%,  42%)'></div>
      <div style='background:hsl(156,   45%,  45%)'></div>
      <div style='background:hsl(168,   48%,  48%)'></div>
      <div style='background:hsl(180,   52%,  52%)'></div>
      <div style='background:hsl(192,   55%,  55%)'></div>
      <div style='background:hsl(204,   58%,  58%)'></div>
      <div style='background:hsl(216,   61%,  61%)'></div>
      <div style='background:hsl(228,   65%,  65%)'></div>
      <div style='background:hsl(240,   68%,  68%)'></div>
      <div style='background:hsl(252,   71%,  71%)'></div>
      <div style='background:hsl(264,   74%,  74%)'></div>
      <div style='background:hsl(276,   78%,  78%)'></div>
      <div style='background:hsl(288,   81%,  81%)'></div>
      <div style='background:hsl(300,   84%,  84%)'></div>
      <div style='background:hsl(312,   87%,  87%)'></div>
      <div style='background:hsl(324,   91%,  91%)'></div>
      <div style='background:hsl(336,   94%,  94%)'></div>
      <div style='background:hsl(348,   97%,  97%)'></div>
      <div style='background:hsl(360,  100%, 100%)'></div>
    </body>
</html>
```

HSLA Colors

To provide even further control over how colors will appear, you can use the `hsla()` function, supplying it with a fourth (or alpha) level for a color, which is a floating point value between 0 and 1. A value of 0 specifies that the color is totally transparent, while 1 means it is fully opaque.

Here's how you would choose a fully saturated yellow color with standard brightness and 30 percent opacity:

```
color:hsla(60, 100%, 50%, 0.3);
```

Or, for a fully saturated but lighter blue color with 82 percent opacity, you might use this declaration:

```
color:hsla(240, 100%, 60%, 0.82);
```

RGB Colors

You will probably be more familiar with the RGB system of selecting a color as it's similar to using the #nnnnnn and #nnn color formats. For example, to apply a yellow color to a property, you can use either of the following declarations (the first supporting about 16 million colors, and the second about 4,000):

```
color:#ffff00;
color:#ff0;
```

You can also use the CSS `rgb()` function to achieve the same result, but you use decimal numbers instead of hexadecimal (where `255` decimal is `ff` hexadecimal):

```
color:rgb(255, 255, 0);
```

But even better than that, you don't even have to think in amounts of up to 256 anymore, because you can specify percentage values, like this:

```
color:rgb(100%, 100%, 0);
```

In fact you can now get very close to a desired color by simply thinking about its primary colors. For example, green and blue make cyan, so to create a color close to cyan, but with more green in it than blue, you could make a good first guess at 0 percent red, 60 percent green, and 40 percent blue, and try a declaration such as this:

```
color:rgb(0%, 60%, 40%);
```

Figure 15-3 shows a selection of colors displayed using this function, created with the accompany example file *rgbcolors.htm*, listed next.

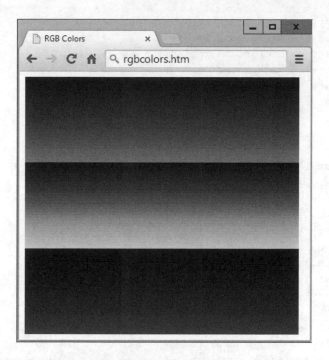

FIGURE 15-3   Using the **rgb()** function to display different colors

```
<!DOCTYPE html>
<html>
  <head>
    <title>RGB Colors</title>
    <style>
      div {
        width :400px;
        height:4px;
      }
    </style>
    <script src='../prefixfree.js'></script>
  </head>
<body>
    <div style='background:rgb(  3%, 0%, 0%)'></div>
    <div style='background:rgb(  6%, 0%, 0%)'></div>
    <div style='background:rgb(  9%, 0%, 0%)'></div>
    <div style='background:rgb( 13%, 0%, 0%)'></div>
    <div style='background:rgb( 16%, 0%, 0%)'></div>
    <div style='background:rgb( 19%, 0%, 0%)'></div>
    <div style='background:rgb( 22%, 0%, 0%)'></div>
    <div style='background:rgb( 26%, 0%, 0%)'></div>
```

```
<div style='background:rgb( 29%, 0%, 0%)'></div>
<div style='background:rgb( 32%, 0%, 0%)'></div>
<div style='background:rgb( 35%, 0%, 0%)'></div>
<div style='background:rgb( 39%, 0%, 0%)'></div>
<div style='background:rgb( 42%, 0%, 0%)'></div>
<div style='background:rgb( 45%, 0%, 0%)'></div>
<div style='background:rgb( 48%, 0%, 0%)'></div>
<div style='background:rgb( 52%, 0%, 0%)'></div>
<div style='background:rgb( 55%, 0%, 0%)'></div>
<div style='background:rgb( 58%, 0%, 0%)'></div>
<div style='background:rgb( 61%, 0%, 0%)'></div>
<div style='background:rgb( 65%, 0%, 0%)'></div>
<div style='background:rgb( 68%, 0%, 0%)'></div>
<div style='background:rgb( 71%, 0%, 0%)'></div>
<div style='background:rgb( 74%, 0%, 0%)'></div>
<div style='background:rgb( 78%, 0%, 0%)'></div>
<div style='background:rgb( 81%, 0%, 0%)'></div>
<div style='background:rgb( 84%, 0%, 0%)'></div>
<div style='background:rgb( 87%, 0%, 0%)'></div>
<div style='background:rgb( 91%, 0%, 0%)'></div>
<div style='background:rgb( 94%, 0%, 0%)'></div>
<div style='background:rgb( 97%, 0%, 0%)'></div>
<div style='background:rgb(100%, 0%, 0%)'></div>

<div style='background:rgb(0%,    3%, 0%)'></div>
<div style='background:rgb(0%,    6%, 0%)'></div>
<div style='background:rgb(0%,    9%, 0%)'></div>
<div style='background:rgb(0%,   13%, 0%)'></div>
<div style='background:rgb(0%,   16%, 0%)'></div>
<div style='background:rgb(0%,   19%, 0%)'></div>
<div style='background:rgb(0%,   22%, 0%)'></div>
<div style='background:rgb(0%,   26%, 0%)'></div>
<div style='background:rgb(0%,   29%, 0%)'></div>
<div style='background:rgb(0%,   32%, 0%)'></div>
<div style='background:rgb(0%,   35%, 0%)'></div>
<div style='background:rgb(0%,   39%, 0%)'></div>
<div style='background:rgb(0%,   42%, 0%)'></div>
<div style='background:rgb(0%,   45%, 0%)'></div>
<div style='background:rgb(0%,   48%, 0%)'></div>
<div style='background:rgb(0%,   52%, 0%)'></div>
<div style='background:rgb(0%,   55%, 0%)'></div>
<div style='background:rgb(0%,   58%, 0%)'></div>
<div style='background:rgb(0%,   61%, 0%)'></div>
<div style='background:rgb(0%,   65%, 0%)'></div>
<div style='background:rgb(0%,   68%, 0%)'></div>
```

```
    <div style='background:rgb(0%,   71%, 0%)'></div>
    <div style='background:rgb(0%,   74%, 0%)'></div>
    <div style='background:rgb(0%,   78%, 0%)'></div>
    <div style='background:rgb(0%,   81%, 0%)'></div>
    <div style='background:rgb(0%,   84%, 0%)'></div>
    <div style='background:rgb(0%,   87%, 0%)'></div>
    <div style='background:rgb(0%,   91%, 0%)'></div>
    <div style='background:rgb(0%,   94%, 0%)'></div>
    <div style='background:rgb(0%,   97%, 0%)'></div>
    <div style='background:rgb(0%,  100%, 0%)'></div>

    <div style='background:rgb(0%, 0%,   3%)'></div>
    <div style='background:rgb(0%, 0%,   6%)'></div>
    <div style='background:rgb(0%, 0%,   9%)'></div>
    <div style='background:rgb(0%, 0%,  13%)'></div>
    <div style='background:rgb(0%, 0%,  16%)'></div>
    <div style='background:rgb(0%, 0%,  19%)'></div>
    <div style='background:rgb(0%, 0%,  22%)'></div>
    <div style='background:rgb(0%, 0%,  26%)'></div>
    <div style='background:rgb(0%, 0%,  29%)'></div>
    <div style='background:rgb(0%, 0%,  32%)'></div>
    <div style='background:rgb(0%, 0%,  35%)'></div>
    <div style='background:rgb(0%, 0%,  39%)'></div>
    <div style='background:rgb(0%, 0%,  42%)'></div>
    <div style='background:rgb(0%, 0%,  45%)'></div>
    <div style='background:rgb(0%, 0%,  48%)'></div>
    <div style='background:rgb(0%, 0%,  52%)'></div>
    <div style='background:rgb(0%, 0%,  55%)'></div>
    <div style='background:rgb(0%, 0%,  58%)'></div>
    <div style='background:rgb(0%, 0%,  61%)'></div>
    <div style='background:rgb(0%, 0%,  65%)'></div>
    <div style='background:rgb(0%, 0%,  68%)'></div>
    <div style='background:rgb(0%, 0%,  71%)'></div>
    <div style='background:rgb(0%, 0%,  74%)'></div>
    <div style='background:rgb(0%, 0%,  78%)'></div>
    <div style='background:rgb(0%, 0%,  81%)'></div>
    <div style='background:rgb(0%, 0%,  84%)'></div>
    <div style='background:rgb(0%, 0%,  87%)'></div>
    <div style='background:rgb(0%, 0%,  91%)'></div>
    <div style='background:rgb(0%, 0%,  94%)'></div>
    <div style='background:rgb(0%, 0%,  97%)'></div>
    <div style='background:rgb(0%, 0%, 100%)'></div>
  </body>
</html>
```

RGBA Colors

As with the `hsla()` function, the `rgba()` function supports a fourth alpha argument, so you can, for example, apply the previous cyan-like color with an opacity of 40 percent, by using declarations such as this:

```
color:rgba(0%, 60%, 40%, 0.4);
```

Now, when elements are given color, the amount of opacity (or conversely the transparency) to also apply can be assigned at the same time, providing the ability to create very subtle blending effects.

The `opacity` Property

The `opacity` property provides the same alpha control as the `hsla()` and `rgba()` functions, but it lets you modify an entire object's opacity (or transparency if you prefer) separately from its color.

To use it, you apply a declaration such as the following to an element (which in this example sets the opacity to 25 percent—or a 75 percent transparency):

```
opacity:0.25;
```

 When opacity is applied (as with all properties), it flows through the cascade. So, all descendant elements will also be given this property value. This, of course, means you don't have to style descendants separately when you want to change the opacity of an element containing sub-elements.

This property works in the latest versions of all major browsers, including iOS and Android, but if you need backward compatibility with older browser versions, you will also need to add the following declaration for Safari and Chrome:

```
-webkit-opacity:0.25;
```

While for backward compatibility with earlier versions of Firefox, you'll need to also add this declaration:

```
-moz-opacity:0.25;
```

And for backward compatibility with releases of Internet Explorer prior to version 9, you should add the following declaration (in which the opacity value is multiplied by 100):

```
filter:alpha(opacity='25');
```

 Most of these cases can be taken care of, however, if you instead simply include the *prefixfree.js* utility in the accompanying archive at *20lessons.com*.

Figure 15-4 shows the values 0.0 through 1.0 in steps of 0.1 applied to elements using this function, created with the document *opacity.htm* from the accompanying archive, and listed next.

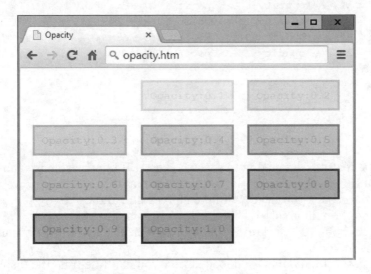

FIGURE 15-4   Using the `opacity` property to choose the opacity of an element

```
<!DOCTYPE html>
<html>
  <head>
    <title>Opacity</title>
    <style>
      div {
        font-family:Monospace;
        font-size  :12pt;
        border     :3px solid #008;
        float      :left;
        margin     :10px;
        padding    :10px;
        background :#f80;
        color      :#f00;
      }
    </style>
    <script src='../prefixfree.js'></script>
  </head>
  <body>
    <div style='opacity:0.0'>Opacity:0.0</div>
    <div style='opacity:0.1'>Opacity:0.1</div>
    <div style='opacity:0.2'>Opacity:0.2</div>
    <div style='opacity:0.3'>Opacity:0.3</div>
```

```
    <div style='opacity:0.4'>Opacity:0.4</div>
    <div style='opacity:0.5'>Opacity:0.5</div>
    <div style='opacity:0.6'>Opacity:0.6</div>
    <div style='opacity:0.7'>Opacity:0.7</div>
    <div style='opacity:0.8'>Opacity:0.8</div>
    <div style='opacity:0.9'>Opacity:0.9</div>
    <div style='opacity:1.0'>Opacity:1.0</div>
  </body>
</html>
```

Summary

Using the features detailed in this lesson, you will now be able to manipulate the colors of HTML elements in the finest of detail and in the subtlest ways to provide exactly the results you need. With the alpha value and `opacity` property, you can also blend them in precisely with other elements on a page. And, as you'll see in Lesson 20, `opacity` is a great property to use in conjunction with transitions to fade elements in and out.

In Lesson 16, though, we'll look at how you can fine-tune the display of written content by using various text effects.

Self-Test Questions

Using these questions, test how much you have learned in this lesson. If you don't know an answer, go back and reread the relevant section until your knowledge is complete. You can find the answers in the appendix.

1. What is the difference between how the `rgb()` and `hsl()` functions work?

2. What range of values is required for the hue value by the `hsl()` function?

3. What range of values is required for the saturation and luminance values by the `hsl()` function?

4. What is different about the `hsla()` function compared to the `hsl()` function?

5. What range of values is required for the alpha value by the `hsla()` function?

6. What values can be supplied to the `rgb()` function?

7. What is different about the `rbga()` function compared to the `rgb()` function?

8. What range of values is required for the alpha value by the `rgba()` function?

9. With which property can you change the transparency of an element?

10. What range of values is required by the `opacity` property?

Creating Text Effects and Changing the Box Model

 To view the accompanying video for this lesson, please visit mhprofessional.com/ nixoncss/.

As with the development of HTML5, CSS3 has been a work in progress for some years, but by now a number of new effects have become standard across all major browsers, and can therefore now be applied to text. These include adding text shadows, getting text to overlap, and selecting how word wrapping occurs.

Plus you now have a choice as to how the box model should be applied, which also affects how your text displays, because you can decide to have padding and borders either subtract from the width and height of an element, or be added onto those dimensions.

In this lesson I explain all these and a couple of other handy features, which allow user-resizing of certain elements, and changing the way the outline of elements in focus is displayed.

The `text-shadow` Property

This property is similar to the `box-shadow` property (covered in Lesson 14) and takes the same set of arguments: a horizontal and vertical offset, an amount for the blur radius, and the color to use. For example, the following declaration offsets the shadow by 3 pixels both horizontally and vertically, and displays the shadow in dark gray, with a blur radius of 4 pixels:

```
text-shadow:3px 3px 4px #444;
```

The result of this declaration looks like Figure 16-1, which also shows an element with a box-shadow for comparison. Created using the file *text-shadow.htm* in the accompanying archive (and listed here), note how the text shadow flows perfectly around the text, while the box shadow encompasses the element, not its contents.

FIGURE 16-1   The CSS3 text-shadow property applied to a sentence

```
<!DOCTYPE html>
<html>
  <head>
    <title>The text-shadow Property</title>
    <style>
      .textshadow {
        font-size  :26pt;
        text-shadow:3px 3px 6px #444;
        margin     :20px;
      }
      .boxshadow {
        font-size  :26pt;
        box-shadow :3px 3px 6px #444;
        width      :325px;
        border     :1px solid #aaa;
        padding    :0 4px;
        margin     :20px;
      }
    </style>
    <script src='../prefixfree.js'></script>
  </head>
  <body>
    <div class='textshadow'>This text has a shadow</div>
    <div class='boxshadow' >This box has a shadow</div>
  </body>
</html>
```

This property works on all major browsers, including recent versions of Internet Explorer. But if you wish to also support earlier versions of IE, you will need to add the following proprietary-to-Microsoft declaration (which will *not* be done for you by the *prefixfree.js* utility):

```
filter:progid:DXImageTransform.Microsoft.Shadow(
  color='#888888', Direction=135, Strength=4);
```

While not being a proper text shadow (as implemented by the other browsers), it provides a reasonable copy of the effect.

The `text-shadow` Supported Values

The `text-shadow` property requires values for the horizontal and vertical offset of the shadow, and it supports optional values supplying the blur radius and color for the shadow.

Negative, zero, or positive values can be supplied for either offset in order to offset the shadow in any direction.

If you would like your shadow to have alpha transparency, you can use either the `hsla()` or `rgba()` function in place of supplying a color name or string, like the following, which creates a dark gray shadow at 50 percent opacity:

```
text-shadow:3px 3px 6px rgba(44, 44, 44, 0.5);
```

You may even use light colors such as white for a text shadow, but these won't display well on light backgrounds, and so are better suited to darker backgrounds.

Unlike the `box-shadow` property, `text-shadow` doesn't support a spread value to spread out the extent of the shadow, nor can you supply the value `inset` to have the shadow display inside the text. To spread a shadow out more, use as contrasting a color as you can with the background and a high blur value.

The `text-overflow` Property

When using any of the CSS overflow properties with a value of hidden, you can also use the `text-overflow` property to place an ellipsis (three dots) just before the cutoff to indicate that some text has been truncated, like this:

```
text-overflow:ellipsis;
```

Without this property, truncated text will look like the top element in Figure 16-2, but with it the result you get is shown in the bottom element of that figure.

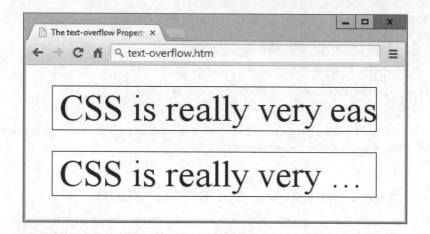

FIGURE 16-2 A phrase displayed without and with the **text-overflow** property

For this to work, three things are required:

1. The element should have an overflow property that is not visible (overflow:hidden is ideal for this).

2. The element must have the white-space:nowrap property set to constrain the text.

3. The width of the element must be less than that of the text to truncate.

Figure 16-2 was created with the file *text-overflow.htm*, available in the accompanying archive, and also listed below:

```
<!DOCTYPE html>
<html>
  <head>
    <title>The text-overflow Property</title>
    <style>
      div {
        font-size    :40pt;
        overflow     :hidden;
        white-space  :nowrap;
        width        :450px;
        border       :1px solid #000;
        padding      :0 10px;
        margin       :30px;
      }
      .textoverflow {
      text-overflow:ellipsis;
```

```
    }
  </style>
  <script src='../prefixfree.js'></script>
</head>
<body>
  <div                    >CSS is really very easy</div>
  <div class='textoverflow'>CSS is really very easy</div>
</body>
</html>
```

If you wish, you can assign a string of your choosing in place of the `ellipsis` value, or simply use the value `clip` (the default) to clip the remainder of text that cannot be displayed.

The `word-wrap` Property

As an alternative to using the `text-overflow` property and truncating text, when you have a really long word that is wider than the element containing it, then it will either overflow or be truncated. But if you use the `word-wrap` property with a value of `break-word`, then you can force long words to always wrap, like this:

`word-wrap:break-word;`

For example, in the top element of Figure 16-3 the word is too wide for the containing box, and because no overflow properties have been applied, it has overflowed its bounds. But in the bottom element the `word-wrap` property of the element has been assigned a value of `break-word`, and so the word has neatly wrapped around to the next line.

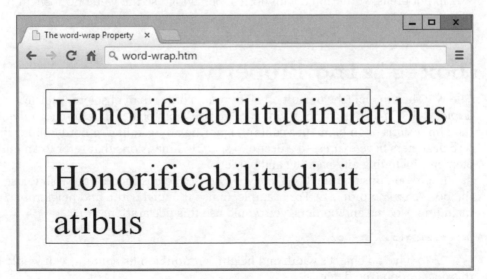

FIGURE 16-3 The word has overflowed in the top element but wrapped in the bottom one.

This property is supported by all the latest versions of all major browsers and the file *word-wrap.htm* in the accompanying archive (and listed here) illustrates this in action.

```html
<!DOCTYPE html>
<html>
  <head>
    <title>The word-wrap Property</title>
    <style>
      div {

        font-size:40pt;
        width    :450px;
        border   :1px solid #000;
        padding  :0 10px;
        margin   :30px;
      }
      .wrap {
        word-wrap:break-word;
      }
    </style>
    <script src='../prefixfree.js'></script>
  </head>
  <body>
    <div            >Honorificabilitudinitatibus</div>
    <div class='wrap'>Honorificabilitudinitatibus</div>
  </body>
</html>
```

To not break words and obtain normal behavior, use the value normal in place of break-word.

The **box-sizing** Property

The W3C box model (the default on all browsers other than obsolete Internet Explorer 5.5) specifies that the width and height of an object should refer only to the dimensions of an element's content, ignoring any padding or border. But some web designers have expressed a desire to specify dimensions that refer to an entire element, including any padding and border.

To provide this feature, CSS3 lets you choose the box model you wish to use with the box-sizing property. For example, to use the total width and height of an object including padding and borders, you would use this declaration:

```
box-sizing:border-box;
```

Or, to have an object's width and height refer only to its content, you would use this declaration (the default):

```
box-sizing:content-box;
```

Let's look at what this means in practice by viewing an object that is of known dimensions, such as Figure 16-4—a 300 × 300-pixel element, created using the file *boxsizing1.htm* in the accompanying archive, and listed next.

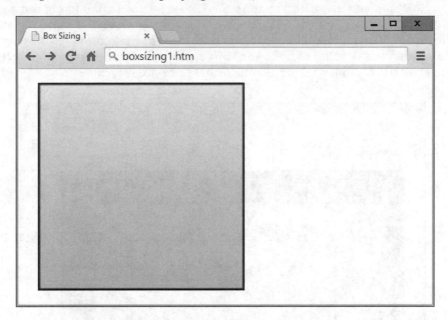

FIGURE 16-4 **An element with width and height of 300 pixels**

```
<!DOCTYPE html>
<html>
  <head>
    <title>Box Sizing 1</title>
    <style>
      div {
        background:#faa;
        margin     :20px;
      }
      .box {
        width      :300px;
        height     :300px;
      }
    </style>
  </head>
  <body>
    <div class='box'>
      <img src='box.jpg' style='width:100%; height:100%'>
    </div>
  </body>
</html>
```

The declaration block applied to all < div> elements simply sets the element up so that we can perform tests on it, the first of which is the two declarations applied to the box class, in which the width and height of the class are set to 300 pixels each.

Now compare that with Figure 16-5, which is an object that has both padding of 50 pixels and a border of 50 pixels, but which is also given the same 300 × 300 dimensions. In this case, though, because no box-sizing property is assigned (or, rather, the default value of content-box is assumed for the property), the element has substantially enlarged to the tune of 100 extra pixels at each edge.

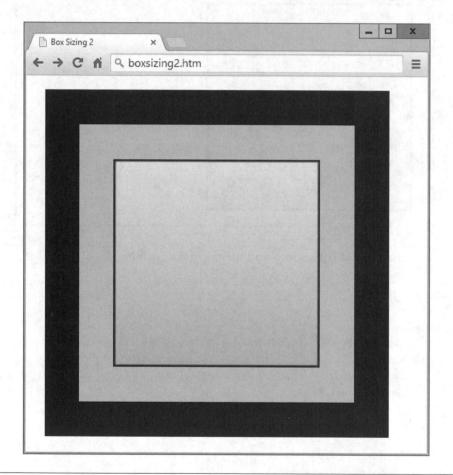

FIGURE 16-5 Assuming the default **box-sizing** method of **content-box**

In this instance the two following lines have simply been added to the box class of the previous example:

```
border :50px solid black;
padding:50px;
```

Now take a look at Figure 16-6, in which the following additional declaration is added to the box class of the example:

```
box-sizing:border-box;
```

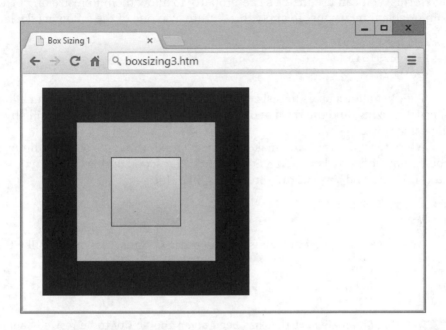

FIGURE 16-6 Setting **box-sizing** to **border-box**

Here, the border and padding have now been taken from the given width and height of 300 pixels, such that both the border and the padding are applied inside the given width and height, resulting in a reduced content area of just 100 × 100 pixels—exactly the effect that some web developers dislike.

As you can imagine, there's a lot of discussion over which of these is better, but armed with this property, whichever side of the fence you stand on, you can now build your web pages using the box model that seems the most intuitive to you.

To save you typing them in, the files *boxsizing2.htm* and *boxsizing3.htm*, used to create Figures 16-5 and 16-6, can be found in the accompanying archive at *20lessons.com*.

Browser Compatibility

The standard box-sizing name for this property has only recently become used by browsers other than Opera and Android. Therefore, for this feature to work on older web browsers, you'll need to use the browser-specific prefixes for this property (such as -webkit- and -moz-), or include the *prefixfree.js* utility in your web pages that access this property.

The `resize` Property

If you wish to give your users a little more control over the way they input information into forms, you can use the `resize` property to allow them to resize an object to more comfortable dimensions. To apply this feature, use one of the following declarations:

```
resize:horizontal;
resize:vertical;
resize:both;
```

The first allows users to resize objects only horizontally, the second allows only vertical resizing, and the third allows both. You can also disallow resizing by assigning the value none.

When resizing, you can't make an object smaller than its original dimensions, but you can make it any larger size. So to restrict the scope of this feature, you can use the `max-height` and `max-width` properties, like this:

```
max-height:500px;
max-width :300px;
```

Or you can use percent values (or any other CSS measurements), like this:

```
max-height:200%;
max-width :200%;
```

 Although an element that has been given the ability to be resized cannot be made smaller than its initial dimensions, it's still worth telling you about the inverse properties to `max-height` and `max-width`, which are `min-height` and `min-width`. You might not need to use them in the preceding example, but they can be handy to prevent JavaScript or browser-resizing of elements down below certain values.

Currently, probably due to the ability of web pages on touch devices to be resized by pinching, this feature is not enabled on either iOS or Android, but it does work on the latest versions of all desktop browsers except IE. When enabled, a small resize handle is placed at the lower right of any resizable object that you can grab and drag, as shown in Figure 16-7, in which the element's bottom right handle is shown highlighted.

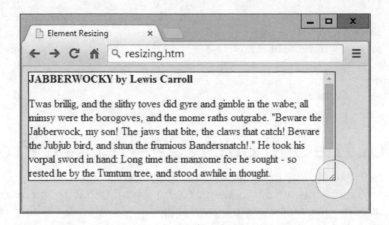

FIGURE 16-7   This object can be resized using the bottom right drag handle.

The file *resizing.htm* in the accompanying archive, and listed here, illustrates this in action:

```
<!DOCTYPE html>
<html>
  <head>
    <title>Element Resizing</title>
    <style>
      .resize {
        resize     :both;
        width      :300px;
        height     :150px;
        max-width  :600px;
        max-height :300px;
        overflow   :auto;
        border     :1px solid black;
      }
    </style>
    <script src='../prefixfree.js'></script>
  </head>
<body>
  <div class='resize'>
    <b>JABBERWOCKY by Lewis Carroll</b>
    <p>Twas brillig, and the slithy toves did gyre and gimble in the
    wabe; all mimsy were the borogoves, and the mome raths outgrabe.
    "Beware the Jabberwock, my son! The jaws that bite, the claws that
    catch! Beware the Jubjub bird, and shun the frumious
```

```
Bandersnatch!." He took his vorpal sword in hand: Long time the
manxome foe he sought - so rested he by the Tumtum tree, and stood
awhile in thought.</p>
        </div>
    </body>
</html>
```

The `outline` and `outline-offset` Properties

If you don't like the way the outline box is applied to an object when it gains focus, you can use the `outline` and `outline-offset` properties to style and resize it, as follows, which, for example, creates a dark gray, thin, dashed outline, which is then extended out from the object by 10 pixels (as shown in Figure 16-8):

```
outline         :#444 thin dashed;
outline-offset:10px;
```

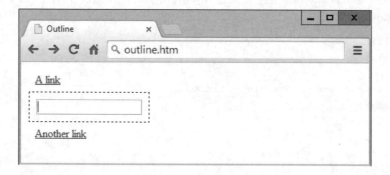

FIGURE 16-8 The outline (showing the input field has focus) is enlarged.

The color value supplied to the `outline` shorthand property can be any legal CSS color or color function, the style can be any of `auto`, `none`, `dotted`, `dashed`, `solid`, `double`, `groove`, `ridge`, `inset`, or `outset`, and the width can be `thin`, `medium`, `thick`, or a length. The value supplied to `outline-offset` can be any legal CSS length.

These features work on the latest versions of all browsers, except for Internet Explorer (which only supports the `outline` property, and not the `outline-offset` property), and can be seen in action below and in the file *outline.htm* in the accompanying archive of files:

```
<!DOCTYPE html>
<html>
    <head>
        <title>Outline</title>
        <style>
```

```
      body {
        margin-left   :20px;
      }
      html *:focus {
        outline        :dashed thin;
        outline-offset:10px;
      }
    </style>
    <script src='../prefixfree.js'></script>
  </head>
  <body>
    <p>
      <a href='nowhere'>A link</a>
    </p>
    <p>
      <input type='text'>
    </p>
    <p>
      <a href='alsonowhere'>Another link</a>
    </p>
  </body>
</html>
```

When you open this document in a browser, press the TAB key to give focus to different elements, and you will see the outline surround them.

To style them separately, you can also use the longhand outline properties of `outline-color`, `outline-style`, and `outline-width`.

Summary

Now that you have a variety of methods for styling your text in interesting ways and making its presentation as eye-catching and easy-to-read as possible, in Lesson 17 we'll further extend your repertoire by looking at how to access the hundreds of free (and premium) quality web fonts now available.

Self-Test Questions

Using these questions, test how much you have learned in this lesson. If you don't know an answer, go back and reread the relevant section until your knowledge is complete. You can find the answers in the appendix.

1. Which two values are required by the `text-shadow` property?

2. What optional values does the `text-shadow` property accept?

3. How can you give alpha transparency to a text shadow?

4. When text overflows an element, which property can you use to specify whether the extra text is to be clipped or replaced with an indicator that text is missing?

5. How can you force words to wrap around when they are too large to fit?

6. What does the box-sizing property do?

7. Which three values are accepted by the box-sizing property, and which value has which action?

8. Which property enables input and textarea elements to become user resizable, and what values are supported by it?

9. How can you restrict the amount of resizing a user can apply to an element?

10. Which two properties can be used to modify the appearance of the outline applied by browsers to elements that gain focus?

Linking to Web Fonts

 To view the accompanying video for this lesson, please visit mhprofessional.com/ nixoncss/.

More than images, audio, or even video, text is probably the most important part of any web page. Not only does it provide information about whatever is on the web page to you, the reader, it also enables search engine spiders to understand and rank pages to better match web searches.

And web typography has continually evolved as Internet technologies have improved, with one of the biggest leaps being the development of downloadable fonts to vastly expand the basic repertoire of just a dozen or so "web safe" fonts.

During its development, a few different competing standards fought a battle for dominance, with the eventual winners now pretty much decided and available for use on all major platforms and browsers.

In this lesson I explain the current state of play and show you how to make the most use of web fonts in your own web pages.

Loading a Web Font

The use of CSS3 web fonts vastly increases the typography available to web designers by allowing fonts to be loaded in and displayed from across the Web, not just from the user's computer. To achieve this, you declare a web font using the @font-face at-rule (so named because of the @ preface), like this:

```
@font-face
{
  font-family:FontName;
  src:url('FontName.otf');
}
```

The url() function requires a value containing the path or URL of a font. On most browsers you can use TrueType (*.ttf*), OpenType (*.otf*), or WOFF (*.wof*) fonts, but be aware that older versions of Internet Explorer restrict you to only TrueType fonts that have been converted to EOT (*.eot*).

The Main Types of Web Fonts

There are three main types of web font, as follows:

- **TrueType** An outline font standard developed by Apple and Microsoft as a competitor to Adobe's Type 1 fonts, as used in PostScript. It is the most common format for fonts on both Mac OS and Microsoft Windows.
- **OpenType** A format for scalable computer fonts. It was built on its predecessor TrueType, retaining TrueType's basic structure but adding new data structures that extended typographic behavior.
- **Web Open Font Format** Developed only as recently as 2009, WOFF is now a World Wide Web Consortium (W3C) recommendation. Essentially it comprises either OpenType or TrueType, but with compression and additional metadata.

Loading a Web Font

To tell the browser the type of font you wish to use, you also supply an argument to the format() function, as with the following for OpenType fonts (where *FontName* is the name of the font to load):

```
@font-face
{
  font-family:FontName;
  src        :url('FontName.otf') format('opentype');
}
```

This is how you load a TrueType font:

```
@font-face
{
  font-family:FontName;
  src        :url('FontName.ttf') format('truetype');
}
```

And this is how you load a Web Open Format font:

```
@font-face
{
  font-family:FontName;
  src        :url('FontName.woff') format('woff');
}
```

Older Versions of Internet Explorer

Because older versions of IE accept only Embedded Open Type (EOT) fonts, they will ignore `@font-face` at-rules that contain the `format()` function. In fact, it seems that when using EOT fonts, you should never use a `format()` function or IE will probably not even load the font in the first place.

Here is the syntax for loading an EOT font:

```
@font-face
{
  font-family: FontName;
  src        :url('FontName.eot');
}
```

And the Winner Is...

In the introduction I mentioned there was a format war. Well, let me announce the winner in my view, which is WOFF. Standing for Web Open Format Fonts, this isn't actually a format of its own. Rather it's a compressed file that contains both the font data and the information required to enable browsers to display it.

This combination overcomes all the previous browser compatibility issues and makes the format my recommended choice for the greatest browser compatibility. It is also the format used by the vast archive of Google fonts (see the following section), and it's the officially recommended format of the W3C.

 I don't supply any example HTML or web font file in the accompanying archive because Google and many other providers offer a wealth of web fonts totally free and hosted on their servers.

Google Web Fonts

As long as you are creating an Internet-enabled (rather than standalone) app or web page, one of the best ways to use web fonts is to load them in for free from Google's servers. To find out more about this, you should check out the Google Fonts website (*google.com/ fonts*—shown in Figure 17-1), where you can get access to 638 font families, and counting! To show you how easy it is, here's how you load one in using a `<link>` tag:

```
<link href='http://fonts.googleapis.com/css?family=Lobster' rel='stylesheet'
type='text/css'>
```

Then to use the font, just apply it in a CSS rule, like this:

```
h1 { font-family:"Lobster", Arial, serif; }
```

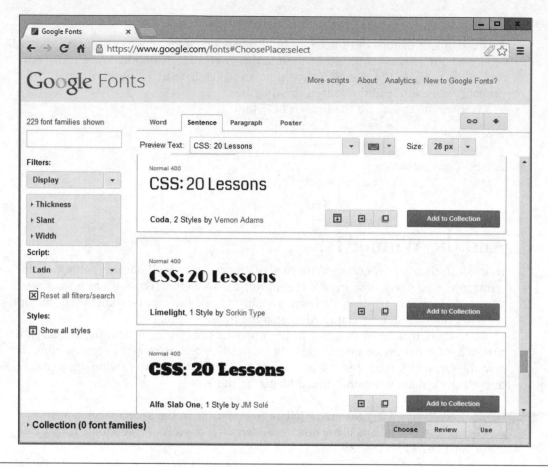

FIGURE 17-1 The Google Fonts website

Figure 17-2 shows just a few of the hundreds of fonts and font variants provided by Google. You can try a sample out for yourself using the file *webfonts.htm* in the accompanying archive of example files, as listed here:

```
<!DOCTYPE html>
<html>
  <head>
    <title>Google Fonts</title>
    <style>
      body      { font-size  :22pt;
                  margin      :15px 20px;                              }
```

```
      .cantarell { font-family:"Cantarell", sans-serif;        }
      .droidsans { font-family:"Droid Sans", sans-serif;       }
      .imfell    { font-family:"IM Fell English", serif;       }
      .lobster   { font-family:"Lobster", fantasy, serif;      }
      .reenie    { font-family:"Reenie Beanie", cursive, serif; }
      .tangerine { font-family:"Tangerine", cursive, serif;    }
      .vollkorn  { font-family:"Vollkorn", serif;              }
      .yanone    { font-family:"Yanone Kaffeesatz", sans-serif; }
    </style>
    <script src='../prefixfree.js'></script>
    <link rel='stylesheet' type='text/css'
      href='http://fonts.googleapis.com/css?family=Cantarell'>
    <link rel='stylesheet' type='text/css'
      href='http://fonts.googleapis.com/css?family=Droid+Sans'>
    <link rel='stylesheet' type='text/css'
      href='http://fonts.googleapis.com/css?family=IM+Fell+English'>
    <link rel='stylesheet' type='text/css'
      href='http://fonts.googleapis.com/css?family=Lobster'>
    <link rel='stylesheet' type='text/css'
      href='http://fonts.googleapis.com/css?family=Reenie+Beanie'>
    <link rel='stylesheet' type='text/css'
      href='http://fonts.googleapis.com/css?family=Tangerine'>
    <link rel='stylesheet' type='text/css'
      href='http://fonts.googleapis.com/css?family=Vollkorn'>
    <link rel='stylesheet' type='text/css'
      href='http://fonts.googleapis.com/css?family=Yanone+Kaffeesatz'>
  </head>
  <body>
    <div class='cantarell'>Cantarell</div>
    <div class='droidsans'>Droid Sans</div>
    <div class='imfell'   >IM Fell English</div>
    <div class='lobster'  >Lobster</div>
    <div class='reenie'   >Reenie Beanie</div>
    <div class='tangerine'>Tangerine</div>
    <div class='vollkorn' >Vollkorn</div>
    <div class='yanone'   >Yanone Kaffeesatz</div>
  </body>
</html>
```

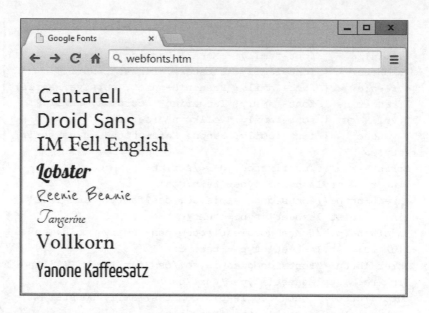

FIGURE 17-2 Incorporating Google fonts in a web page is easy.

Browser Differences

The various main browsers handle web fonts in slightly different ways. For example, Google Chrome, Apple Safari, and Opera first render the rest of a web page and then only render a web font once it has loaded. On the other hand, Firefox initially displays web fonts in a native font and then re-renders the text once the web font has loaded. This causes the text to flicker and has been given the name "flash of unstyled text."

Internet Explorer, however, is similar in action to the other non-Firefox browsers but you must be careful. For example, if the <link> tag to select the web font is placed after any <script> elements, the entire page will not display anything until the font has loaded.

If you wish for consistency across all browsers, you may want to look into the Web Font Loader utility that was jointly developed by Google and Typekit. With it you can ensure all browsers will behave in a similar manner, for example, all just like Firefox. You can get more information on this free program at the following URL: *developers .google.com/fonts/docs/webfont_loader*.

Other Font Sources

As well as Google there are other free and premium web font services available, of which the following are just a few examples to get you started (availability and quantities were correct at the time of writing):

- **fonts.com** 3,000 free fonts for up to 25,000 monthly page views, and 20,000 premium web fonts at various paid levels.
- **typekit.com** 800 free fonts for up to 25,000 monthly page views, and 4,000 premium web fonts at various paid levels, as shown in Figure 17-3.
- **myfonts.com** 85,000 premium fonts for purchase, with a free trial available.

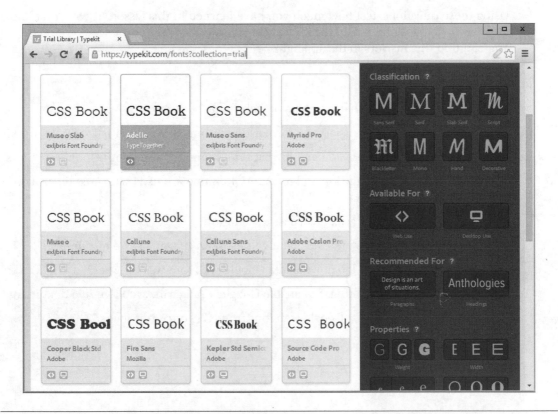

FIGURE 17-3 Some of the trial fonts at *typekit.com*

Summary

Using the information in this lesson you now have access to not only the immense archive of free fonts at Google, but also an enormous variety of other free and low-cost fonts from a wide range of other companies—all from a quick web search.

This lesson marks the end of the basics of what's new in CSS3. In the final three lessons we'll be exploring the more advanced and exciting new features in CSS3, including 2D and 3D transformations and other powerful effects.

Self-Test Questions

Using these questions, test how much you have learned in this lesson. If you don't know an answer, go back and reread the relevant section until your knowledge is complete. You can find the answers in the appendix.

1. What is a web font?

2. What are the three main formats of web fonts?

3. What font name extension and format type name are used with TrueType fonts?

4. What font name extension and format type name are used with OpenType fonts?

5. What font name extension and format type name are used with Web Open Font Format fonts?

6. Which CSS at-rule is used to access a web font?

7. What two properties must be given values in an @font-face at-rule?

8. What method is used to download a Google web font to a browser?

9. What syntax would you use to enable Google's Tangerine web font in a document?

10. How can you access a Google web font from CSS once it is loaded?

Making 2D Transformations

 To view the accompanying video for this lesson, please visit mhprofessional.com/ nixoncss/.

I've saved some of the best new additions to CSS for last because they are fun, and they can generally be applied in conjunction with other CSS declarations to provide animation effects such as transformations and transitions.

As with some other CSS3 enhancements, certain properties have only recently been implemented in some browsers, and older versions will employ the browser-specific prefixes of `-moz-` for Mozilla Firefox, `-webkit-` for browsers such as Safari, and so on. Therefore, I recommend using the *prefixfree.js* utility (a copy of which is in the accompanying archive of example files) to take the worry out of determining when and where these prefixes are required.

Also, these features are *not* implemented by pre—version 9 releases of Microsoft's Internet Explorer browser, although (as you'll see), there are ways of emulating some of these effects, while versions 9 and higher of IE do now support many of these features.

2D Transformations

There is a wide range of different types of transformations you can apply to HTML elements using CSS3, all of which can be achieved using the information in this lesson (although simpler functions to make the process even easier are explained in Lesson 19).

The `none` Transformation Type

The none transformation type is generally used dynamically from JavaScript to remove a transformation that was previously applied. Its syntax is as follows:

```
transform:none;
```

However, to ensure that the declaration works in as many older browsers as possible, you may wish to apply all the browser-specific prefixes:

```
-moz-transform    :none;
-webkit-transform:none;
-o-transform      :none;
-ms-transform     :none;
transform         :none;
```

In the preceding set of declarations, first Mozilla-based browsers such as Firefox are covered, followed by webkit ones such as Apple Safari and Google Chrome (and recently new Opera), and then the older Opera browser. Finally, there is no equivalent property for Microsoft's Internet Explorer versions below IE9, but version 9 and above of the browser supports the -ms- prefix, so that is used. Last, the generic version of the declaration is applied.

 Of course, the *prefixfree.js* utility obviates the need to include all browser-specific prefixed properties, except when applying them via JavaScript (as follows); then you're back to having to perform your own research and applying the various prefixed properties according to the browsers you must support.

Applying Properties with JavaScript

Because you will most often apply the none value to remove a previously specified transform, it is likely you will be doing so with JavaScript, in which case (assuming the object element refers to an existing HTML element) your code for doing so may look something like this:

```
<script>
  element.style.MozTransform    = 'none'
  element.style.webkitTransform = 'none'
  element.style.OTransform      = 'none'
  element.style.msTransform     = 'none'
  element.style.transform       = 'none'
</script>
```

 Because the - symbol is reserved by JavaScript for use as the mathematical subtraction operator, when accessing these properties from JavaScript, the - symbol is omitted and the letter after it is capitalized, but only older versions of Opera (OTransform) and all versions of Firefox (MozTransform) use this scheme for the entire property name. Webkit (used in Safari, Chrome, and the latest Opera browsers) and Microsoft's Internet Explorer have opted to keep the first letter of the prefix part of the property name in lowercase (using the property names webkitTransform and msTransform). Therefore, bear this in mind as it could catch out the unwary.

Due to what appears to be a bug, or perhaps because Microsoft often does things its own way, in earlier versions of Internet Explorer you may *not* use the following JavaScript syntax to define a transformation:

```
<script>
  element.style.msTransform = 'none'; // Don't use this in earlier IE
</script>
```

Instead, if you need to support these older versions, you should use the more long-winded but easier to comprehend setAttribute() function, like this (which also shows how to use the function across the other main browsers):

```
<script>
  element.style.setAttribute('style', '-moz-transform:none')
  element.style.setAttribute('style', '-webkit-transform:none')
  element.style.setAttribute('style', '-o-transform:none')
  element.style.setAttribute('style', '-ms-transform:none')
  element.style.setAttribute('style', 'transform:none')
</script>
```

Now that you know how to remove or turn off a transformation, let's look at how you get them going in the first place.

The `matrix(w,s1,s2,h,x,y)` Function

The matrix() CSS function provides a means of directly accessing transformation parameters. With it you can achieve some of the ready-made function effects such as skew() and scale() (see Lesson 19), and many others too.

For example, let's style an image, to which we'll apply some matrix transforms, using this CSS and HTML (saved as *matrix.htm* in the accompanying archive):

```
<!DOCTYPE html>
<html>
  <head>
    <title>CSS Matrix Example</title>
    <style>
      #image {
        position  :absolute;
        border    :1px solid #000;
        top       :100px;
        left      :55px;
        transition:all .5s ease-in-out;
      }
```

```
       #b1, #b2, #b3, #b4, #b5, #b6 {
         width      :40px;
         height     :30px;
         margin     :20px 0 0 20px;
       }
       #b1:hover ~ #image { transform:matrix(1.2, 0,   0,   1,   0,   0);}
       #b2:hover ~ #image { transform:matrix(1,   0.2, 0,   1,   0,   0);}
       #b3:hover ~ #image { transform:matrix(1,   0,   0.2, 1,   0,   0);}
       #b4:hover ~ #image { transform:matrix(1,   0,   0,   1.2, 0,   0);}
       #b5:hover ~ #image { transform:matrix(1,   0,   0,   1,   20,  0);}
       #b6:hover ~ #image { transform:matrix(1,   0,   0,   1,   0,   20);}
     </style>
     <script src='../prefixfree.js'></script>
   </head>
   <body>
     <input id='b1' type='button' value='1'>
     <input id='b2' type='button' value='2'>
     <input id='b3' type='button' value='3'>
     <input id='b4' type='button' value='4'>
     <input id='b5' type='button' value='5'>
     <input id='b6' type='button' value='6'>
     <img id='image' src='image.jpg'>
   </body>
</html>
```

Looking at the `<style>` section, what this starts with is setting the properties for an element with the ID of image such that it is offset from the top and left of the browser by 100 and 55 pixels. The image being used is given absolute positioning so that it can be manipulated, and also has a 1-pixel border added to it.

The only new declaration at this point is the following, which uses the `transition` property (explained in Lesson 20). It is used here to animate the change between image transformations as a smooth transition, rather than have an instant flip occur when the mouse passes over.

```
transition:all .5s ease-in-out;
```

Then there is one rule to set the style properties for the buttons, followed by six rules to apply the `matrix()` function (with differing values) to the image, according to which of the buttons the mouse hovers over. This is achieved using the general sibling selector symbol (~) in such a way that, although the mouse hovers over one element (such as a button with the ID of b4), it's the sibling element (with the ID of image) which gets modified. In its initial state this document results in Figure 18-1.

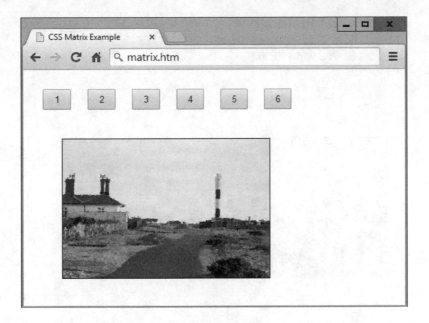

FIGURE 18-1 A photo is loaded and buttons are ready to manipulate it.

So now, let's look at the result of applying different values to these arguments by doing just that. As you hover the mouse over each of the six buttons, a different matrix is applied to the image, as shown in the following sections.

Argument 1

```
transform:matrix(1.2, 0, 0, 1, 0, 0);
```

This `matrix` function stretches the image along its horizontal axis by 20 percent. It looks like Figure 18-2. To shrink an element, use a value less than 1 but greater than 0. The default value at which there is no stretching is 1.

FIGURE 18-2 The image has been horizontally stretched by 20 percent.

If you use a negative value, you can horizontally mirror an object by the amount specified. To fully mirror an object, use a value of −1, or to mirror an object but scale it down in size by half, use a value of −0.5, and so on.

Argument 2

```
transform:matrix(1, 0.2, 0, 1, 0, 0);
```

This example applies a vertical skew such that the *left* of the image moves *up* by 10 percent, and the right moves down also by 10 percent, giving a combined skew of 20 percent. If supplied with a negative value, the left of the image moves down and the right moves up.

It looks like Figure 18-3. A value of 0.5 skews by 50 percent, 1 skews by 100 percent, 2 by 200 percent, and so on. To skew in the other direction, use a negative value. The default value at which there is no skew is 0.

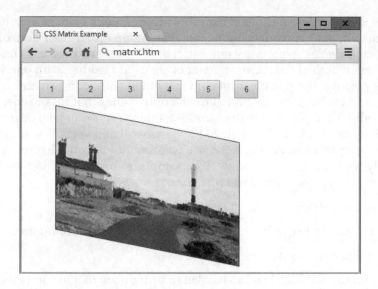

FIGURE 18-3   The image has been skewed vertically in a clockwise direction.

Argument 3

```
transform:matrix(1, 0, 0.2, 1, 0, 0);
```

This example applies a horizontal skew such that the *bottom* moves to the *right* by 10 percent, while top of the image moves to the left by 10 percent, giving a combined skew of 20 percent, as shown in Figure 18-4. If a negative value is supplied, the bottom moves to the left and the top moves to the right.

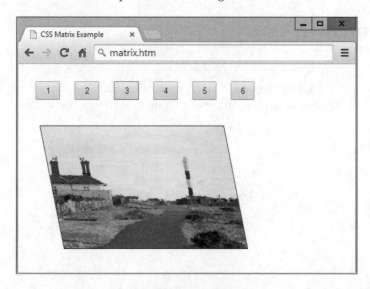

FIGURE 18-4   The image has been skewed horizontally and counterclockwise.

One way to think of this and the previous argument's effects is as if the image is being rotated, but the corners are forced to maintain either their horizontal or their vertical coordinates (with every other part of the element similarly constrained). In fact, when both of these two arguments are used together, with one value negative and one positive, the result is a rotation combined with enlargement.

When skewing to create a rotation, the only values that make sense are between 0 and 1, and 0 and −1, where the 1 and −1 values represent a 90-degree rotation. Values between 0 and 1 also apply to the horizontal and vertical scaling factors because, to keep an object the same size when rotating, you must reduce the scaling inversely with the amount of skew. For example, to rotate an object 90 degrees counterclockwise, you would use this matrix:

```
transform:matrix(0, -1, 1, 0, 0, 0);
```

Or to rotate it 90 degrees in a clockwise direction, you would use:

```
transform:matrix(0, 1, -1, 0, 0, 0);
```

In both cases the scaling has needed to be reduced to 0 to compensate for the increases in size caused by the skewing. However, the rate of scaling compensation is not linear. For example, to rotate an object clockwise by 45 degrees, although you use values of 0.5 and −0.5 for the skew arguments, in this instance scaling should be 0.88:

```
transform:matrix(0.88, 0.5, -0.5, 0.88, 0, 0);
```

 Combining arguments to the `matrix()` function can be tricky, so you may prefer to use the simpler functions in Lesson 19, each of which concentrates on a single type of transformation.

Argument 4

```
transform:matrix(1, 0, 0, 1.2, 0, 0);
```

This example stretches the image along its vertical axis by 20 percent. It looks like Figure 18-5. To shrink an element, use a value less than 1 but greater than 0.

FIGURE 18-5   The image has been stretched vertically.

If you use a negative value, you can vertically flip an object by the amount specified. To fully flip an object, use a value of −1, or to flip an object but scale it down in size by half, use a value of −0.5, and so on.

If you use negative values for both arguments 1 and 4, you can rotate an object by 180 degrees. The amount of each negative value then represents the scaling of the final object, where values of −1 and −1 perform the rotation while retaining the same size.

Argument 5

```
transform:matrix(1, 0, 0, 1, 20, 0);
```

This example offsets the image to the right by 20 pixels, as shown in Figure 18-6. To offset to the left, use a negative value.

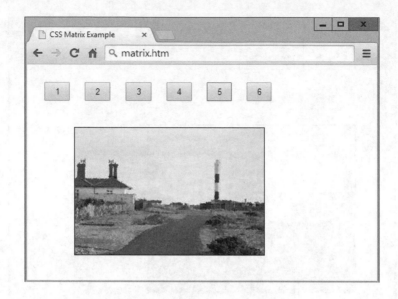

FIGURE 18-6 The image has been moved to the right by 20 pixels.

Argument 6

```
transform:(1, 0, 0, 1, 0, 20);
```

This example offsets the image down by 20 pixels, as shown in Figure 18-7. To offset upward, use a negative value.

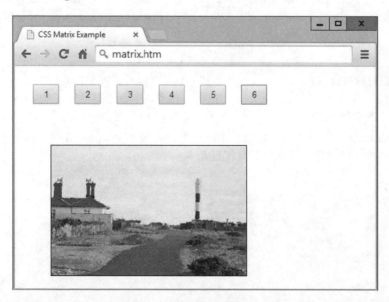

FIGURE 18-7 The image has been moved down by 20 pixels.

By combining these arguments, you can create more interesting effects. For example, by increasing both arguments 1 and 4 by the same amount, you can scale an element up in size. In the same way, by reducing the values for these two arguments to a number less than 1 (but greater than 0), you can scale elements down too.

Or, by skewing an element in the same direction both horizontally and vertically, you can rotate it, as shown in Figure 18-8, in which the square has been rotated by 45 degrees using the following transform (modifying arguments 2 and 3):

```
transform:matrix(1, 1, -1, 1, 0, 0);
```

FIGURE 18-8   The element has been rotated clockwise by 45 degrees and enlarged.

As you can see, this has the side effect of increasing the image in size. So it's at this point I have to confess that what I've explained here isn't strictly true, because what is going on is that the elements are actually multiplied by the values supplied in the matrix in a rather complex manner, which is beyond the scope of this discussion. To counteract the enlargement, you also need to decrease the vertical and horizontal scales by suitable values.

But the explanation I have given will enable you to at least use the `matrix()` function without having to understand all the mathematics, by simply tweaking the various values until you get the desired effect. However, if you are interested, a full explanation of matrix multiplication and CSS transforms can be found at *tinyurl.com/ css3matrix*.

Note If you have any difficulties using the `matrix()` function, don't worry, because most of the main transformations it can apply are replicated for you, but in a much simpler fashion with functions such as `rotate()`, `scale()`, and `skew()`, as you'll learn in Lesson 19.

Internet Explorer Prior to IE9

The CSS3 `matrix()` function is not supported by versions of Internet Explorer earlier than 9, but for these browsers you can use an alternative, which is the Microsoft-specific `filter` property. You only get access to the first four arguments (you cannot supply either an X or Y offset as arguments 5 and 6), and you use it like this:

```
filter:progid:DXImageTransform.Microsoft.Matrix(
  SizingMethod='auto expand', M11=1, M12=0.2, M21=0, M22=1);
```

The `SizingMethod='auto expand'` argument is essential because otherwise IE will simply apply the transform within the current bounds of an element, without resizing it accordingly, even if the element is specifically to be resized.

The arguments M11, M12, M21, and M22 are the direct equivalents of arguments 1 through 4 in the `matrix()` CSS function and are used in the same way, with the same values, except that you need only mention the value(s) that are to be changed (or no values if everything is to be restored to its default). For example, to skew horizontally, you might use the following declaration, which accesses just the M12 argument:

```
filter:progid:DXImageTransform.Microsoft.Matrix(
  SizingMethod='auto expand', M12=0.2);
```

Internet Explorer doesn't apply the matrix using the center of an element, around which the transform is made with other browsers. Rather it uses the top, left-hand corner, and therefore elements will move down and to the right in IE if they need to expand (or will simply shrink only the right and/or bottom edge if reducing), instead of neatly transforming in situ.

Therefore, if you need your web page to look good in older versions of IE using a matrix transform, you will have to play with directly moving elements in IE as necessary, possibly by setting their position property to relative and then providing negative values to their `left` and `top` attributes.

Most likely you would use conditional style sheets for this, in which you load in a modified style sheet specifically for IE users. A good article on using tricks such as this can be found at *tinyurl.com/condstyles*.

Interestingly, the `filter` property is making a comeback as a recommendation by the W3C for all browsers. When ready, it will work differently to Microsoft's original version, and will provide blurring and many other very useful effects, with just a single declaration. However it's currently only supported by Chrome and Opera (which uses Chrome as its base), but do keep an eye out for it.

Summary

Armed with the `matrix()` function, you now have an amazing variety of tools you can use to manipulate elements at your disposal. However, `matrix()` is not exactly an easy function to fully understand, so some simpler functions that stick to specific tasks (such as rotation or skew) have also been made available, and are detailed in Lesson 19.

Self-Test Questions

Using these questions, test how much you have learned in this lesson. If you don't know an answer, go back and reread the relevant section until your knowledge is complete. You can find the answers in the appendix.

1. With which function can CSS perform transformations on elements such as skewing, scaling, and rotation?

2. Which argument (1–6) to the `matrix()` function moves an element horizontally?

3. Which argument (1–6) to the `matrix()` function moves an element vertically?

4. With which argument (1–6) to the `matrix()` function can you scale an element horizontally?

5. With which argument (1–6) to the `matrix()` function can you scale an element vertically?

6. Which argument (1–6) to the `matrix()` function skews an element horizontally?

7. Which argument (1–6) to the `matrix()` function skews an element vertically?

8. What value can you supply to the `transform` property to remove or cancel a transformation?

9. What values would you supply to the `matrix()` function to rotate an object 90 degrees counterclockwise, without any change in size?

10. What values would you supply to the `matrix()` function to mirror an object horizontally, without any change in size?

Applying Specific Transformations

 To view the accompanying video for this lesson, please visit mhprofessional.com/nixoncss/.

Having learned how to make good use of the `matrix()` function when you need to perform a number of transformations at a time, in this lesson we'll look at the more specific functions that concentrate on single tasks, and are therefore easier to use and understand.

These include the facility to translate elements to different locations by changing their vertical and horizontal offsets, rotating elements about their center, scaling them up and down in size, and skewing them to form them into a rhombus shape.

The `translate(x,y)` Function

The `translate()` function lets you move an object to a new position by supplying a horizontal and vertical offset. This is the same as using arguments 5 and 6 in the `matrix()` function, as described in Lesson 18.

For example, the following two declarations have the same effect as that shown in Figures 18-6 and 18-7:

```
transform:translate(20px, 0px);
transform:translate(0px, 20px);
```

Figure 19-1 shows an image translated to the right by 20 pixels using the document *translate.htm*, listed here and available in the accompanying archive at *20lessons.com*:

```
<!DOCTYPE html>
<html>
  <head>
```

```
<title>CSS Translate Example</title>
<style>
  #image {
    position  :absolute;
    border    :1px solid #000;
    top       :120px;
    left      :55px;
    transition:all .5s ease-in-out;
  }
  input {
    width     :40px;
    height    :30px;
    margin    :20px 0 0 20px;
  }
  #b1:hover ~ #image { transform:translate(20px, 0px); }
  #b2:hover ~ #image { transform:translate(0px, 20px); }
</style>
<script src='../prefixfree.js'></script>
</head>
<body>
  <input id='b1' type='button' value='X'>
  <input id='b2' type='button' value='Y'>
  <img id='image' src='image.jpg'>
</body>
</html>
```

FIGURE 19-1 The image has been moved to the right by 20 pixels.

The amount of translation must be specified. In this instance it's pixels, but it could be points or other units of measurement. If the second argument is omitted, then the Y offset is 0.

You can also use the `translateX()` and `translateY()` functions to modify just the vertical or horizontal translation. All properties support negative, zero, and positive values to enable translation of objects in all directions.

 This function is not supported by earlier versions of Microsoft's Internet Explorer, and the only way to easily accomplish the same effect is to use a separate style sheet for such versions of IE in which you specify the offset values required.

Why `translate` Is More Efficient

If you have used the `top` and `left` properties of an object to animate it and are unimpressed with the results due to less than perfectly smooth movement, try using the `translate` property instead, and you may well find you get more eye-pleasing results.

This is because transforms can generally be fully rendered using the computer's graphical processing unit (GPU), whereas changes to elements' `top` and `left` properties normally cause page re-rendering that can only be performed on the central processing unit (CPU), which is a lot slower.

The `scale(x,y)` Function

With the `scale()` function, you can scale an element either up or down in size and by different horizontal and vertical amounts. This works in the same way as modifying arguments 1 and 4 in the `matrix()` function.

For example, the following two declarations have the same effect as that shown in Figures 18-2 and 18-5:

```
transform:scale(1.2, 1  );
transform:scale(1,   1.2);
```

In Figure 19-2, the image has been scaled up vertically by 20 percent, using the document *scale.htm* in the accompanying archive, and listed next:

```
<!DOCTYPE html>
<html>
  <head>
    <title>CSS Scale Example</title>
    <style>
      #image {
        position  :absolute;
        border    :1px solid #000;
```

```
      top       :120px;
      left      :55px;
      transition:all .5s ease-in-out;
    }
    input {
      width     :40px;
      height    :30px;
      margin    :20px 0 0 20px;
    }
    #b1:hover ~ #image { transform:scale(1.2, 1); }
    #b2:hover ~ #image { transform:scale(1, 1.2); }
  </style>
  <script src='../prefixfree.js'></script>
</head>
<body>
  <input id='b1' type='button' value='W'>
  <input id='b2' type='button' value='H'>
  <img id='image' src='image.jpg'>
</body>
</html>
```

FIGURE 19-2   The image has been vertically stretched by 20 percent.

A value of 1 keeps a dimension unscaled, less than 1 (but greater than 0) reduces it, and greater than 1 increases it. If no second argument is supplied, the Y axis scaling will be the same as the X axis.

You can also use the functions `scaleX()` and `scaleY()` to change only a single dimension of an element.

A negative value for any of these arguments causes the object to mirror (or flip) in that axis. If you supply two negative values to the `scale()` function, the combination of mirror and flip will result in a 180-degree rotation.

Older Versions of IE

On Internet Explorer browsers prior to IE9, you can use the following alternative declarations with the `Matrix()` function to achieve the same effect by modifying the `M11` and `M22` arguments (but remember that the scaling is from the top-left corner, not the element's center).

The `rotate (n)` Function

To rotate an object while retaining the same dimensions (a feat requiring complex math when using the `matrix()` function), simply specify the number of degrees by which an object should be rotated, like this:

```
transform:rotate(45deg);
```

Figure 19-3 shows the example file *rotate.htm* from the accompanying archive (and listed next), in which the mouse is over the 45-degree button. When you use the `rotate()` function, the element being rotated does so about its center.

```
<!DOCTYPE html>
<html>
  <head>
    <title>CSS Rotate Example</title>
    <style>
      #image {
        position  :absolute;
        border    :1px solid #000;
        top       :120px;
        left      :55px;
        transition:all .5s ease-in-out;
      }
      input {
        width     :40px;
        height    :30px;
        margin    :20px 0 0 20px;
      }
```

```
          #b1:hover ~ #image { transform:rotate(45deg);  }
          #b2:hover ~ #image { transform:rotate(90deg);  }
          #b3:hover ~ #image { transform:rotate(135deg); }
          #b4:hover ~ #image { transform:rotate(180deg); }
          #b5:hover ~ #image { transform:rotate(225deg); }
          #b6:hover ~ #image { transform:rotate(270deg); }
          #b7:hover ~ #image { transform:rotate(315deg); }
       </style>
       <script src='../prefixfree.js'></script>
     </head>
     <body>
       <input id='b1' type='button' value='45' >
       <input id='b2' type='button' value='90' >
       <input id='b3' type='button' value='135'>
       <input id='b4' type='button' value='180'>
       <input id='b5' type='button' value='225'>
       <input id='b6' type='button' value='270'>
       <input id='b7' type='button' value='315'>
       <img id='image' src='image.jpg'>
     </body>
   </html>
```

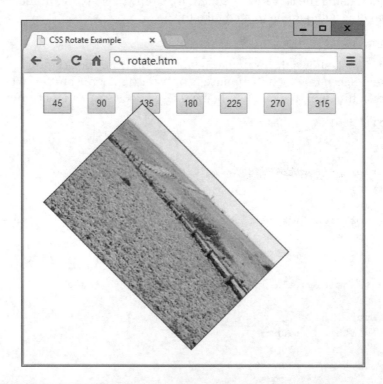

FIGURE 19-3   The element has been rotated clockwise by 45 degrees.

When specifying rotations, you may use values in either degrees or radians (a radian being equal to about 57.3 degrees, because there are 2π radians in 360 degrees), so both the following declarations are acceptable:

```
transform:rotate(57deg);
transform:rotate(1rad);
```

You may also supply negative values to rotate counterclockwise. Also, if you select values greater than 360 degrees (or less than -360) or the equivalent in radians, the value *does* apply because you can rotate objects more than once. If you also enable transitions (as described in Lesson 20), you will see that objects rotate as many times as necessary. For example, a value of 720 degrees will cause a double rotation and so on.

Older Versions of IE

You can achieve the same effect in Internet Explorer browser versions prior to IE9, but it requires using matrix multiplication of sine and cosine values. However, to get you started with a few declarations, here are the values to use for the four diagonal rotations of 45, 135, 225, and 315 degrees:

```
filter:progid:DXImageTransform.Microsoft.Matrix(SizingMethod='auto expand',
  M11= 0.7071, M12=-0.7071, M21= 0.7071, M22= 0.7071);
filter:progid:DXImageTransform.Microsoft.Matrix(SizingMethod='auto expand',
  M11=-0.7071, M12=-0.7071, M21= 0.7071, M22=-0.7071);
filter:progid:DXImageTransform.Microsoft.Matrix(SizingMethod='auto expand',
  M11=-0.7071, M12= 0.7071, M21=-0.7071, M22=-0.7071);
filter:progid:DXImageTransform.Microsoft.Matrix(SizingMethod='auto expand',
  M11= 0.7071, M12= 0.7071, M21=-0.7071, M22= 0.7071);
```

And here are IE declarations for 90-, 180-, and 270-degree rotations, which are much easier to set up, because the `BasicImage()` function can handle these rotations, with simple values for the rotation argument of just 1, 2, and 3:

```
filter:progid:DXImageTransform.Microsoft.BasicImage(rotation=1);
filter:progid:DXImageTransform.Microsoft.BasicImage(rotation=2);
filter:progid:DXImageTransform.Microsoft.BasicImage(rotation=3);
```

Remember, though, that IE uses the top-left corner as the point of rotation and therefore an element will be offset down and/or to the right if a rotation increases any dimensions. To fix this, you will need to use a trick such as a separate style sheet for Internet Explorer users of versions less than 9, to offset the rotated element back so that it is centered again on its initial location.

The `skew(x,y)` Function

The `skew()` function will skew an element in either the horizontal or vertical plane, either clockwise or counterclockwise. It works in a similar way to arguments 2 and 3 in the `matrix()` function, except that values must be supplied in degrees, and the arguments to this function affect the horizontal, then vertical skew in order (as opposed to arguments 2 and 3 of `matrix()` affecting the vertical, then horizontal skew, in that order) so that the following two declarations give similar results to Figures 18-3 and 18-4:

```
transform:skew(10deg, 0deg);
transform:skew(0deg, 10deg);
```

By assigning values as follows to both arguments, you can create either a diamond effect as shown in Figure 19-4, or a rotation, as shown in Figure 19-5:

```
transform:skew(10deg, 10deg);
transform:skew(10deg, -10deg);
```

FIGURE 19-4   Using the same value for each argument to `skew()`

FIGURE 19-5   Using the opposite values for each argument to `skew()`

These figures were created with the document *skew.htm* from the accompanying archive, and listed here:

```
<!DOCTYPE html>
<html>
  <head>
    <title>CSS Skew Example</title>
    <style>
      #image {
        position  :absolute;
        border    :1px solid #000;
        top       :120px;
        left      :55px;
        transition:all .5s ease-in-out;
      }
      input {
        width     :70px;
        height    :30px;
        margin    :20px 0 0 20px;
      }
      #b1:hover ~ #image { transform:skew(10deg,  0deg); }
      #b2:hover ~ #image { transform:skew(0deg,  10deg); }
      #b3:hover ~ #image { transform:skew(10deg, 10deg); }
```

```
      #b4:hover ~ #image { transform:skew(10deg, -10deg); }
    </style>
    <script src='../prefixfree.js'></script>
  </head>
  <body>
    <input id='b1' type='button' value='V'       >
    <input id='b2' type='button' value='H'       >
    <input id='b3' type='button' value='Same'    >
    <input id='b4' type='button' value='Opposite'>
    <img id='image' src='image.jpg'>
  </body>
</html>
```

You can also use the functions skewX() and skewY() to modify on the horizontal or vertical skew of an element.

At the time of writing, Chrome and Opera (due to using the Chrome engine) both have a serious bug when it comes to using the skew() function together with the transition property, which (for a change) Internet Explorer and the other main browsers do not exhibit. The problem is that when both horizontal and vertical skews are selected, Chrome moves the horizontal skews at a different rate (often vastly different) to the vertical skews, so the animation shape gets distorted, and this is only rectified once the transition ends, resulting in a very ugly and sudden collapse to the shape the object should have been.

Older Versions of IE

Using Internet Explorer browser versions prior to IE9, you can emulate this effect with the Matrix() function, so that the following four declarations are similar to the four preceding ones:

```
filter:progid:DXImageTransform.Microsoft.Matrix(
  SizingMethod='auto expand', M21=0.2);
filter:progid:DXImageTransform.Microsoft.Matrix(
  SizingMethod='auto expand', M12=0.2);
filter:progid:DXImageTransform.Microsoft.Matrix(
  SizingMethod='auto expand', M21=0.2, M12= 0.2);
filter:progid:DXImageTransform.Microsoft.Matrix(
  SizingMethod='auto expand', M21=0.2, M12=-0.2);
```

Remember that because the skew() function uses arguments in degrees, it will take different values than those supplied to either the CSS matrix() or Internet Explorer Matrix() functions.

Summary

At this point you have now learned just about everything you need to know about CSS and CSS3, up to and including advanced transformations. But there's one goody left to explore, which is taking transformations one step further, into the world of 3D, which we'll do in Lesson 20 (the final lesson).

Self-Test Questions

Using these questions, test how much you have learned in this lesson. If you don't know an answer, go back and reread the relevant section until your knowledge is complete. You can find the answers in the appendix.

1. With which `transform` function can you move an element to a different location?

2. Which two `transform` functions can be used to move an element just horizontally or vertically?

3. What range of values is supported by the `translate()` function?

4. With which function can you scale an element up and down in size?

5. Which two functions can scale an element just horizontally or vertically?

6. With which function can you rotate an element?

7. What types and ranges of values are supported by the `rotate()` function?

8. With which function can you skew an element?

9. Which two functions support skewing only horizontally or vertically?

10. What range of values is supported by the `skew()` function?

Directing 3D Transformations

To view the accompanying video for this lesson, please visit mhprofessional.com/nixoncss/.

Not only can you transform elements using CSS in an infinite variety of two-dimensional ways, you can also introduce the third dimension and transform them in that too, bringing a whole new level of depth to your web pages.

This is achieved by introducing depth using the `perspective` property, and then, using slightly different versions of the transformation functions I have already shown you, to manipulate elements in three (instead of two) dimensions.

If the concept seems difficult to get your head around, don't worry, it will all become quite clear very soon, and you'll be creating 3D transformations in next to no time.

The **perspective** Property

The `perspective` property releases an element from 2D space and creates a third dimension within which it can move. The property can be applied to unique elements, which will then have their own perspective view, but if you wish to have several elements on a page sharing the same perspective, then you must apply the `perspective` property to a parent object.

The value assigned to the property is any accepted CSS measurement, but pixels are good to use. It represents the distance between the viewer and the object. High values place the object farther away (but not reduced in size), and therefore it will show only a subtle 3D effect. A lower number places the object closer to the viewer (although still retaining the same size), and therefore any 3D effect is much more intense.

To rotate an object through the three dimensions, you use the `rotate3d()` function, or the `rotateX()`, `rotateY()`, and `rotateZ()` functions (explained later in this lesson). Similarly, other functions such as `skew()` and `translate()` have their own 3D versions too.

Figure 20-1 was created using the file *perspective.htm* from the accompanying archive, and it is listed next. In it a `perspective` value of 400 pixels has been assigned to the image's parent `<div>` (named `outer`), with this rule:

```
#b2:hover ~ #outer { perspective:400px; }
```

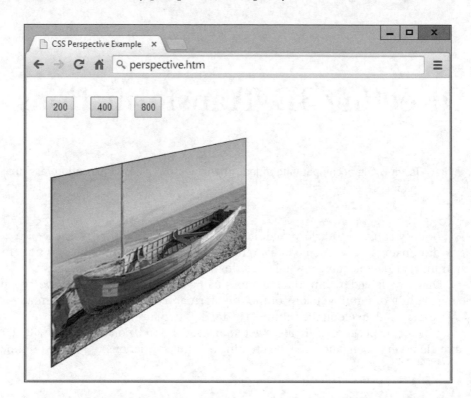

FIGURE 20-1 The image has been rotated using a **perspective** value of 400 pixels.

```
<!DOCTYPE html>
<html>
  <head>
    <title>CSS perspective Example</title>
    <style>
      #image {
        position   :absolute;
        border     :1px solid #000;
        top        :60px;
        left       :55px;
        transform  :rotateY(45deg);
      }
      #b1, #b2, #b3 {
```

```
    width      :40px;
    height     :30px;
    margin     :20px 0 0 20px;
  }
  #outer {
    transition :all .5s ease-in-out;
    perspective:10000px;
  }
  #b1:hover ~ #outer { perspective:200px; }
  #b2:hover ~ #outer { perspective:400px; }
  #b3:hover ~ #outer { perspective:800px; }
  </style>
  <script src='../prefixfree.js'></script>
</head>
<body>
  <input id='b1' type='button' value='200'>
  <input id='b2' type='button' value='400'>
  <input id='b3' type='button' value='800'>
  <div id='outer'>
    <img id='image' src='image.jpg'>
  </div>
</body>
</html>
```

When the mouse passes over one of the three buttons, a value of 200px, 400px, or 800px is assigned to the image's parent object's perspective property.

 At the time of writing, all the Webkit-based browsers are still using the -webkit-prefix for this property, so ensure you include additional declarations for it (particularly, if accessing CSS from JavaScript). Or, if you are only accessing the properties from CSS, you can use the *prefixfree.js* utility to take care of the browser-specific prefixes for you.

The transform-origin Property

By default, the point of origin for an element (or group of elements) is its center point. This is like the vanishing point you see in a photograph or painting—the location at which all lines converge to a single point. You can change the location of this point to anywhere within the 3D space of an element that has been given perspective, like this:

```
transform-origin:20% 30% 40%;
```

This sets the vanishing point to 20 percent in the X dimension, 30 percent in Y, and 40 percent in Z. Figure 20-2 illustrates an image in the process of being rotated around the Z axis with the X and Y origins transformed by 60 percent each, using the file *transform-origin.htm* (listed next) from the accompanying archive. Try passing your mouse over the buttons quickly to keep the rotation in place, and you'll see that the image simply shifts location according to the offset values.

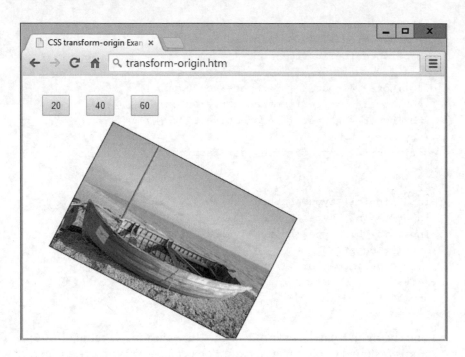

FIGURE 20-2 The rotation is offset by 60 percent in the X and Y dimensions.

```
<!DOCTYPE html>
<html>
  <head>
    <title>CSS transform-origin Example</title>
    <style>
      #image {
        position        :absolute;
        border          :1px solid #000;
        top             :120px;
        left            :55px;
        transition      :all .5s ease-in-out;
      }
      #b1, #b2, #b3 {
        width           :40px;
        height          :30px;
        margin          :20px 0 0 20px;
      }
```

```
    #outer {
      perspective      :300px;
    }
    #b1:hover ~ #image {
      transform        :rotateZ(90deg);
      transform-origin:20% 20%;
    }
    #b2:hover ~ #image {
      transform        :rotateZ(90deg);
      transform-origin:40% 40%;
    }
    #b3:hover ~ #image {
      transform        :rotateZ(90deg);
      transform-origin:60% 60%;
    }
    </style>
    <script src='../prefixfree.js'></script>
  </head>
  <body>
    <div id='outer'>
      <input id='b1' type='button' value='20'>
      <input id='b2' type='button' value='40'>
      <input id='b3' type='button' value='60'>
      <img id='image' src='image.jpg'>
    </div>
  </body>
</html>
```

Only two values are supplied to the `transform-origin` property, to give X and Y (horizontal and vertical) offsets. Providing a third value for Z (depth) would be meaningless because the image is being rotated in the Z dimension, and it would have no effect. In fact, when a third value is supplied to the preceding example, it actually seems to stop the other values from being accepted. The following section should clarify things for you if they are not yet fully clear.

About the Three Dimensions

When using 3D transforms, you can view the three dimensions as lines, along which transforms such as scaling and translation are applied, and around which rotations are applied, as follows:

- **X** This line stretches from left to right. An object rotated around this axis will have either the top or bottom edge move toward the viewer, and the other edge will move away behind the line.

- **Y** This line stretches up and down. An object rotated around this axis will have either the left or right edge move toward the viewer, and the other edge will move away behind the line.
- **Z** This line stretches in and out. An object rotated around this axis will simply rotate either clockwise or counterclockwise, maintaining the same profile toward the viewer.

Any combination of transforms can be applied at the same time, resulting in the ability to move, scale, rotate, and otherwise manipulate an element anywhere in the 3D space it occupies.

The **translate3d(x,y,z)** Function

This function moves an element to another location in its 3D space, while still retaining its dimensions and rotation. The file *translate3d.htm* in the accompanying archive features three buttons over which you can hover the mouse (remember to use Google Chrome or Apple Safari) to move an element by 30 pixels in any of the three dimensions, as shown in Figure 20-3, in which an element has been moved toward the viewer, using this CSS transform declaration:

```
transform:translate3d(0px, 0px, 60px)
```

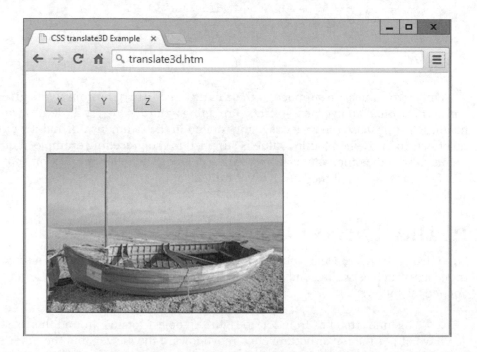

FIGURE 20-3 The element is moved 60 pixels toward the viewer along the Z axis.

The figure was created with the following HTML (saved as *translate3d.htm* in the accompanying archive):

```
<!DOCTYPE html>
<html>
  <head>
    <title>CSS translate3d Example</title>
    <style>
      #image {
        position    :absolute;
        border      :1px solid #000;
        top         :100px;
        left        :55px;
        transition  :all .5s ease-in-out;
      }
      #b1, #b2, #b3 {
        width       :40px;
        height      :30px;
        margin      :20px 0 0 20px;
      }
      #outer {
        perspective:500px;
      }
      #b1:hover ~ #image { transform:translate3d(60px, 0px, 0px); }
      #b2:hover ~ #image { transform:translate3d(0px, 60px, 0px); }
      #b3:hover ~ #image { transform:translate3d(0px, 0px, 60px); }
    </style>
    <script src='../prefixfree.js'></script>
  </head>
  <body>
    <div id='outer'>
      <input id='b1' type='button' value='X'>
      <input id='b2' type='button' value='Y'>
      <input id='b3' type='button' value='Z'>
      <img id='image' src='image.jpg'>
    </div>
  </body>
</html>
```

To move left, up, or away from the viewer, simply change the positive pixel values to negative, like this:

```
transform:translate3d(0px, 0px, -60px)
```

To change only a single dimension at a time, you can use one of the `translateX()`, `translateY()`, or `translateZ()` functions instead of the `translate3d()` function.

The `scale3d(x,y,z)` Function

You can scale elements up or down in size, in any or all three dimensions, like the following, which enlarges in X by 20 percent, keeps Y the same, and reduces Z by 20 percent:

```
transform:scale3d(1.2, 1, .8)
```

 Because elements are two-dimensional to begin with, when you stretch them in the third dimension, they have no depth to either shrink or grow, so nothing will seem to happen. However, once an element has been rotated a little either horizontally or vertically, it will then extend into the Z dimension, and so scaling and other transformations in that dimension will have an observable effect.

The *scale3d.htm* example file in the accompanying archive (and listed next) has three buttons over which you can hover the mouse to scale an element in any of the X, Y, or Z dimensions, as shown in Figure 20-4, in which the element used in the earlier `translate3d()` section is being scaled in the Y dimension, while also being rotated by 45 degrees in all dimensions (see the following section on `rotate3d()` for further details).

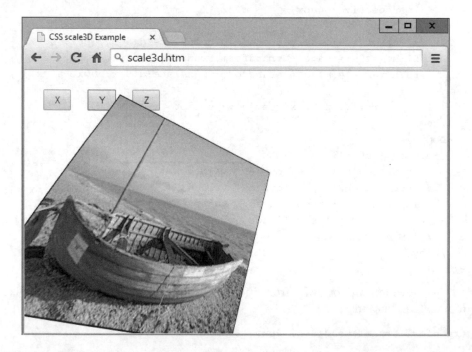

FIGURE 20-4   A 45-degree rotation in all dimensions with 20 percent upscaling in the Y dimension

```html
<!DOCTYPE html>
<html>
  <head>
    <title>CSS scale3d Example</title>
    <style>
      #image {
        position    :absolute;
        border      :1px solid #000;
        top         :100px;
        left        :55px;
        transition  :all .5s ease-in-out;
      }
      #b1, #b2, #b3 {
        width       :40px;
        height      :30px;
        margin      :20px 0 0 20px;
      }
      #outer {
        perspective:300px;
      }
      #b1:hover ~ #image {
        transform   :rotate3d(1, 1, 1, 45deg) scale3d(1.2, 1,   1  );
      }
      #b2:hover ~ #image {
        transform   :rotate3d(1, 1, 1, 45deg) scale3d(1,   1.2, 1  );
      }
      #b3:hover ~ #image {
        transform   :rotate3d(1, 1, 1, 45deg) scale3d(1,   1,   1.2);
      }
    </style>
    <script src='../prefixfree.js'></script>
  </head>
  <body>
    <div id='outer'>
      <input id='b1' type='button' value='X'>
      <input id='b2' type='button' value='Y'>
      <input id='b3' type='button' value='Z'>
      <img id='image' src='image.jpg'>
    </div>
  </body>
</html>
```

This is a good example of combining multiple transformation functions in a single declaration. For example, the one used in the figure (because the second button has been hovered over) is as follows:

```
transform:rotate3d(1, 1, 1, 45deg) scale3d(1, 1.2, 1);
```

You may add as many functions as you like after the `transform` property by separating them with spaces. This provides a particular fluid effect when animating because all scaling, rotation, and other manipulations will occur together.

To change only a single dimension at a time, you can use one of the `scaleX()`, `scaleY()`, or `scaleZ()` functions instead of the `scale3d()` function.

The `rotate3d(x,y,z,r)` Function

Using the `rotate3d()` function, you can also rotate an element around any of the X, Y, and Z axes. To use it, you must provide a value of either 0 or 1 for each of the axes to use, and then a fourth argument is required, supplying the number of degrees to rotate the object.

If only one axis is set to 1, the rotation will be simply around that line (left to right, up to down, or in to out). But if two or three axes are set to 1, then a new axis of rotation is created that combines them.

The file *rotate3d.htm* in the accompanying archive (and listed next) provides three buttons over which you can pass the mouse to rotate around the X, Y, or Z axis, as shown in Figure 20-5, in which the element from the previous section is being rotated around the X axis, with the top going away from the viewer and the bottom coming toward the viewer.

```
<!DOCTYPE html>
<html>
  <head>
    <title>CSS rotate3d Example</title>
    <style>
      #image {
        position  :absolute;
        border    :1px solid #000;
        top       :100px;
        left      :55px;
        transition:all .5s ease-in-out;
      }
      #b1, #b2, #b3 {
        width     :40px;
        height    :30px;
        margin    :20px 0 0 20px;
      }
```

```
      #outer {
        perspective:500px;
      }
      #b1:hover ~ #image { transform:rotate3d(1, 0, 0, 75deg); }
      #b2:hover ~ #image { transform:rotate3d(0, 1, 0, 75deg); }
      #b3:hover ~ #image { transform:rotate3d(0, 0, 1, 75deg); }
    </style>
    <script src='../prefixfree.js'></script>
  </head>
  <body>
    <div id='outer'>
      <input id='b1' type='button' value='X'>
      <input id='b2' type='button' value='Y'>
      <input id='b3' type='button' value='Z'>
      <img id='image' src='image.jpg'>
    </div>
  </body>
</html>
```

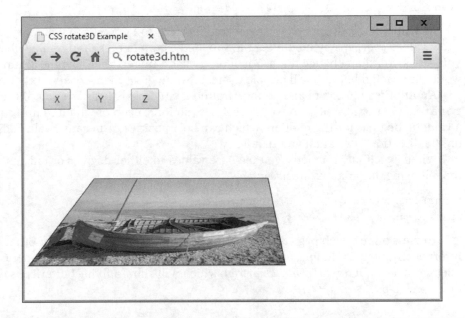

FIGURE 20-5   The element has been rotated around the X axis by 75 degrees.

To rotate in the other directions, replace the value 1 with −1, like this:

```
transform:rotate3d(0, 0, -1, 75deg)
```

Or you can keep the values of 1 and replace the rotation value with its inverse, like this:

```
transform:rotate3d(0, 0, 1, -75deg)
```

As I mentioned you may combine any of the three axes in this function call to achieve a rotation about any possible line in an element's three-dimensional space. To do this, rather than using values of 1 for each of the first three arguments, you can specify relational values.

For example, the following declaration specifies that the amount of rotation in X should be half that in Y, which should be half that in Z:

```
transform:rotate3d(5, 10, 20, 30deg);
```

You can also write this declaration as follows, or use any other sets of numbers that have the same ratio:

```
transform:rotate3d(1, 2, 4, 30deg);
```

You can also combine negative values for either the ratios or the degrees of rotation, so the following is a valid declaration:

```
transform:rotate3d(3, -11, 14, -30deg);
```

As with using matrices, this can get complicated, so I encourage you to try entering a few values (perhaps by modifying the supplied example files) and seeing what results you get as you then change them. You'll pretty soon understand how the arguments all work with each other and will be able to create some great mouseover or other effects.

Another way to rotate an element around a single axis is to use any of the rotateX(), rotateY(), and rotateZ() functions, each of which requires simply a value in degrees for the rotation, which can be a positive or negative value depending on the direction of rotation you require.

When specifying rotations, you may use values in either degrees or radians, so both the following declarations are acceptable:

```
transform:rotate3d(3, 2, 5, 100deg);
transform:rotate3d(7, 9, 4, 2rad );
```

To view a great web page displaying these 3D effects in any browser other than Internet Explorer (including, at the time of writing, not even the IE Developer Channel release), check out *tinyurl.com/3dbutterfly*, which will show a flying butterfly as depicted in Figure 20-6.

FIGURE 20-6 The butterfly flies around the browser window using 3D transforms.

The `backface-visibility` Property

When rotating elements, the back face (the inverse of the element) will be displayed when the front is turned away from the viewer. Sometimes you do not want this behavior if, for example, you have placed two elements back to back like a playing card and wish to view only the face that's toward you.

To ensure this happens, you can set the `backface-visibility` property to hidden, like this:

```
backface-visibility:hidden;
```

To cause the back face to reappear, use the following declaration (or the browser-specific one(s) you need):

```
backface-visibility:visible;
```

Figure 20-7 was created using the file *backface-visibility.htm* from the accompanying archive (and listed next). In it the second button employs the backface-visibility attribute so that when you hover the mouse over the first button, the image turns upside down and you see its back (which is the image turned upside down). But when you hover the mouse over the second button, and the image flips, it disappears after 90 degrees of rotation is reached, because the back of the image is not being displayed.

```
<!DOCTYPE html>
<html>
  <head>
    <title>CSS backface-visibility Example</title>
    <style>
      #image {
        position                :absolute;
        border                  :1px solid #000;
        top                     :100px;
        left                    :55px;
        transition              :all .5s ease-in-out;
      }
      #b1, #b2 {
        width                   :40px;
        height                  :30px;
        margin                  :20px 0 0 20px;
      }
      #outer {
        perspective             :500px;
      }
      #b1:hover ~ #image {
        transform               :rotate3d(1, 0, 0, 180deg);
      }
      #b2:hover ~ #image {
        backface-visibility:hidden;
        transform               :rotate3d(1, 0, 0, 180deg);
      }
    </style>
    <script src='../prefixfree.js'></script>
  </head>
  <body>
    <div id='outer'>
      <input id='b1' type='button' value='A'>
      <input id='b2' type='button' value='B'>
      <img id='image' src='image.jpg'>
    </div>
  </body>
</html>
```

FIGURE 20-7   The back of the element is not hidden.

The `transform-style` Property

Using this property, you can specify whether a child or nested element inherits the 3D space of its parent (if it has one) which is the default, or if it should restrict itself to 2D, for example, to act as a texture mapped onto the parent. The two values you can assign to this property are as follows (where `flat` is the default uninherited value):

```
transform-style:preserve-3d;
transform-style:flat;
```

Transitions

Also appearing on all the latest versions of the major browsers is a fantastic new feature called transitions. Using it, you can specify a type of animation effect you want to occur when an element is transformed, and the browser will automatically take care of all the in-between frames for you.

There are up to four properties you can use to set up a transition, as follows:

```
transition-property        :property;
transition-duration        :time;
transition-delay           :time;
transition-timing-function:type;
```

Remember, of course, to also preface these properties with the relevant browser prefixes, like this (or use the *prefixfree.js* utility to do this for you) to ensure maximum cross-browser compatibility:

```
-moz-transition-property    :width;
-webkit-transition-property:width;
-o-transition-property      :width;
-ms-transition-property     :width;
transition-property         :width;
```

The `transition-property` Property

This is the property to which you assign the property or properties that are to be animated, like this:

```
transition-property:width;
```

Here the `width` property is the only one supplied, but if more properties are required, they can be added by separating them with commas, like this:

```
transition-property:width, height, opacity;
```

Or, if you want absolutely everything about an element to transition (including colors, borders, width, height, and, well everything that happens to get changed and that can be animated), use the value `all`, like this:

```
transition-property:all;
```

 If you list a shorthand property such as `border` or `background`, then all of its sub-properties such as `border-width` or `background-color` that can be animated, will be animated. For a comprehensive breakdown of the properties that may and may not be animated, check out *tinyurl.com/animproperties*.

The `transition-duration` Property

The `transition-duration` property sets the length of time during which the animation should occur, in other words the length of the transition.

The property requires a value of 0 seconds or greater, like the following, which specifies that the transition should take 1.25 seconds to complete:

```
transition-duration:1.25s;
```

The `transition-delay` Property

You can choose to delay the start of a transition by a specified amount by assigning that delay to the `transition-delay` property.

If the property is given a value of 0 seconds or higher (as follows), it specifies that the transition should start only after a delay, which is 0.1 seconds in the following example:

```
transition-delay:0.1s;
```

If the `transition-delay` property is given a value of less than 0 seconds (in other words a negative value), then the transition will execute the moment the property is changed, but it will appear to have begun execution at the specified offset, partway through its cycle.

The `transition-timing-function` Property

With the `transition-timing-function` property, you can specify the animation timing that should be used by choosing a function representing the way the animation speeds up and slows down during its presentation.

This property requires one of the following values:

- **ease**   Start slowly, get faster, then end slowly
- **linear**   Transition at constant speed (the default)
- **ease-in**   Start slowly, then go quickly until finished
- **ease-out**   Start quickly, stay fast, then end slowly
- **ease-in-out**   Start slowly, go fast, then end slowly

Using any of the values with the word `ease` in it ensures that the transition looks extra fluid and natural, unlike linear transitions, which somehow seem more mechanical.

The `cubic-bezier()` Function

If the previous timing functions aren't sufficiently varied for you, you can create your own transitions with the `cubic-bezier()` function, which you assign to the property.

For example, following are the declarations used to create the preceding five transition types, and they are identical in action to them (illustrating how easily you can create new ones):

```
transition-timing-function:cubic-bezier(0.25, 0.10, 0.25, 1.00);
transition-timing-function:cubic-bezier(0.00, 0.00, 1.00, 1.00);
transition-timing-function:cubic-bezier(0.42, 0.00, 1.00, 1.00);
transition-timing-function:cubic-bezier(0.00, 0.00, 0.58, 1.00);
transition-timing-function:cubic-bezier(0.42, 0.00, 0.58, 1.00);
```

Basically the arguments represent two pairs of numbers occurring on a two-dimensional graph charting a diagonal line (pointing in a northeasterly direction), and which shows change in property over time. The coordinate pairs work like attractors that pull this line (as if it is old-fashioned cassette audio tape being attracted by magnets) into an S shape.

So, for example, in the following function call (which performs the `ease` function) the pair 0.25, 0.10 is at the start and a little to the right of the diagonal line, while 0.25, 1.00 is pulled a long way to the left of the line point. The result is a slightly slower start-up, then a rapid speed-up, followed by a smoothly slowing ending.

```
cubic-bezier(0.25, 0.10, 0.25, 1.00)
```

For a detailed explanation of how this function works, check out the website at *tinyurl.com/cubicbezier*, where you can click the graph that shows this S-shaped line to call up a utility to dynamically create and test your own timings. Figure 20-8 illustrates using this program. In it I have captured the screen with the five test squares in the middle of a test transition.

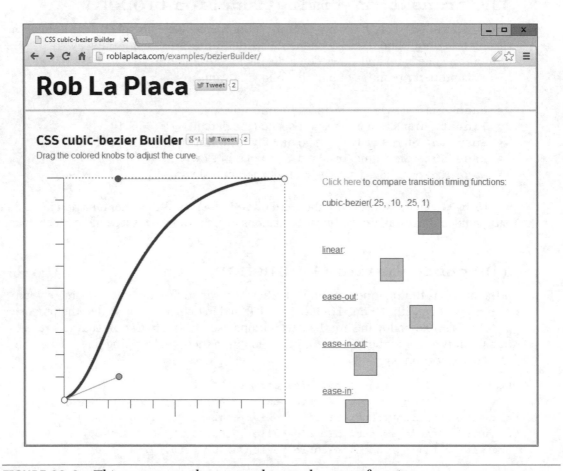

FIGURE 20-8 This curve uses the same values as the **ease** function.

Shorthand `transition` Property Syntax

You may find it easier to use the shorthand version of the `transition` property and include all the values in a single declaration such as the following, which will transition all properties in a linear fashion, over a period of .3 seconds (the first time value is the duration), but only after an initial delay of .2 seconds (the second time value is the delay):

```
transition:all .3s linear .2s;
```

Assigning the values this way will save on entering many very similar declarations, particularly if you are supporting all the major browser prefixes.

To animate a selection of properties, separate each property name (plus any timing declarations) with a comma, like this example which eases the width and height over 1 second each and, after an initial delay of half a second, linearly transitions the background over 2 seconds:

```
transition:width 1s ease, height 1s ease, 2s background .5s linear;
```

 You can see a great example incorporating 3D transforms and transitions, as well as back face hiding, at *tinyurl.com/css3cube3d*. When you load the page in any browser other than Internet Explorer (or even the IE Developer Channel release—at the time of this writing), you will be able to manipulate a three-dimensional cube using only CSS transformations and transitions, as shown in Figure 20-9.

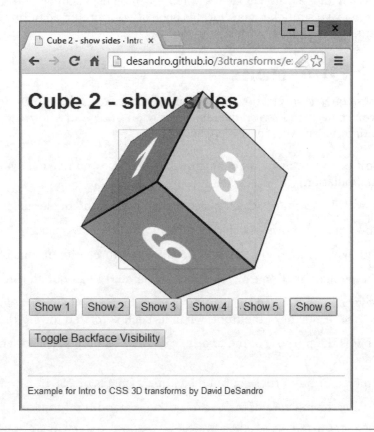

FIGURE 20-9   Combining 3D transformations and transitions to animate a rotating cube

Summary

And that's it. You now know all the most important things there are to learn about using CSS and CSS3, although there are a number of other additions to CSS that for one reason or another I haven't mentioned, usually because they are still only a draft proposal, their application is experimental, they don't work in enough browsers yet, or features might be subject to change.

Some examples of this may include style sheets for speech, generated content, constants and variables to enable CSS to work more like a programming language, the ability to flow content into nonrectangular shapes, support for orienting text in different directions, and a new way of blending background images together to provide Photoshop-quality backgrounds.

Once these (and other newer) goodies become widely available, I intend to cover their use in a future edition of this course. In the meantime, though, I hope you've enjoyed reading this book and, if you haven't already, I do urge you to test your new knowledge with the self-test questions at the end of each chapter, to ensure you've remembered as much as possible.

And, as ever, all comments and suggestions are always welcome via the website at *20lessons.com* and, if you feel so motivated, I will be especially grateful if you have a moment to leave a quick review for this book at your preferred online book retailer.

Thanks again and good luck with your web designing!

Self-Test Questions

Using these questions, test how much you have learned in this lesson. If you don't know an answer, go back and reread the relevant section until your knowledge is complete. You can find the answers in the appendix.

1. How can you release an element from 2D space and make it available for 3D manipulation?

2. How can you change the transformational center of an element?

3. How can you move an object to a new location in 3D space?

4. With which function can you scale any or all three dimensions of an element?

5. With which function can you rotate an element in any or all three dimensions?

6. How can you prevent the back of an element being displayed (generally the inverse or mirror of the front) when its back is rotated toward the viewer?

7. What is the purpose of the `transform-style` property, and what values does it accept?

8. Which four properties control the various aspects of CSS transitions?

9. What is the purpose of the `transition-property` property?

10. What shorthand declaration can you use to transition all of an element's properties to ease in and out over 1.5 seconds?

Answers to the Self-Test Questions

This appendix contains the answers to all the questions posed at the end of the lessons in this book. To ensure you have understood everything, try to refrain from checking these answers until you have attempted to answer all the questions in a lesson.

If you don't know an answer, try to find it in the book before you look here if you can, as this will help you to remember it next time.

Lesson 1 Answers

1. HTML is based on the Document Object Model (DOM).

2. The main purpose of style sheets is to enable the separation of content from styling in web documents.

3. The outermost object in the DOM is the browser window (which can also be a tab, iframe, or pop-up window).

4. The two main sections of an HTML document are the head and the body.

5. In the head of a document you will typically find the title, meta elements, style sections, and sometimes scripts.

6. CSS rules are often placed between `<style>` and `</style>` tags in the head of a document.

7. To import an external style sheet into the style section of an HTML document, you use the @import directive—for example: `@import url('styles.css');`.

8. An external style sheet can be imported into the HTML of a web document using the `<link>` tag—for example: `<link rel='stylesheet' type='text/css' href='styles.css'>`.

9. A CSS style can be directly applied to an element by assigning a value to its style attribute—for example: `<h1 style='color:red;'>Hello</h1>`.

10. A CSS class can apply to multiple HTML elements, whereas an ID may apply only to a single element.

Lesson 2 Answers

1. A CSS selector is the element or group of elements being selected by a rule for styling. Selectors may include element types, IDs, or classes.

2. You use { and } symbols to contain the rules that are to apply to one or more selectors.

3. In CSS rules, a colon is used to separate properties and values—for example: `color:green;`.

4. A semicolon is not required after the final rule in a set, or if there is only one rule, but because rules are often copied, pasted, and moved, it is recommended to always place a semicolon after all rules.

5. To apply more than one CSS rule to a selector, separate them with semicolons. They do not have to be on separate lines, but can be for readability.

6. To give the ID of `item1` to an element, assign it to the element's `id` attribute—for example: `<div id='item1'>First item</div>`.

7. To give the class `news` to an element, assign it to the element's `class` attribute—for example: `<h1 class='news'>Headlines</h1>`.

8. To mark a section of CSS as a comment, enclose it within `/*` and `*/` tags. You may also use the `//` tag to comment out to the end of a line, but it is not a recommended standard.

9. Ignoring default and user styles, the main types of CSS rules are external style sheets, internal styles in a `<style>` section, and inline styles assigned to an element's `style` attribute.

10. To set the font size for `<h1>` text to 300 percent the standard size, you could use this selector and rule: `h1 { font-size:300%; }`.

Lesson 3 Answers

1. In CSS and HTML, IDs are given to elements so that they can be uniquely identified by either CSS rules or JavaScript commands.

2. In CSS the purposes of classes is to define a set of rules that can then be applied to multiple elements, not just a single element. In JavaScript, classes are of less use than IDs because extra code must be written to deal with them.

3. In certain circumstances some browsers allow IDs to be used in a similar manner to classes. However, this is nonstandard and the behavior could be easily removed at any time. Also, because classes are available, there is no need to treat IDs as classes. The answer to this question is, therefore, yes you *can* (sometimes) reuse IDs, but you shouldn't.

4. The `float` property can align elements to the left or right such that they line up with other elements—for example: `float:left`.

5. The `border` property lets you add borders to elements—for example: `border:1px solid #888;`.

6. You can change the background color of an element with the `background` property—for example: `background:blue;`.

7. You can specify the width of an element using its `width` property—for example: `width:320px;`.

8. To set an element's text style to italic, you can use its `font-style` property—for example: `font-style:italic;`.

9. To center text within an element, use its `text-align` property—for example: `text-align:center;`.

10. You can apply a shadow to an element through its `box-shadow` property—for example: `box-shadow:4px 4px 4px #888;`.

Lesson 4 Answers

1. The type selector is where a type of element such as `<div>`, `<table>`, or `<img>` is selected—for example: `img { border:1px solid black; }`.

2. The descendant selector applies to children and their children (and so on) of parent elements and is created by placing elements next to each other, separated by a space—for example: `p em { font-style:italic; }`.

3. The child selector applies only to direct children of parent elements and is created with the `>` symbol—for example: `div > p { text-indent:30px; }`.

4. The ID selector applies only to a single element and is created using the `#` symbol—for example: `#myid { color:red; }`.

5. The class selector applies to any elements that use the class and is created using the `.` (period) symbol—for example: `.myclass { color:green; }`.

6. You can narrow the scope of ID and class selectors by prefacing them with element types—for example: `p#myid { font-weight:bold; }`, or `p.myclass { text-indent:30px; }`.

7. The attribute selector is where you apply rules according to whether an element has a particular attribute and is contained within square brackets—for example: `[type='submit'] { width:100px; }`.

8. You can achieve the same result as using the class selector `.classname` with the attribute selector: `[class='classname']`.

9. The universal selector matches absolutely anything and is represented with the `*` symbol—for example: `body * { color:#444; }`.

10. To select groups of elements, you can separate selectors with commas so that the rules will apply to all selectors that match—for example: `div > p, span b, .myclass { font-size:150%; }`.

Lesson 5 Answers

1. The three types of style sheet are: those created by a document's author, those created by the user, and those created by the browser.

2. The three methods of applying styles are: as inline styles, in an embedded style sheet, as an external style sheet. Additionally, styles may also be applied using JavaScript.

3. The three ways in which elements can be selected for styling are: referencing by an individual ID, referencing in groups by class, referencing by element types.

4. A descendant rule is one in which two or more selectors follow each other separated by spaces, and in which each new selector further narrows down the element(s) to be selected.

5. In general, a descendant rule is more specific when it has more selectors, but this does depend on the selector types and is not always the case.

6. To prevent later rules overriding the current one, follow it with the `!important` modifier. Unless another rule is applied on the property that also uses `!important`, the property will be unchangeable—for example: `.myclass { font-weight:bold !important; }`.

7. The biggest difference between a `<div>` and a `<span>` element is that `<div>` elements are block elements, which (by default) assume the document width, and therefore, force other elements to appear beneath them, while `<span>` elements are inline, and they therefore flow with text and (by default) assume only the width of their content.

8. A `<span>` element is best suited for containing portions of text because it assumes the width and height of its contents, in the form of inline text, and therefore can flow over multiple lines. On the other hand, `<div>` elements are rectangular and cannot flow over multiple lines.

9. The measurement types best suited for making relative property size changes are percent (using the `%` symbol) and em—for example: `font-size:200%;`, or `line-height:1.5em;`.

10. The CSS ex measurement type is the odd-one out, because it is not based on a standard measurement or on a global scaling amount. Instead it is calculated from the height of a lowercase *x*, and therefore does not scale by the same amount as the other measurement types when the user scales the browser contents up or down.

Lesson 6 Answers

1. To change font family, use the `font-family` property—for example: `font-family:Arial;`.

2. To display a font in italic, use its `font-style` property—for example: `font-style:italic;`.

3. To change the size of a font, use its `font-size` property—for example: `font-size:16pt;`.

4. To display a font in bold, use its `font-weight` property—for example: `font-weight:bold;`.

5. To choose the Helvetica font with a fallback of sans serif, you would use CSS such as `font-family:Helvetica, sans-serif;`.

6. To underline text with CSS, use the `text-decoration` property—for example: `text-decoration:underline;`.

7. To change the vertical spacing of lines, you can modify the `line-height` property—for example: `line-height:25px;`.

8. To change word and letter spacing of a font, use the `word-spacing` and `letter-spacing` properties—for example: `word-spacing:5px; letter-spacing:1px;`.

9. To specify an indent for text, use its `text-indent` property—for example: `text-indent:30px;`.

10. To capitalize a section of text, you can use its `text-transform` property—for example: `text-transform:uppercase;`.

Lesson 7 Answers

1. Without using a CSS function, you can supply colors to CSS properties using color names (such as `color:black;`), long color strings (such as `color:#012345;`) and short color strings (such as `color:#678;`).

2. To assign the color yellow to a property using the CSS `rgb()` function and base 256 numbers, you could create a rule such as `color:rgb(255, 255, 0);`.

3. To assign the color blue to a property using the CSS `rgb()` function and percentage values, you could create a rule such as `color:rgb(0%, 0%, 100%);`.

4. To assign a linear vertical gradient from white to black to the background of an object, you could use the rule `background:linear-gradient(#fff, #000);`, or you could also use `background:linear-gradient(white, black);`.

5. To assign a linear horizontal gradient from yellow to green to blue, to the background of an object, you could use the rule `background:linear-gradient (90deg, #f00, #0f0, #00f);`, or `background:linear-gradient (90deg, red, green, blue);`, or a combination.

6. To create a linear background gradient from color #345 to color #678, you could use the rule `background:radial-gradient(#345, #678);`.

7. The `position` property supports values `static`, `absolute`, `fixed`, and `relative`.

8. To place an element in a set location at the top left of the browser such that it is not subject to scrolling, you might use these rules: `position:fixed; top:0px; left:0px;`.

9. To remove an element from view without altering its opacity, dimensions, or other visibility properties, you could simply give it an absolute position off-screen—for example: `position:absolute; top:-1000px; left:-1000px;`.

10. To give a color alpha transparency when assigning it to a property, you can use the `rgba()` function supplying the transparency level as a fourth argument—for example: `background:rgba(100%, 100%, 0%, 0.5);`.

Lesson 8 Answers

1. You can modify just the first letter of an element using the `first-letter` pseudo-class—for example: `#text:first-letter { font-size:200%; }`.

2. You can modify just the first line of an element using the `first-line` pseudo-class—for example: `#text:first-line { text-indent:20px; }`.

3. To make all previously visited links display in navy, you could use the rule `a:visited { color:navy; }`.

4. To style only the first child of an element, use its `first-child` pseudo-class—for example: `div p:first-child { text-indent:20px; }`.

5. To select just the third child of a parent, use a rule such as `div p:nth-child(3) { color:red; }`, and to select every odd-numbered child, use either a rule like this: `div p:nth-child(odd) { color:red; }`, or one like this: `div p:nth-child(2n+1) { color:red; }`.

6. To add content before an element, use a rule such as `elem:before { content:'I am before'; }`, and to add it after, use a rule such as `elem:after { content:'I am after'; }`.

7. A shorthand rule to create a 2-pixel-dotted red border is `border:2px dotted red;`.

8. A shorthand rule to create a nonrepeating background from the image *picture.jpg*, with a default background color of yellow, is `background:yellow url('picture.jpg') no-repeat;`.

9. To set an italic Courier New font, in 14 point using shorthand CSS, you could use `font:italic 14pt 'Courier New';`.

10. To set the top and bottom margins of an element to 10 pixels, its left and right margins to 20 pixels, its top padding to 5 pixels, its left and right padding to 10 pixels, and its bottom padding to 15 pixels, you could use these two shorthand rules: `margin:10px 20px; padding:5px 10px 15px;`.

Lesson 9 Answers

1. The term *CSS Box Model* refers to a method of representing the attributes of HTML elements affecting their size, spacing, and borders, in the form of a box model from the outside to the inside (or vice versa).

2. The four levels of the box model are content, padding, border, and margin.

3. Because the smaller margin collapses, the distance in pixels between an element with a margin of 40 pixels, placed directly below one with a margin of 20 pixels, is 40 pixels.

4. When one value is supplied to the `margin`, `padding`, or `border-width` properties, all edges are modified. When two values are supplied, the first alters the top and bottom edges, and the second alters the left and right edges. When three values are supplied, the first alters the top edge, the second alters the left and right edges, and the third alters the bottom edge. When four values are supplied, in turn each value alters the top, right, bottom, and then left edge.

5. To make a block element such as a `<div>` display inline with other elements, change its `display` property to `inline-block`.

6. The main difference between assigning a `<div>` element's `display` property of the value `inline-block`, compared with simply assigning it the value `inline`, is that the `inline-block` value respects top and bottom margins, whereas `inline` does not.

7. One way to ensure the top edges of inline elements align is to assign the value `top` to the `vertical-align` property of the elements—for example: `vertical-align:top;`. You could also supply the values `baseline`, `sub`, `super`, `text-top`, `middle`, and `bottom` for other types of vertical alignment.

8. The default value of the `box-sizing` property is `content-box`, in which padding and borders are added to an element's dimensions.

9. To make an element's padding and border widths get taken from its width and height, assign the value `border-box` to the `box-sizing` property—for example: `box-sizing:border-box;`.

10. When changing the box sizing of a document, it makes sense to also alter the before and after pseudo-elements to ensure they also follow the same rules—for example: `*:before, *:after { box-sizing:border-box; }`.

Lesson 10 Answers

1. Features were still being proposed for CSS3 as recently as 2012.

2. Multiple background images can be added to an element simply by listing them one at a time as values for the `background` property, separated with commas, and optional location and repetition specifiers.

3. The major new enhancement to CSS borders is the ability to create rounded corners.

4. You can create rounded borders using the `border-radius` property.

5. The `box-shadow` property lets you add box shadows to elements.

6. The `text-shadow` property lets you add shadows to text.

7. To control how overflowing content is handled you can use the `overflow` property.

8. The three properties concerned with supporting multiple columns are `column-count`, `column-gap`, and `column-rule`.

9. At the time of writing, the Google Fonts service currently offers in excess of 600 free fonts.

10. The `rotate3d()` function is used to rotate elements in three dimensions.

Lesson 11 Answers

1. The universal selector lets you style any elements. While this makes it very powerful, the downside is that it breaks the cascade of CSS, and therefore, it should be used with caution.

2. A type selector is one that enables styling of HTML elements by element type name—for example: `p { font-style:italic; }`.

3. ID selectors allow styling of a single element, while class selectors can be reused multiple times with multiple elements.

4. A descendant selector selects elements by their parent–child relationship, and by grandchildren and their descendants too. An element that is any type of descendant of the reference (or parent) element is selected. The selector is specified by separating selectors with a space—for example: `div p { color:red; }`.

5. A child selector styles only elements that are a direct child of a parent. Grandchildren and so on are not styled. The symbol used by the child selector is the > (greater than) sign—for example: `span > i { border-bottom:1px dotted green; }`.

6. Adjacent sibling selectors style only those elements that are next to the reference. The two may be directly next to each other or separated by unstyled content, but any HTML tags between the two will prevent selection from occurring. This selector uses the + symbol—for example: `p + p { text-indent:20px; }`.

7. A general sibling selector works in the same way to the adjacent sibling selector except that it is less strict, requiring only that both the reference and the element are direct siblings of a parent, and they can be separated by other HTML elements. The symbol used by this selector is ~ (a tilde)—for example: `#brother:hover ~ #sister { font-weight:bold; }`.

8. An attribute selector selects elements by the contents of their attributes by placing an attribute name and a string to match between square brackets—for example: `img[src='myphoto.jpg'] { border:2px solid black; }`.

9. Using an attribute selector, you can search for a match at the start of a string using the ^ symbol placed directly before the = sign, in this manner: `a[href^='http://']:after { content:' (External link)'; }`. To match at the end of a string, you use the $ symbol, like this: `a[href$='.pdf']:after { content:' (PDF file)'; }`.

10. Using an attribute selector, you can search for a match anywhere in a string using the * symbol before the = sign, as in the following example: `a[href*='google']:after { content:' (At Google)'; }`.

Lesson 12 Answers

1. The `border-box` value refers to the outer edge of an element's border.

2. The `padding-box` value refers to the outer edge of an element's padding area.

3. The `content-box` value refers to the outer edge of an element's content area.

4. The `background-clip` property specifies whether the background should be clipped outside a given area.

5. You can supply any of the values `border-box` (the default), `padding-box`, or `content-box` to the `background-clip` property—for example: `background-clip:padding-box;`.

6. The `background-origin` property specifies where the top-left corner of the background should be located.

7. You can supply any of the values `border-box`, `padding-box` (the default), or `content-box` to the `background-origin` property—for example: `background-origin:content-box;`.

8. You can alter the size of a background image using the `background-size` property—for example: `background-size:500px 300px;`.

9. You can use the `auto` value to scale one background image dimension and have the other scale automatically to match—for example: `background-size:400px auto;`.

10. To load the background image *corner.gif* into the top right-hand corner of an element without repetition, you could use a rule such as `background: url('corner.gif') top right no-repeat;`.

Lesson 13 Answers

1. You can change all the borders of an element to the same color using the `border-color` property—for example: `border-color:red;`, as part of a shorthand border rule—for example: `border:1px solid red;`, or uniquely addressing each corner using the properties `border-top-color`, `border-left-color`, `border-right-color`, and `border-bottom-color`.

2. To set all four borders of an element to different colors with a single rule, you can assign values to the `border-color` property, which are applied clockwise from top to left—for example: `border-color:red green blue orange;`.

3. To change the color of just one border of an element, assign a value to one of the following properties: `border-top-color`, `border-left-color`, `border-right-color`, or `border-bottom-color`—for example: `border-bottom-color:navy;`.

4. You can set all four borders of an element to different styles with a single rule such as `border-style:inset solid outside dotted;`.

5. The three properties that are often used together to assemble multiple border images to make up an element's border are `border-image-source`, `border-image-width`, and `border-image-slice`.

6. The `border-image-width` property assigns either a single width for all borders, or different widths for each. When more than one value is given, in clockwise from top to left, each value represents the width of that edge's border.

7. The `border-image-slice` property assigns either a width and height at which to clip all corner images from the main image, or a different clip width for each edge to be applied separately to each corner of the image. When more than one value is given, in clockwise from top to left, each value represents the clip width for that border.

8. To give all four corners of an element the same border radius, assign the radius amount to the `border-radius` property—for example: `border-radius:10px;`.

9. To assign a radius to just a single corner of an element, give a value to one of these properties: `border-top-left-radius`, `border-top-right-radius`, `border-bottom-left-radius`, and `border-bottom-right-radius`—for example: `border-bottom-right-radius:20px;`.

10. To apply a different radius to each corner of an element using a single CSS rule, assign the four values in a clockwise direction (from top left to bottom left) to the `border-radius` property—for example: `border-radius:20px 40px 60px 80px;`.

Lesson 14 Answers

1. You can add a shadow to an element using the `box-shadow` property.

2. The two values required by the `box-shadow` property are the vertical and horizontal offset of the shadow—for example: `box-shadow:2px 2px;`.

3. The two values that change the blur and spread of a box shadow follow the vertical and horizontal values, blur first, followed by spread—for example: `box-shadow:2px 2px 5px 8px;`.

4. To change the color of a box shadow, simply supply a color value to the `box-shadow` property—for example: `box-shadow:2px 2px red;`.

5. To make a shadow display within an element instead of outside, supply the value `inset` to the `box-shadow` property—for example: `box-shadow:2px 2px red inset;`.

6. In CSS3 the overflow property comes with two new properties, `overflow-x` and `overflow-y`, to handle the vertical and horizontal overflow separately.

7. The four values that the `overflow`, `overflow-x`, and `overflow-y` properties accept are `hidden`, `visible`, `scroll`, and `auto`.

8. You can flow text over columns using the `column-count` property—for example: `column-count:3;`.

9. To change the gap between multiple columns, assign the gap value to the `column-gap` property—for example: `column-gap:15px;`.

10. To place a vertical rule between columns, assign the `column-rule` property the same values you would to a border—for example: `column-rule:1px dotted #888;`.

Lesson 15 Answers

1. The difference between the `rgb()` and `hsl()` functions is that the `rgb()` function requires values of red, blue, and green to describe a color, while `hsl()` needs values for hue, saturation, and luminance.

2. The `hsl()` function requires a value between 0 and 359 for the hue, where 0 is red, green is 120, blue is 240, and other values are created by mixing the prime colors either side (with 360 also being red).

3. The `hsl()` function requires percentage values between `0%` and `100%` for the saturation and luminance values.

4. The `hsla()` function supports the inclusion of alpha transparency when setting a color, which the `hsl()` function does not.

5. The `hsla()` function requires percentage values between `0%` and `100%` for its alpha value.

6. The `rgb()` function accepts three values representing the red, green, and blue portions of a color. The values may be supplied as percentages between `0%` and `100%`, or values between 0 and 255 (or a combination).

7. The `rgba()` function supports the inclusion of alpha transparency when setting a color, which the `rgb()` function does not.

8. The `rgba()` function requires a floating point value between `0.00` and `1.00` for its alpha value.

9. To change the global transparency of an element, you can use its `opacity` property.

10. The `opacity` property requires a floating point value between `0.00` and `1.00`.

Lesson 16 Answers

1. The `text-shadow` property requires the horizontal and vertical offset for the shadow to be supplied—for example: `text-shadow:2px 2px;`.

2. Optionally, the `text-shadow` property accepts a value indicating the amount of blur to apply, and a color—for example: `text-shadow:2px 2px 4px #444;`.

3. To give alpha transparency to a text shadow, you can use either of the `hsla()` or `rgba()` functions, like this: `text-shadow:2px 2px 4px rgba(25%, 25%, 25%, 0.5);`.

4. To deal with overflowing text, you can use the `text-overflow` property. The default value it supports is `clip`, but you can also give values of `ellipsis`, or as string of characters of your choosing—for example: `text-overflow:ellipsis;`.

5. To force words to wrap around when they are too large to fit, you can use the `word-wrap` property—for example: `word-wrap:break-word;`.

6. The `box-sizing` property specifies whether padding and borders are to be added to the width and height of an element, or subtracted from these dimensions.

7. The two values accepted by the `box-sizing` property are `content-box` (the default), which extends the width and height of an element when padding and borders are added, and `border-box`, which takes the space it needs for padding and borders from the current dimensions of the content.

8. The `resize` property enables input and textarea elements to become user resizable. It supports the values `horizontal`, `vertical`, and `both`—for example: `resize:both;`.

9. To restrict the amount of resizing a user can apply to an element, you can specify maximum sizes to the `max-width` and/or `max-height` properties—for example: `max-width:150%; max-height:200%;`.

10. The outline applied by browsers to elements that gain focus can be modified with the `outline` property, which takes color, style and size values, and the `outline-offset` property, which requires a standard CSS measurement value—for example: `outline:red dashed thick; outline-offset:5px;`.

Lesson 17 Answers

1. A web font is one that is not stored locally on the user's computer, but is downloaded on demand over the Internet when a browser requires it.

2. The three main formats of web fonts are TrueType, OpenType, and Web Open format.

3. The font name extension for TrueType fonts is *.ttf*, and the format type name is `truetype`.

4. The font name extension for OpenType fonts is *.otf*, and the format type name is `opentype`.

5. The font name extension for Web Open Format fonts is *.woff*, and the format type name is `woff`.

6. The CSS rule used to access a web font is `@font-face`.

7. The two properties that must be given values in an `@font-face` rule are `font-family` and `src`—for example: `@font-face { font-family:MyFont; src:url('myfont.woff') format('woff');`.

8. To download a Google web font to a browser, you include a style sheet as listed at the Google Fonts website using a `<link>` tag.

9. To enable Google's Tangerine web font in a document, you would load the relevant style sheet—for example: `<link rel = 'stylesheet' type = 'text/css' href = 'http://fonts.googleapis.com/css? family=Tangerine'>`.

10. To access a Google web font once it has loaded, you can pass its name as the value for any `font-family` property assignment, as you would with any locally stored font—for example: `font-family:Tangerine;`.

Lesson 18 Answers

1. CSS can perform transformations such as skewing, scaling, and rotation on elements using the `matrix()` function—for example: `transform:matrix(1.2, 0, 0, 1.2, 0, 0);`.

2. The fifth argument to `matrix()` moves an element horizontally—for example: `transform:matrix(1, 0, 0, 1, **20**, 0);`.

3. The sixth argument to `matrix()` moves an element vertically—for example: `transform:matrix(1, 0, 0, 1, 0, **20**);`.

4. The first argument to `matrix()` scales an element horizontally—for example: `transform:matrix(**2**, 0, 0, 1, 0, 0);`.

5. The fourth argument to `matrix()` scales an element vertically—for example: `transform:matrix(1, 0, 0, **2**, 0, 0);`.

6. The third argument to `matrix()` skews an element horizontally—for example: `transform:matrix(1, 0, **0.5**, 1, 0, 0);`.

7. The second argument to `matrix()` skews an element vertically—for example: `transform:matrix(1, **0.5**, 0, 1, 0, 0);`.

8. To remove or cancel a transformation, you can assign the value none to the transform property—for example: `transform:none;`.

9. To rotate an object 90 degrees counterclockwise, without any change in size, you could use these values: `transform:matrix(0, -1, 1, 0, 0, 0);`.

10. To horizontally mirror an object without any change in size, you could use these values: `transform:matrix(-1, 0, 0, 1, 0, 0);`.

Lesson 19 Answers

1. You can move an element to a different location using the `translate()` function—for example: `transform:translate(10px, 20px);`.

2. To move an element just horizontally or vertically, you can use either the `translateX()` or `translateY()` function—for example: `transform: translateX(50px);` or `transform:translateY(35px);`.

3. The `translate()` function supports any negative, zero, or positive CSS measurement values—for example: `transform:translate(1.2em, 1.5em);`.

4. You can scale an element up and down in size with the `scale()` function—for example: `transform:scale(1.5, 1.5);`.

5. You can scale an object horizontally with the `scaleX()` function, and vertically with the `scaleY()` function—for example: `transform: scaleX(1.5); transform:scaleY(1.8);`.

6. You can rotate an element using the `rotate()` function—for example: `transform:rotate(45deg);`.

7. The `rotate()` function accepts values in either degrees or radians, which can be negative, zero, or positive—for example: `transform: rotate(-2rad);` or `transform:rotate(180deg);`.

8. You can skew an element with the `skew()` function—for example: `transform:skew(15deg, 20deg);`.

9. To skew an object horizontally use the `skewX()` function, or to skew vertically use the `skewY()` function—for example: `transform:skewX(-20deg);` or `transform:skewY(45deg);`.

10. The `skew()` function accepts values in either degrees or radians, which can be negative, zero, or positive—for example: `transform:skew(1rad, 1rad);` or `transform:skew(-25deg, 25deg);`.

Lesson 20 Answers

1. To release an element from 2D space and make it available for 3D manipulation, you can use the `perspective` property on the element or its parent—for example: `perspective:2000px;`.

2. To change the transformational center of an element, you can use the `transform-origin` property—for example: `transform-origin:10% 20% 30%;`.

3. To move an object to a new location in 3D space, you can use the `translate3d()` function—for example: `transform: translate3d(0px, 0px, 60px);`.

4. You can scale any or all three dimensions of an element using the `scale3d()` function—for example: `transform:scale3d(1, 2, 1.5);`.

5. You can scale an element in any or all three dimensions with the `rotate3d()` function—for example: `transform:rotate3d(1, 0, -1, 25deg);`.

6. To prevent the back of an element being displayed when its back is rotated toward the viewer, you can use the `backface-visibility` property—for example: `backface-visibility:hidden;`.

7. The `transform-style` property specifies whether or not children inherit the 3D space of their parent element—for example: `transform-style: preserve-3d;` or `transform-style:flat;`.

8. The four CSS transition properties are `transition-property`, `transition-delay`, `transition-duration`, and `transition-timing-function`.

9. The `transition-property` property specifies which properties of an element (such as width, height, color, location, and so on) will be animated during transitions (any that are not listed will simply change instantly from one state to the new one). The values can be property names or the universal property name `all` to animate all possible properties—for example: `transition-property:width, height, top, left;`.

10. To animate all properties of an element with a 1.5-second ease in and out transition using a shorthand rule, you could make this declaration: `transition:all 1.5s ease-in-out;`.

Index